The Life of Samuel Johnson, LL.D.

SAMUEL JOHNSON
Painted from life by John Opie

The Life of
Samuel Johnson, LL.D.

by

Sir John Hawkins, Knt.

Edited, Abridged, and with an Introduction by

Bertram H. Davis

New York

The Macmillan Company

1961

First Printing

The Macmillan Company, New York
Brett-Macmillan Ltd., Galt, Ontario

Printed in the United States of America

Library of Congress catalog card number: 61-10764

ACKNOWLEDGMENTS

FOR ASSISTANCE of various kinds I wish to express my thanks to Donald J. Greene, Allen T. Hazen, Herman Liebert, Jr., Lawrence F. Powell, Arthur Sherbo, and Marshall Waingrow. W. S. Lewis of Farmington, Connecticut, has kindly granted permission to quote some of the comments made by Horace Walpole in his copy of Hawkins' *Life of Johnson*, now in Mr. Lewis' possession. With James L. Clifford I have consulted at various points during the progress of this edition, and I owe him a special note of thanks for his encouragement and advice. My wife has assisted me in many ways, particularly in the tedious job of proofreading; but I am most grateful for her unfailing patience throughout an association with Sir John Hawkins now in its eighth year. To her this book is dedicated.

The Editor

60574

INTRODUCTION

FOR EVERY person who remembers Sir John Hawkins as the author of the first full-length biography of Samuel Johnson, many remember him as the man Johnson once described as "unclubbable." Had Johnson been aware that this brand would in time become Hawkins' chief mark of identification, he might have resisted the impulse to indulge his talent for ridicule at Hawkins' expense. For Johnson knew very well that Hawkins, whatever his shortcomings as a clubmate, could not be dismissed so simply. Indeed, it seems quite possible that Johnson's final judgment of his friend would have given hardly more than passing recognition to that social ineptitude which subsequent generations have settled upon as Hawkins' dominant trait. "As we were returning from the meadows that day," wrote Miss Frances Reynolds, recalling a Sunday walk with Johnson, "I remember we met Sir John Hawkins, whom Dr. Johnson seemed much rejoiced to see; and no wonder, for I have often heard him speak of Sir John in terms expressive of great esteem and much cordiality of friendship." [1]

Hawkins distinguished himself, to be sure, by withdrawing from Johnson's famous "Literary Club" following an argument in which he is said to have behaved rudely to Edmund Burke. But from a lifetime of many distinctions it has been an injustice to Hawkins to single out for remembrance, as some have done, only the most dubious. Hawkins' life, in fact, provides the materials of one of the eighteenth century's most remarkable success stories. Revealing of his character though his withdrawal from the club was, it may prove on the whole more informative to examine just why men of the eminence of Johnson and Burke, Sir Joshua Reynolds, and Oliver Goldsmith should have been ready to join with him in the first place.

Genealogists have not confirmed Sir John Hawkins' claim to have been descended from his illustrious namesake, the Elizabethan admiral. It is known only that he was born on March 30, 1719, to John and Elizabeth Hawkins, and that his father was in the building trades—a carpenter, according to Boswell, an architect and surveyor, according to Hawkins' daughter. No record of the young John Hawkins' schooling remains; but, not being favored with a university education, he was articled as a clerk to an attorney and solicitor, and in due time became a practicing attorney in the city of London.

The attorney's was not an eminent calling in eighteenth century England. Whereas the solicitor, who was university-educated, practiced in the courts of civil law, the attorney, who was not, practiced in the courts of common law. Johnson once remarked, of a person unnamed in Boswell's account, that "he did not care to speak ill of any man behind his back, but he believed the gentleman was an *attorney*"; and when Boswell in his *Life of Johnson* referred to "Mr. John Hawkins, an attorney," the identification was undoubtedly intended as much for ridicule as for information.[2] In mature reflection, Hawkins could himself admit that the profession of the common law accepted "all whose broken fortunes drive, or a confidence in their abilities tempts to seek a maintenance in it"—men "of low extraction, domestic servants, and clerks to eminent lawyers."

The common law, however, afforded many opportunities for an ambitious young man, and Hawkins seems to have pursued his studies vigorously. At the same time his interests were developing in other directions. He followed closely the events leading up to the demand in parliament that Sir Robert Walpole be removed as Prime Minister. On occasion he contributed poems and moral essays to a number of periodicals, most notably the *Gentleman's Magazine*, which published his "Essay on Honesty" in 1739. He read widely in literature and theology, and there is some evidence that he studied architecture and cultivated a taste for art. He joined the Academy of Ancient Music and, as lyricist, collaborated with the blind composer, John Stanley, in a number of songs which were sung at Vauxhall and published in two collections in the early 1740's. Throughout the decade he made sporadic contributions to the *Gentleman's Magazine*, his most pretentious effort being a criticism of Thomas Otway's tragedy, *The Orphan*, which the magazine printed in 1748.

No evidence has been uncovered to document the time of Hawkins' first meeting with Johnson. It can be said with assurance only that, in the winter of 1749, fifteen years before the founding of the Literary Club, Hawkins joined with Johnson and eight others in a club which met weekly at the King's Head in Ivy Lane. In all likelihood, however, Johnson would not have invited a stranger to contribute to the intellectual enjoyment these meetings were intended to provide him. Numerous hints in Hawkins' *Life* suggest that he and Johnson had become acquainted very early in the decade, perhaps even as early as 1739. Certainly they had ample opportunity to meet each other on the common ground of the *Gentleman's Magazine*. Johnson was the editor's chief support during much of this period, and Hawkins, besides being a contributor, was a frequent visitor at the magazine's offices in St. John's Gate. His *Life* is, in fact, the prime source of information about the many minor figures who were helping to fill the magazine's pages in these first years of its existence. And Hawkins' knowledge of Johnson's political development suggests the intimacy of first-hand experience; a Walpole supporter himself, he seems to have stood by, fascinated, as the violence of Johnson's anti-Walpole bias abated, to be replaced in time by sincere admiration. Johnson's last known attack on Walpole was published in 1739.

The members of the Ivy Lane, the first of Johnson's clubs, were largely men with literary and professional interests, and their fortunes still to make. Johnson, it is true, had already written *London*, the *Life of Savage*, and his play *Irene*. His journalistic efforts had raised the *Gentleman's Magazine* to an eminence no other periodical was to attain throughout the rest of the century, and he had attracted sufficient notice for the booksellers to come to him with a request that he compile an English dictionary. But ahead of him lay the completion of the *Dictionary*, the *Rambler* and *Idler*, *Rasselas*, his edition of Shakespeare, his major political tracts, the *Lives of the Poets*—in short, most of the work on which his reputation is based. Fourteen years were to pass before his first meeting with James Boswell, who in 1749 was still in the lower forms of a schoolboy's drudgery.

Except for Johnson and perhaps John Hawkesworth, who is remembered as the editor of a collection of famous voyages, none of the club members was to go on to as many accomplishments as John Hawkins. Doubtless the very practical Hawkins would not have considered it the least of his accomplishments that he removed the threat of poverty from his life by winning the favor of a wealthy and elderly lawyer, who offered him a position and a daughter's hand. In 1753 he married Sidney Storer, whose inheritance of twenty thousand pounds, added to her dowry of ten thousand, enabled him in 1760 to purchase a substantial dwelling on the Thames at Twickenham, close to his friend Horace Walpole. In 1760 Hawkins published an edition of Izaak Walton's *Compleat Angler*, which proved so successful that it was reprinted frequently during the next hundred years. With his appointment to the magistrate's bench in 1761, he began a career as public servant which was climaxed by his election, in 1765, to the important post of Chairman of the Quarter Sessions for the County of Middlesex. Early in the 1760's he undertook the first research on his monumental history of music, a major preoccupation during the years preceding its publication in 1776.

Thus, by the winter of 1764, when the Literary Club was established, Hawkins would have recommended himself to Johnson and the other club members both by his achievements and his promise. A practicing magistrate, widely read in the works of the English poets and divines, would have been a rarity in himself. In Hawkins the club members acquired in addition an amateur musicologist more learned than the professionals, a student, if not a connoisseur, of art and architecture, and an acute political observer. There could be no doubt that he was amply qualified for the company he was asked to keep. Indeed, for sheer breadth of learning probably none of the club members but Johnson could have claimed a superiority.

Although his career in the club was brief, Hawkins went on to fulfill much of the promise of his early years. He was knighted in 1772 and, as Sir John, continued to serve as Chairman of the

Quarter Sessions until 1781. He published occasional articles of antiquarian interest. His study of music culminated in the publication of a massive five-volume work entitled A *General History of the Science and Practice of Music,* the first of its kind that English scholars had produced. In 1784, following a long period during which Johnson had turned to him frequently for consolation and advice, he was appointed one of Johnson's executors; and shortly after Johnson's death a group of booksellers invited him to direct their edition of Johnson's works and write an account of his life.

The bare enumeration of Hawkins' achievements, however, distorts the picture of these years of fulfillment, for almost none of Hawkins' successes was unqualified. He himself appealed to the king for the honor of knighthood, and his appeal seems to have been prompted in part by a desire for a recognition equal to that accorded his rival and better known magistrate, Sir John Fielding, brother of the novelist. His neglect of duty during the Gordon riots of 1780 may have hastened his departure as Chairman of the Quarter Sessions. His history of music drew the fire of critics, and the wounds they inflicted helped drop it into the shadows of a similar history by Dr. Charles Burney, the first volume of which was published the same year as Hawkins'. His conduct as executor was sharply criticized by other intimate friends of Johnson. His work as Johnson's editor and biographer released an avalanche of abuse under which he has lain effectually buried ever since.

Hawkins' resignation from the Literary Club occurred some years before he had risen high in the public view. But it was an earnest of things to come. It may in fact be taken almost as a symbol of the aloofness from the literary world which his unpopularity forced upon him. The man whose rudeness could drive him from the company of such men as Edmund Burke and Sir Joshua Reynolds was indeed unclubbable. More important still, in dissociating himself from this segment of the Johnson circle, Hawkins was alienating the very men who could have been most helpful to him when he took up his pen to inscribe his memorial of his dead friend. Instead of encouragement, Hawkins met hostility at almost every turn.

II

Nothing attests more graphically to the profound impression which Johnson had made on his age than the number of writers who set about recording his life immediately following his death on December 13, 1784. Within hours, Thomas Cadell and William Strahan, representing a large group of London booksellers, called upon Sir John Hawkins with their proposals for a biography and an edition of Johnson's works. On December 16, four days before Johnson's funeral, the influential *St. James's Chronicle* was already giving recognition to the crowded field and announcing that the principal candidates in Johnsonian biography were Sir John Hawkins and James Boswell. The day following the funeral, Hawkins' publishers advertised their projected edition in a number of newspapers, called attention to the "authentick" life by one of Johnson's executors which was to accompany it, and cautioned the public against giving credit to any particulars of Johnson's life which might issue from less competent pens.

The first honors, limited though they were, thus went to Hawkins. But for a time they were to be practically his last. Early in the new year, an anonymous correspondent of the *St. James's Chronicle* began a series of letters with the undisguised purpose of exalting James Boswell's qualifications above those of Hawkins:

It is evident from the Conduct of the late Dr. Johnson, that he designed Mr. Boswell for the sole Writer of his Life. Why else did he furnish him with such Materials for it as were withheld from every other Friend? . . . Little indeed did he suppose that a Person whom he had made one of his Executors would have instantly claimed the Office of his Biographer. Still less could he have imagined that this Self-Appointment would have been precipitately confirmed by the Booksellers.

The anonymous correspondent, as James Boswell was quick to discover, was George Steevens, Johnson's collaborator in the revision of his edition of Shakespeare. In Steevens, whose malicious nature had earned him the nickname "The Asp," Hawkins was not encountering a new adversary. The *Memoirs* of Laetitia-Matilda

Hawkins, which recounts in some detail the history of her father's quarrelsome relationship with Steevens, corroborates Hawkins' own charge that in 1775 Steevens had carried from his house "a paper of a public nature, and of great importance," and had published it without Hawkins' knowledge or consent; and one tradition attributes the disappointing sale of Hawkins' history of music to the severity of Steevens' criticism.

It is difficult to estimate the effect of Steevens' letters, which, in a newspaper of only four pages, could hardly have gone unnoticed. Eloquently written as they were, and based on what seemed an intimate knowledge of Johnson, they may well have prejudiced a number of readers against Hawkins' forthcoming volume. Whatever else may be said, their scornful and apparently unchallenged dismissal of Hawkins, two years before his qualifications could be fairly assessed, makes clear that his volume was not likely to fall among critics kindly disposed toward it. The ink in Steevens' pen, at least, had many years to run.

The months following Johnson's death were troubled ones for Hawkins. A rumor circulated that he had slandered Johnson. He was accused of presuming upon his office as executor to claim some of Johnson's effects for himself. As most active of the executors, he was blamed for withholding the full service at Johnson's funeral. Of graver concern to Hawkins, his house in Queen's Square burned to the ground on the night of February 23, 1785, and he barely managed to rescue the materials—including portions of Johnson's diaries—which were to be foundation stones of his work. After this calamity, the publication in June, 1785, of the satirical *Probationary Odes for the Laureateship* must have come as only a minor shock to him. The title page of the *Probationary Odes*, with its bold announcement that the "preliminary discourse" was by "Sir John Hawkins, Knt.," could hardly have deceived anyone who took the trouble to look further, since the entire discourse was a rollicking parody of Hawkins' style in the history of music. Popular enough to justify eight editions before the publication of Hawkins' *Life*, the book served to nurture the doubts of Hawkins' competence already raised in the Steevens' letters.

Hawkins seems to have endured both criticism and adversity

without complaint. With no time to rebuild what the fire had destroyed, he moved quickly into a new residence and, ignoring his critics, concentrated upon pushing his work to completion. It was made available to the public, both as a separate work and as the first volume of the edition of Johnson's works, early in March, 1787.

III

In the first two months of its existence the *Life of Johnson* enjoyed a popularity it was not to enjoy again. With the exception of John Nichols, who was concerned primarily to point out Hawkins' indebtedness to the *Gentleman's Magazine*, no reviewer appeared to dull the first success of the book. And a considerable success it was. The Dublin booksellers, as was their custom, quickly met the demand with a pirated edition. Following the practice of the day, the *St. James's Chronicle* and the *London Chronicle* spent several weeks publishing extracts from the *Life of Johnson*. Most of the London magazines—and there were a good many in 1787—devoted a number of their pages to the same undertaking, and two of them, the *Universal Magazine* and the *Political Magazine*, initiated series of extracts chronologically arranged and continuing for months to come. No other book published in 1787 was plundered so flatteringly. By mid-April the extensive sale of the first edition had sent the publishers back to Hawkins with a request that he prepare a second.

But by the time the second edition, with its numerous additions and corrections, could be printed, reviewers in the *Monthly Review*, the *Critical Review*, the *English Review*, and the *European Magazine* had given the public an entirely new perspective on the *Life of Johnson*. Here, they contended, was a malevolent and spiteful account of Johnson's life, grossly inaccurate, and rendered utterly ridiculous by its pompous legalisms and its digressions on every conceivable subject. The book, if they were to be believed, was less a biography than a polemic, less a work of art than a collection of senile gossip. The reviewers, moreover, were persuasive; they fell to their task, which most of them seemed to look upon as the defense of Johnson's good name, with all the zest they would have given to a defense of London against an invading armada. The second edition seems to have languished in the book-stalls, and it is seldom seen today.

The quality of the reviews, some of which were continued through several monthly issues of the magazines in which they appeared, may be suggested by one or two brief extracts. An anonymous writer in the *Critical Review* complained that in the *Life of Johnson* "we often lose Dr. Johnson. . . . The knight sinks under the weight of his subject, and is glad to escape to scenes more congenial to his disposition, and more suitable to his talents, the garrulity of a literary old man." The dramatist Arthur Murphy, writing anonymously in the *Monthly Review*, amused his readers with a parody of Hawkins' style:

Sir John most probably acquired his notions of language at his master's desk: he admired the phraseology of deeds and parchments, *whereof*, to speak in his own manner, he read so much, that in consequence *thereof*, he has been chiefly conversant *therein*; and by the help of the parchments *aforesaid*, missed the elegance *abovementioned*, and uses words, that *in them* we sometimes meet with, and being bred an attorney, he caught the language of the *said* trade, *whereof* he retains so much, that he is now rendered an incompetent critic *thereby*, and in consequence *thereof*.

It was hardly to be expected, he remarked, that a person whose reading had been confined to "old homilies and the statute-book, should have a true relish for the beauties of composition." In the *European Magazine*, two articles by "Philo Johnson," almost certainly a pseudonym for George Steevens, gave vigorous expression to a charge which has clung to the *Life of Johnson* ever since:

the great solid principle that secures its condemnation, is the spirit of malevolence to the dead, which breathes all through it. Sir John Hawkins, with all the humanity and very little of the dexterity of a Clare-Market butcher, has raised his blunt axe to deface the image of his friend.

Johnson's executor had become his executioner.[3]

Sensing a good thing, the newspapers turned their wits loose upon Hawkins. It is not true, asserted the *St. James's Chronicle* on the second of June, "that Mrs. Hobart had an intention of reading Sir John Hawkins' book. The late hours at which people of rank go to bed, renders it wholly unnecessary to force a sleep in public places." A writer for an unidentified newspaper reported that a "gentleman, lately arrived in town, has been for several days past afflicted with a *lethargy*, owing to the perusal of three chapters in Hawkins' *Life of Johnson*." Another writer suggested an appropriate use for the famous willow tree planted at Lichfield by Johnson: "The branches only should be lopped off, and tied in bundles, . . . and properly applied to the naked backs of his various biographers, taking care, that the largest bundle be appropriated unto the use and behoof of Sir John Hawkins, Knight." [4]

Had nothing more ambitious followed the reviews than these amusing sallies, Hawkins might have considered himself fortunate. But the end was not in sight. In May, James Boswell inserted an advertisement in at least three London newspapers, in which he assured the public that his own *Life of Johnson* was "in great forwardness," but had been delayed in the expectation that the various promised works on Johnson might add significantly "to the large store of materials which he had already accumulated." Disappointed in this expectation, he cautioned the public against permitting "unfavourable impressions to be made on their minds," either "by the light effusions of carelessness and pique, or the ponderous labours of solemn inaccuracy and dark uncharitable conjecture"—the light effusions undoubtedly being a reference to Mrs. Piozzi's *Anecdotes of Dr. Johnson*, published in 1786, and the ponderous labours to Hawkins' *Life*. In September, the *Gentleman's Magazine* published the first installment of a three-part "Panegyric Epistle" on Hawkins' *Life*, which kept the town in laughter by ironically praising all the faults to which the reviewers had given their attention. The mock solemnity with which the author, the classical scholar Richard Porson, closed his panegyric is typical of the entire satire: "I do hereby assure his Worship [Hawkins], that when any other friends of his die, whether he be disposed *to carve them as a dish fit for the gods, or hew them like a carcase for the hounds,* I shall be ready to exert my utmost powers in his behalf against all his enemies open or secret." After Porson's severe but subtle rebuke, the outhouse obscenity of *More Last Words of Dr. Johnson,* an anonymous attack upon Hawkins published as a separate volume in November, provided at best a disgusting anticlimax. By no means typical of the reaction to Hawkins' book, it may nevertheless be cited as evidence of the extent to which at least one of his critics was willing to go. In the short span of a few months the fall from favor was virtually complete, with the result that few persons would have disputed the terse opinion which Lady Eleanor Butler confided to her diary on February 9 of the following year: "Sir John Hawkins' life of Johnson. Wretched performance." [5]

IV

Most of the charges against Hawkins' *Life of Johnson* were not to find their most cogent expression until 1791, when Boswell's long-awaited biography was published. Sir John Hawkins does not himself come to life in Boswell's pages (Boswell seldom saw him in Johnson's company), but Boswell relinquished few opportunities to compare his own work favorably with Hawkins', and his introductory statement on the Hawkins biography has become the classic indictment, widely read and accepted. Indeed, many people know of Hawkins' *Life of Johnson* only as Boswell has presented it to them:

Since my work was announced, several Lives and Memoirs of Dr. Johnson have been published, the most voluminous of which is one compiled for the booksellers of London, by Sir John Hawkins, Knight, a man, whom, during my long intimacy with Dr. Johnson, I never saw in his company, I think but once, and I am sure not above twice. Johnson might have esteemed him for his decent, religious demeanour, and his knowledge of books and literary history; but from the rigid formality of his manners, it is evident that they never could have lived together with companionable ease and familiarity; nor had Sir John Hawkins that nice perception which was necessary to mark the finer and less obvious parts of Johnson's character. His being appointed one of his executors, gave him an opportunity of taking possession of such fragments of a diary and other papers as were left; of which, before delivering them up to the residuary legatee, whose property they were, he endeavoured to extract the substance. In this he has not been very successful, as I have found upon a perusal of those papers, which have been since transferred to me. Sir John Hawkins's ponderous labours, I must acknowledge, exhibit a *farrago*, of which a considerable portion is not devoid of entertainment to the lovers of literary gossipping; but besides its being swelled out with long unnecessary extracts from various works, (even one of several leaves from Osborne's Harleian Catalogue, and those not compiled by Johnson, but by Oldys,) a very small part of it relates to the person who is the subject of the book; and, in that, there is such an inaccuracy in the statement of facts, as in so solemn an authour is hardly excusable, and certainly makes his narrative very unsatisfactory. But what is still worse, there is throughout the whole of it a dark uncharitable cast, by which the most unfavourable construction is put upon almost every circumstance in the character and conduct of my illustrious friend; who, I trust, will, by a true and fair delineation, be vindicated both from the injurious misrepresentation of this authour, and from the slighter aspersions of a lady who once lived in great intimacy with him.[6]

Coming from a man of Boswell's stature, and supported as it is from any number of quarters, such an indictment cannot summarily be dismissed as the jealous effusion of a rival seeking to establish the sole claim in Johnsonian biography. Doubtless Boswell resented any encroachment on what he considered his domain, and doubtless this fact colored his attitude toward the efforts of both Hawkins and Mrs. Piozzi. But Boswell speaks of Johnson with such authority that it is never safe to assume him wrong. The burden of proof falls inevitably upon the challenger.

The charge of earlier critics that Hawkins' volume is filled with digressions was given a new dress and impetus by Boswell's term "farrago," and on the face of it the charge may scarcely seem refutable. Boswell did not elaborate, but he might easily have done so. Hawkins' *Life* contains, among a variety of other things, an account in Latin of a sixteenth century breakfast, a disquisition on the proportions of columns, an essay on the history of taverns, and an enumeration of fourteen ways in which a criminal may avoid being brought to justice. Hawkins, moreover, did swell out his volume with long extracts from Johnson's works, including, in addition to the extract mentioned by Boswell, two lengthy speeches from the parliamentary debates in the body of the text and two in the footnotes.

Boswell's charge goes further, however, than a mere accusation that the book contains digressions: "a very small part of it relates to the person who is the subject of [it]." No doubt Boswell did not put himself to the inconvenience of computing the exact proportion of the book which is directly related to Johnson. Had he undertaken such a computation, it is difficult to believe that he would not have felt impelled to revise his estimate. If one includes Hawkins' criticisms of Johnson's works, which are certainly admissible in literary biography, he finds that a good half of the book is devoted explicitly to narrating and interpreting the events of Johnson's life. Even by themselves, these three hundred pages of the original edition would have stood as a substantial monument to the memory of Johnson.

On the other hand, three hundred pages of digressions, if we are to consider them digressions, are themselves substantial and hardly speak well for Hawkins' ability to keep his mind on his subject. Many of these pages, however, could be considered digressive only by one who failed to recognize the value of the background supplied by Hawkins in what has sneeringly been referred to as his "miscellaneous matter." The book is not merely the life of Johnson. Like Boswell's biography, it is the life and times of Johnson. A contemporary of Hawkins, Dr. Samuel Parr, once remarked that, if he had written his projected life of Johnson, he would "have related not only everything important about Johnson, but many things about the men who flourished at the same time." [7] Like Parr, Hawkins recognized Johnson's central position, and he perceived that Johnson could be displayed with greatest luster in the elaborate setting of his age. Hawkins knew also that much of Johnson's work (the *Dictionary*, the edition of Shakespeare, and the moral essays, for example) could be properly appreciated only if one knew something of similar undertakings which had preceded them, just as the phenomenal rise of the *Gentleman's Magazine* took on additional meaning when viewed against the background of earlier periodicals and the political ferment of the times.

One would not wish to go as far as Austin Dobson and say that the "abiding and original side" of Hawkins' labors is just those "divagations" which the eighteenth century critics deplored.[8] But they give to Hawkins' biography a dimension to be found in no other contemporary account of Johnson except Boswell's. Hawkins' purpose was laudable, and to a large extent it was achieved. What he lacked was the ability to see when his purpose was being defeated by excessive attention to some of Johnson's contemporaries, by too lengthy illustration from Johnson's works, or by a pedantic overindulgence in reminiscences only vaguely, if at all, related to Johnson. The slashes of an editorial pencil might not have spared Hawkins the rebukes of his critics, but they would have removed those sections of the book which were easiest to ridicule, and they might have helped the book to a more favorable consideration once the first heated assaults upon it had expended their energies.

The second object of Boswell's criticism was Hawkins' inaccuracy, which, according to Boswell, "makes his narrative very unsatisfactory." A modern biographer who relied solely upon Hawkins for many of his facts of Johnson's life would compile a very unsatisfactory narrative indeed, and would properly be rebuked by his critics. But Hawkins did not have the benefit of 175 years of research. Many of his misstatements had been accepted as fact before their appearance in his biography, and they were not to be corrected until men like George Birkbeck Hill and Aleyn Lyell Reade gave their best efforts to digging in the Johnson earth. An unsympathetic critic might declare other mistakes "hardly excusable," as Boswell did. Hawkins overlooked some materials in the *Gentleman's Magazine* which contained more accurate accounts of brief episodes in Johnson's life than he was otherwise able to obtain; his memory occasionally betrayed him; he badly misread Johnson's handwriting in a few manuscripts; and he did not take ample pains in proofreading his book. Of similar errors, however, even the best biographies are seldom free: from Boswell's itself an imposing list might be compiled. And scholars, as they have searched these early memorials in an effort to piece together all the available facts of Johnson's life, have been discovering not only that Hawkins' *Life* contains much authentic information not to be found in Boswell, but that his accounts of a number of incidents in Johnson's life are either more reliable than Boswell's or must be studied in conjunction with his if a reasonably accurate picture is to be obtained.

It can be demonstrated, for example, that Hawkins provided a more accurate account than Boswell of Johnson's brief career as undermaster of Market Bosworth School. It is clear that each biographer incorporated errors into his accounts of Johnson's undergraduate days at Oxford, of the length of time Johnson composed the parliamentary debates for the *Gentleman's Magazine*, of Johnson's translation of a work by Crousaz; but it is equally clear that each managed to find some grains of truth in all these accounts which the other overlooked. Boswell documented with much greater fullness the efforts of Johnson to obtain mercy for the condemned forger Dr. Dodd; but Hawkins' account of Mrs. Dodd's activity in her husband's behalf and of the attempts to bribe the turnkey and the Keeper of Newgate afford an insight into this episode not available in the series of letters and petitions by means of which Boswell recounted it. In its accounts of Johnson's early years—through the founding of the Ivy Lane Club— and of Johnson's dying months, Hawkins' *Life* contains much information which Boswell's cannot duplicate.

Admittedly Hawkins' *Life* would be improved if it contained fewer errors of fact. But Hawkins, who was striking out for information across a wilderness through which only a few narrow paths had been cut, can hardly be held to the standard of accuracy we would set for a modern biographer. Even Boswell, who had four years to correct the mistakes of his predecessor, could not close his volume to a sizable number of errors. Our judgment of Boswell, it is clear, has been reached, not by totaling his mistakes but by assessing his portrait of Johnson, and thus it seems only fair to Hawkins that we should judge his book in the same way. To attempt to do so, however, is to run headlong into Boswell's final and most serious criticism—the same, in fact, which earlier critics had made central to their thesis—that there is throughout the whole of Hawkins' book a "dark uncharitable cast, by which the most unfavourable construction is put upon almost every circumstance in the character and conduct" of Johnson. If Boswell's charge is well founded, then Hawkins' book must be set aside as a rancorous diatribe, to be read with satisfaction only by those few persons who share his "uncharitable" view of one of the eighteenth century's best loved figures.

V

Like Boswell, Hawkins did not profess to be Johnson's panegyrist. "In the performance of the engagement I am under," he wrote, "I find myself compelled to make public, as well those particulars of Johnson that may be thought to abase as those that exalt his character." Such an approach to biography would have had the approval of Johnson, who once remarked that if "nothing but the bright side of characters should be shown, we should sit down in despondency, and think it utterly impossible to imitate them in *any thing*." [9] It has, of course, almost universal approval today, and thus the question which must be answered here is whether, in carrying out his plan, Hawkins failed to strike a reasonable balance between those particulars which abased Johnson's character and those which exalted it.

Those aspects of Johnson of which Hawkins was most critical were his table manners, his dress, his indolence, the political cant of his early years, and what Hawkins termed his "indiscriminate bounty." Of the first two of these Boswell was equally critical; he once caused trouble for himself, in fact, by suggesting to Johnson that he might do well to dress a little better than was his custom. Boswell also refers frequently to Johnson's "constitutional indolence," although he did not make quite such an object lesson of it as Hawkins, who considered it his duty to point out the evils of idleness to the "rising generation." In discussing Johnson's early political activity, Boswell, who had no personal knowledge of the London of 1738 and 1739, merely echoed Hawkins' conclusion that Johnson, in attacking the Walpole ministry, was repeating the common cant of the opposition and raising fears that were quite ill founded.

When Hawkins criticized Johnson's indiscriminate bounty— to beggars, felons, wastrels of every kind—he was doubtless recalling some of the many appearances these unfortunates had made before his magistrate's bench. It was not that Hawkins condemned the giving of alms. But in misdirecting his charity, Johnson was merely lending encouragement to vice, while at the same time his extreme generosity was endangering his own welfare. Johnson himself once admitted that one could give away five hundred pounds a year and do no good, and Henry Fielding, who had like Hawkins a magistrate's experience to support him, denounced bounty to beggars as "a crime against the public." "It is assisting," he said, "in the continuance and promotion of a nuisance." [10]

Although candor compelled him to be outspoken on this subject, we would be unjust to Hawkins if we failed to record his profound admiration for the man who could empty his pockets for the benefit of the undeserving with no expectation of either thanks or repayment. Indeed, says Hawkins, "they were such creatures as were incapable of being awed by a sense of his worth, or of discerning the motives that actuated him." Had Hawkins' admiration ended here, it would of course be useless to attempt a reply to Boswell. But one can go as far as to say that Hawkins' admiration for Johnson's many remarkable qualities makes itself felt again and again, beginning with the very first page of the book, and that Boswell's charge of his lack of charity could not even be sustained if we ignored much of the book and considered only those events of Johnson's life to which he and Hawkins gave different interpretations.

For the truth is that some of Boswell's interpretations do not withstand analysis as well as Hawkins'. One might cite, for example, Boswell's weak attempt to reconcile Johnson's definition of *pension* in his *Dictionary* ("pay given to a state hireling for treason to his country") and his acceptance of a pension; Hawkins makes much better sense with his candid acknowledgment of Johnson's obvious indiscretion in the *Dictionary* and with his accompanying defense of Johnson's integrity. One might compare Boswell's sentimentalized account of Johnson's marriage with the forthright account by Hawkins, which shocked Johnson's friends and has continued to shock many readers. The only proper defense of Hawkins' account is that it is closer to the truth than Boswell's. Johnson's marriage was not an ideal one by any means. Boswell

suppressed some evidence to achieve his picture, whereas if Hawkins erred he erred quite unintentionally. "Though Hawkins's remarks in this instance may have sounded uncharitable," writes
a leading Johnson authority, "they impressed me as representing
a more probable condition." [11]

Far from putting an unfavorable construction on almost every
circumstance in Johnson's character and conduct, Hawkins almost
always gave Johnson every credit which candor would allow. While
asserting that Johnson, in his early political writing, had merely
fallen under the spell of the opposition, Hawkins insisted that
there was no hypocrisy in his heated attacks upon the ministry.
His sympathetic and trenchant analysis of Johnson's political tracts
of the 1770's rejects the attacks of Johnson's enemies upon his
motives and concentrates upon the arguments and principles which
made the tracts so effective. Hawkins came to Johnson's defense
in a number of matters—his attack upon the bookseller Osborne,
his prayers for the dead, his support of the charlatan William
Lauder—which had subjected him to public ridicule. And for much
of Johnson's conduct Hawkins voiced unqualified admiration.

Hawkins was deeply moved, for example, by Johnson's behavior
in the difficult days preceding his death, and his comment is typical
of his reverence for his almost lifelong friend: "As Johnson lived
the life of the righteous, his end was that of a Christian: he strictly
fulfilled the injunction of the apostle, to work out his salvation
with fear and trembling." There were no captious reservations.
Death brought to a close the life of a man "endued with a capacity
for the highest offices, a philosopher, a poet, an orator, and, if
fortune had so ordered, a chancellor, a prelate, a statesman. . . ."
If Hawkins found some faults in Johnson, he was not deluded
into thinking that they marred his essential greatness.

The conclusion seems inescapable that what Hawkins' detractors
interpreted as lack of charity was frequently no more than a sincere
attempt to see Johnson as he was. In the tradition of the magistrate, Hawkins considered it necessary to cast up the account of
good and bad, of pro and con, and to base his judgment, not
on some preconceived notion, but on the evidence as it was presented to him. It is true that on occasion he reached conclusions
which few others have been able to share; witness, for example,
his unfeeling attack on Johnson's servant for being an un-

worthy object of Johnson's "ostentatious bounty." Like the
magistrate, moreover, Hawkins did not hesitate to call attention
to any departure from what he looked upon as exemplary conduct. But to accuse Hawkins of attempting to deface Johnson's
image, as Philo Johnson did, or of putting an unfavorable construction on almost every circumstance in Johnson's character and
conduct, as Boswell did, is to read into his book what no truly
dispassionate examination of it will discover.

This is not to say that most of those who accused Hawkins of
a lack of charity did so purely out of a spirit of perversity. George
Steevens, to be sure, seems to have had an overweening desire
to play the dragon's role. But many of Johnson's friends were
genuinely distressed to find the weaknesses of their idol displayed
in full color before the public. Placed on the defensive, they rallied
for a counterattack, and, ignoring many of the book's virtues, they
singled out those parts which were truly vulnerable, or which
could not be fitted into the picture of Johnson their memories
retained. By the time Boswell was ready to publish, he needed no
objective analysis of Hawkins' *Life* to support his various accusa-
tions against it, since most of the public had long before accepted
the judgment of the critics who had preceded him.

Today, so many years after Johnson's death, Hawkins' readers
will not be disturbed by his attention to Johnson's shortcomings.
Warm though Johnson's memory remains, his weaknesses have
long since passed into the public record, as vital a part of him as
his many strengths. Indeed, Hawkins' first virtue as a biographer
is that he saw Johnson's strengths and weaknesses in perspective,
and thus he has been able to record him for posterity very much
as he was. His is not an account of a man "utterly impossible to
imitate in *any thing*," but rather of a man who, for all his greatness, was beset by many of the same evils that have dogged the
rest of mankind since the first fall from grace.

VI

The poet William Cowper predicted in 1789 that perhaps in
fifty years the world would consider itself obliged to Sir John
Hawkins for his *Life of Johnson*. But the odds were against the

fulfillment of this prediction. A book written by a man of Hawkins' austere nature had to fight its way to recognition not only over its own defects but over the defects of its author as well. No critic could properly ignore Hawkins' indisputably irrelevant passages or his inelegancies of style, which would have been apparent to the most casual reader; and those who felt that Johnson's weaknesses should be hidden from public view were understandably offended by his candor. But the severity of the abuse heaped upon Hawkins, even before his book was published, suggests that the book was not the sole object of the critics' attack. Unclubbable, dignified Sir John Hawkins—here was a morsel substantial enough for any number of critics. "Boswell, and Co. will torture the poor Knight, half an inch at a time, to literary death," wrote Sir Herbert Croft to John Nichols on March 11, 1787, several weeks before the first review of the *Life of Johnson* appeared. The man who had withdrawn from the Literary Club was paying the price of his unsociability.[12]

What William Cowper could not foresee was the extent to which Boswell's *Life of Johnson* would eclipse all previous efforts; nor could he foresee that Boswell's indictment of Hawkins would be accepted on faith by almost all his readers. All Cowper knew was that, having read Hawkins' *Life of Johnson* and Boswell's *Journal of a Tour to the Hebrides,* he considered himself "almost as much a master of Johnson's character, as if . . . [he] had known him personally," and it must have seemed reasonably safe to predict that a book which brought one into such intimate association with greatness would survive the jeers of its first reception.

Modern biographers have found it impossible to construct their pictures of Johnson without quoting liberally from Boswell. It will therefore come as a surprise to many that, without the benefit of Boswell's *Life,* Hawkins has left us a portrait which is not only full-length but which captures the real quality of its subject. It is true that Hawkins does not pull up a chair for his readers in Johnson's company, as Boswell so frequently does; but on the other hand the reader of Hawkins may become as much a master of Johnson's character as Cowper believed himself to be. In almost no essential does Hawkins' portrait differ from Boswell's. Whether he is recounting Johnson's varied knowledge ("he could describe,

with great accuracy, the process of malting; and, had necessity
driven him to it, could have thatched a dwelling"), his love of
tavern life ("I have heard him assert, that a tavern-chair was the
throne of human felicity"), or the stubborn defiance with which
he yielded to death, Hawkins reveals himself as a man of acute
observation, prepared to relinquish no detail of the complex character which was Johnson's.

And if Hawkins' *Life* is remarkable for the accuracy with which
it depicts Johnson's character, it is no less remarkable for the penetrating judgment which it brings to bear upon many of Johnson's
qualities and actions. Only in our time have Hawkins' insights
into Johnson's political principles and writings begun to be appreciated. His comments on Johnson's friendship with the vagrant
poet Richard Savage, on his fear of madness, or on his relationships
with the group of ne'er-do-wells that hung about his household
bore into some of the springs buried deep in Johnson's character.
He was the first to recognize the tincture of enthusiasm in Johnson's religion, or to comment in depth on Johnson's ideas of departed spirits. In ignoring his comments on Johnson's humor ("In
the talent of humour there hardly ever was his equal"), a number
of later biographers have left untouched one of the most engaging
aspects of Johnson's character. It may be too much to say, with
Harold Nicolson, that to no slight extent Boswell had to fear
comparison with Hawkins.[13] But if one had to single out any
quality of Hawkins' book which gives it at times an advantage
over Boswell's, he could not go wrong in mentioning the shrewd-
ness of some of the insights Hawkins brought to it. Hawkins has
repelled some readers by his judicial approach to almost everything. But it was just the magistrate in Hawkins which was his
greatest source of strength, since it compelled him to examine
carefully all the relevant evidence and to reach conclusions which
were not only supportable but which cut to the heart of his subject.

Obviously, no book can replace Boswell's. Boswell's thorough-
ness, his skill in re-creating the everyday drama of Johnson's life,
and the easy, familiar style which graces his entire book, have
rightly lifted his *Life of Johnson* to a position of supremacy among
works of its kind. In these things Hawkins was no match for the
younger biographer. But greatness can endure scrutiny from many

directions. The totally different temperaments of Boswell and Hawkins, and their many differences in point of view, have provided us with complementary accounts of the same great man, and it would be as foolish to continue our neglect of the Hawkins biography as it would be to discard all other portraits of Johnson because one of Sir Joshua Reynolds' is most to our taste.

Sir John Hawkins brought to his task an unusual ability to turn up out-of-the-way information, an acquaintance with Johnson that spanned almost half a century, and a lifelong intimacy with the London that was Johnson's milieu. As executor, he had access to Johnson's private papers, including substantial portions of his diaries; and during the two years his book was in the making he was able to examine the numerous Johnsoniana that poured from the press. In the alembic of a thoughtful mind, Hawkins' resources were transmuted into a biography of Johnson which is second in authority only to Boswell's. If William Cowper's prediction was premature, it grew nonetheless out of a sincere conviction that the hubbub of criticism would shortly subside, and the book's many virtues would at last be recognized. "Such a biography of Milton or Shakespeare," Cowper exclaimed. "O how desirable!" [14] Here in these pages is a painstaking memorial of one of England's greatest men, and we may be obliged to Hawkins for not following the easy path of publishing only his personal recollections, but for availing himself instead of almost every material that a biographer could profitably put to use.

A NOTE ON THE TEXT

THE FIRST edition of Hawkins' *Life of Johnson* was published in March, 1787, and the second, containing Hawkins' additions and corrections, was published three months later. The book has not been reprinted since that time. The present text is based on the second edition, with occasional modifications to take advantage of more correct readings in the first edition.

In abridging the text, I have tried to bear in mind the need to retain, first, all the fullness of Hawkins' portrait of Johnson, and, second, enough of Hawkins' background material to make this, like both the first and second editions, the "life and times" of Johnson. Thus, although I have omitted or abridged some of the longer excerpts from Johnson's works, and have abridged some of Hawkins' comments on Johnson's works, I have included all other material which bears directly upon Johnson. In addition, I have abridged some of the accounts of Johnson's close associates and of eighteenth century phenomena, but have omitted entirely only those accounts which seemed to me largely to defeat their purpose as background material by being either too long or dubiously relevant. Brief omissions from the text have been indicated by an asterisk, and all others by a note; but a number of Hawkins' footnotes have been dropped without any notice to that effect.

Capitalization and spelling, in which Hawkins was not always consistent, have been modernized throughout, but I have retained Hawkins' spelling of proper names. Book titles have been printed in italics instead of the quotation marks used by Hawkins, and quotations of several lines length have been set in extract type. I have changed Hawkins' punctuation only for the purpose of setting quotations in accordance with modern practice, and to achieve uniformity in dates and appositives.

For convenience in reading, I have divided the book into chapters at points which seemed to mark logical divisions. The notes are not intended to provide a thorough annotation of Hawkins' text, which must await the first modern reprinting of the entire work. I hope merely that they will serve to correct Hawkins' errors, point out some of the relevant discoveries of recent scholarship, and answer the more obvious questions the reader is likely to have.

Those who wish additional information about Hawkins will find it in Percy A. Scholes' *The Life and Activities of Sir John Hawkins*, published in 1953 by the Oxford University Press. My own detailed study of Hawkins' *Life of Johnson* was published in 1960 by the Yale University Press under the title *Johnson Before Boswell*.

B. H. D.

Washington, D.C.
May 31, 1961

CONTENTS

I

T
HE GENERAL sense of mankind and the practice of the learned in all ages, have given a sanction to biographical history, and concurred to recommend that precept of the wise son of Sirach, in which we are exhorted to 'praise famous men, such as by their counsels and by their knowledge of learning were meet for the people,—and were wise and eloquent in their instructions, —and such as recited verses in writing.' [1] In each of these faculties did the person, whose history I am about to write, so greatly excel, that, except for my presumption in the attempt to display his worth, the undertaking may be thought to need no apology; especially if we contemplate, together with his mental endowments, those moral qualities which distinguished him, and reflect that, in an age when literary acquisitions and scientific improvements are rated at their utmost value, he rested not in the applause which these procured him; but adorned the character of a scholar and a philosopher with that of a Christian.

Justified, as I trust, thus far in the opinion of the reader, I may, nevertheless, stand in need of his excuse; for that, in the narration of facts that respect others, I have oftener spoke of myself, and in my own person, than the practice of some writers will warrant. To this objection, if any shall please to make it, I answer, that the reverse of wrong is not always right. By the office I have undertaken I stand engaged to relate facts to which I was a witness, conversations in which I was a party, and to record memorable sayings uttered only to myself. Whoever attends to these circumstances, must, besides the disgust which such an affectation of humility would excite, be convinced, that in some instances, the avoiding of egotisms had been extremely difficult, and in many impossible.

Samuel Johnson, the subject of the following memoirs, was the elder of the two sons of Michael Johnson, of the city of Lichfield, bookseller, and of Sarah his wife, a sister of Dr. Joseph Ford, a physician of great eminence, and father of the famous Cornelius otherwise called Parson Ford.[2] He was born, as I find it noted in his diary, on the seventh day of September, 1709: his brother, named Nathanael, was born some years after.[3] Mr. Johnson was a man of eminence in his trade, and of such reputation in the city above-mentioned, that he, more than once, bore, for a year, the office of bailiff or chief magistrate thereof, and discharged the duties of that exalted station with honour and applause. It may here be proper, as it will account for some particulars respecting the character of his son Samuel, to mention, that his political principles led him to favour the pretensions of the exiled family, and that though a very honest and sensible man, he, like many others inhabiting the county of Stafford, was a Jacobite.[4]

It may farther be supposed, that he was possessed of some amiable qualities either moral or personal, from a circumstance in his early life, of which evidence is yet remaining. While he was an apprentice at Leek in Staffordshire, a young woman of the same town fell in love with him, and upon his removal to Lichfield followed him, and took lodgings opposite his house. Her passion was not unknown to Mr. Johnson, but he had no inclination to return it, till he heard that it so affected her mind that her life was in danger, when he visited her, and made her a tender of his hand, but feeling the approach of death, she declined it, and shortly after died, and was interred in Lichfield cathedral. In pity to her sufferings, Mr. Johnson caused a stone to be placed over her grave with this inscription:

Here lies the body of
Mrs. ELIZABETH BLANEY, a stranger.
She departed this life,
2d of September, 1694.[5]

The first born child of Mr. Johnson and his wife, their son Samuel, had the misfortune to receive, together with its nutriment derived from a hired nurse, the seeds of that disease which troubled him through life, the struma, or, as it is called, the king's-evil; for the cure whereof his mother, agreeable to the opinion then entertained of the efficacy of the royal touch, presented him to Queen Anne, who, for the last time, as it is said, that she ever performed that office, with her accustomed grace and benignity administered to the child as much of that healing quality as it was in her power to dispense, and hung about his neck the usual amulet of an angel of gold, with the impress of St. Michael the archangel on the one side, and a ship under full sail on the other.[6] It was probably this disease that deprived him of the sight of his left eye, for he has been heard to say, that he never remembered to have enjoyed the use of it.

It may seem a ridiculous attempt to trace the dawn of his poetical faculty so far back as to his very infancy; but the following incident I am compelled to mention, as it is well attested, and therefore makes part of his history. When he was about three years old, his mother had a brood of eleven ducklings, which she permitted him to call his own. It happened that in playing about he trod on and killed one of them, upon which running to his mother, he, in great emotion bid her write. Write, child? said she, what must I write? Why write, answered he, so:

> Here lies good Master Duck,
> That Samuel Johnson trod on,
> If't had liv'd 'twould have been good luck,
> For then there'd been an odd one.

and she wrote accordingly.[7]

Being arrived at a proper age for grammatical instruction, he was placed in the free school of Lichfield, of which Mr. Hunter was then master.[8] The progress he made in his learning soon attracted the notice of his teachers; and among other discernible qualities that distinguished him from the rest of the school, he was bold, active and enterprising, so that without affecting it, the seniors in the school looked on him as their head and leader, and readily acquiesced in whatever he proposed or did. There dwelt at Lichfield a gentleman of the name of Butt, the father of the Reverend Mr. Butt, now a King's Chaplain, to whose house on holidays and in school vacations he was ever welcome. The children in the family, perhaps offended with the rudeness of his behaviour, would frequently call him the great boy, which the father once overhearing, said, 'You call him the great boy, but take my word for it, he will one day prove a great man.' [9]

A more particular character of him while a schoolboy, and of his behaviour at school, I find in a paper now before me, written by a person yet living,[10] and of which the following is a copy:

Johnson and I were, early in life, schoolfellows at Lichfield, and for many years in the same class. As his uncommon abilities for learning far exceeded us, we endeavoured by every boyish piece of flattery to gain his assistance, and three of us, by turns, used to call on him in a morning, on one of whose backs, supported by the other two, he rode triumphantly to school. He never associated with us in any of our diversions, except in the winter when the ice was firm, to be drawn along by a boy barefooted. His ambition to excel was great, though his application to books, as far as it appeared, was very trifling. I could not oblige him more than by sauntering away every vacation, that occurred, in the fields, during which time he was more engaged in talking to himself than his companion. Verses or themes he would dictate to his favourites, but he would never be at the trouble of writing them. His dislike to business was so great, that he would procrastinate his exercises to the last hour. I have known him after a long vacation, in which we were rather severely tasked, return to school an hour earlier in the morning, and begin one of his exercises, in which he purposely left some faults, in order to gain time to finish the rest.

I never knew him corrected at school, unless it was for talking and diverting other boys from their business, by which, perhaps, he might hope to keep his ascendancy. He was uncommonly inquisitive, and his memory so tenacious, that whatever he read or heard he never forgot. I remember rehearsing to him eighteen verses, which after a little pause he repeated verbatim, except one epithet, which improved the line.

After a long absence from Lichfield, when he returned I was apprehensive of something wrong in his constitution, which might either impair his intellect or endanger his life, but, thanks to Almighty God, my fears have proved false.[11]

In the autumn of the year 1725, he received an invitation from his cousin, Cornelius Ford, to spend a few days with him at his house, which I conjecture to have been on a living of his in one of the counties bordering upon Staffordshire; [12] but it seems that discovering that the boy was possessed of uncommon parts, he was unwilling to let him return, and to make up for the loss he might sustain by his absence from school, became his instructor in the classics, and farther assisted him in his studies; so that it was not till the Whitsuntide following, that Johnson went back to Lichfield. Whether Mr. Hunter was displeased to find a visit of a few days protracted into a vacation of many months, or that he resented the interference of another person in the tuition of one of his scholars, and he one of the most promising of any under his care, cannot now be known; but, it seems, that at Johnson's return to Lichfield, he was not received into the school of that city; on the contrary, I am informed, by a person who was his schoolfellow there, that he was placed in one at Stourbridge in Worcestershire, under the care of a master named Winkworth, but who, affecting to be thought allied to the Strafford family, assumed the name of Wentworth.[13]

When his school education was finished, his father, whose circumstances were far from affluent, was for some time at a loss how to dispose of him: he took him home, probably with a view to bring him up to his own trade; for I have heard Johnson say, that he himself was able to bind a book. This suspense continued about two years, at the end whereof, a neighbouring gentleman, Mr. Andrew Corbet, having a son, who had been educated in the same school with Johnson, whom he was about to send to Pembroke College in Oxford, a proposal was made and accepted, that Johnson should attend his son thither, in quality of assistant in his studies; and accordingly, on the 31st day of October, 1728, they were both entered, Corbet as a gentleman commoner, and Johnson as a commoner.[14]

The college tutor, at that time, was a man named Jordan, whom Johnson, though he loved him for the goodness of his nature, so contemned for the meanness of his abilities, that he would oftener risk the payment of a small fine than attend his lectures; nor was he studious to conceal the reason of his absence. Upon occasion of one such imposition, he said to Jordan, 'Sir, you have sconced me twopence for non-attendance at a lecture not worth a penny.'

Whether it was this discouragement in the outset of their studies, or any other ground of disinclination that moved him to it, is not known, but this is certain, that young Corbet could not brook submission to a man who seemed to be little more learned than himself, and that having a father living, who was able to dispose of him in various other ways, he, after about two years stay, left the college, and went home.

But the case of Johnson was far different: his fortunes were at sea; his title to a stipend was gone, and all that he could obtain from the father of Mr. Corbet, was, an agreement, during his continuance at college, to pay for his commons. With no exhibition, or other means of support in the prosecution of his studies, he had nothing to depend on, save the assistance of a kind and indulgent parent. At that time the trade of a country bookseller, even in a city where was a cathedral and an incorporation of ecclesiastics, was less profitable than it is now; for though it may be said, that during the reign of Queen Anne, multitudes of controversial books and pamphlets were publishing, yet these yielded but small advantage to the mere venders of them: there were then no such publications for the mere amusement of young readers or idle persons as the press now daily sends forth; nor had any bookseller entertained in his mind the project of a circulating library: from hence it is evident, that his father, having no other means of subsisting himself and his children, than the ordinary income of his shop, was but little able to afford him any other than a scanty maintenance.

The want of that assistance, which scholars in general derive from their parents, relations, and friends, soon became visible in the garb and appearance of Johnson, which, though in some degree concealed by a scholar's gown, and that we know is never deemed the less honourable for being old, was so apparent as to excite pity in some that saw and noticed him. Shall I be particular, and relate a circumstance of his distress, that cannot be imputed to him as an effect of his own extravagance or irregularity, and consequently reflects no disgrace on his memory? He had scarce any change of raiment, and, in a short time after Corbet

left him, but one pair of shoes, and those so old, that his feet
were seen through them: a gentleman of his college, the father
of an eminent clergyman now living, directed a servitor one morning to place a new pair at the door of Johnson's chamber, who,
seeing them upon his first going out, so far forgot himself and the
spirit that must have actuated his unknown benefactor, that, with
all the indignation of an insulted man, he threw them away.[15]

He may be supposed to have been under the age of twenty,
when this imaginary indignity was offered him, a period of life at
which, so far as concerns the knowledge of mankind, and the
means of improving adverse circumstances, everyone has much to
learn: he had, doubtless, before this time, experienced 'the proud
man's contumely'; and in this school of affliction might have first
had reason to say,—

> Slow rises worth by poverty deprest.[16]

his spirit was, nevertheless, too great to sink under this depression. His tutor, Jordan, in about a year's space, went off to a living which he had been presented to, upon giving a bond to resign
it in favour of a minor, and Johnson became the pupil of Mr.
Adams, a person of far superior endowments, who afterwards attained a doctor's degree, and is at this time head of his college.
Encouraged, by a change so propitious to his studies, he prosecuted them with diligence, attended both public and private lectures, performed his exercises with alacrity, and in short, neglected
no means or opportunities of improvement. He had at this time
a great emulation, to call it by no worse a name, to excel his competitors in literature. There was a young gentleman of his college,
named Meekes, whose exercises he could not bear to hear commended; and whenever he declaimed or disputed in the hall,
Johnson would retire to the farthest corner thereof, that he might
be out of the reach of his voice.[17]

In this course of learning, his favourite objects were classical
literature, ethics, and theology, in the latter whereof he laid the
foundation by studying the Fathers. If we may judge from the
magnitude of his Adversaria, which I have now by me,[18] his plan
for study was a very extensive one. The heads of science, to the

extent of six folio volumes, are copiously branched throughout it; but, as is generally the case with young students, the blank far exceed in number the written leaves.

To say the truth, the course of his studies was far from regular: he read by fits and starts, and, in the intervals, digested his reading by meditation, to which he was ever prone. Neither did he regard the hours of study, farther than the discipline of the college compelled him. It was the practice in his time, for a servitor, by order of the master, to go round to the rooms of the young men, and knocking at the door, to inquire if they were within, and, if no answer was returned, to report them absent: Johnson could not endure this intrusion, and would frequently be silent, when the utterance of a word would have insured him from censure; and, farther to be revenged for being disturbed when he was as profitably employed as perhaps he could be, would join with others of the young men in the college in hunting, as they called it, the servitor, who was thus diligent in his duty; and this they did with the noise of pots and candlesticks, singing to the tune of 'Chevy Chase,' the words in that old ballad,

To drive the deer with hound and horn, &c.

not seldom to the endangering the life and limbs of the unfortunate victim.

These, and other such levities, marked his behaviour for a short time after his coming to college; but he soon convinced those about him, that he came thither for other purposes than to make sport either for himself or them. His exercises were applauded, and his tutor was not so shallow a man, but that he could discover in Johnson great skill in the classics, and also a talent for Latin versification, by such compositions as few of his standing could equal.[19] Mr. Jordan taking advantage, therefore, of a transgression of this his pupil, the absenting himself from early prayers, imposed on him for a vacation exercise, the task of translating into Latin verse the *Messiah* of Mr. Pope, which being shown to the author of the original, by a son of Dr. Arbuthnot, then a gentleman commoner of Christ Church, and brother of the late Mr. Arbuthnot of the Exchequer Office, was read, and returned with this encomium: 'The writer of this poem will leave it a question for posterity, whether his or mine be the original.' This translation found its way into a miscellany published by subscription at Oxford, in the year 1731, under the name of J. Husbands.[20]

He had but little relish for mathematical learning, and was content with such a degree of knowledge in physics, as he could not but acquire in the ordinary exercises of the place: his fortunes and circumstances had determined him to no particular course of study, and were such as seemed to exclude him from every one of the learned professions. He, more than once, signified to a friend who had been educated at the same school with him, then at Christ Church, and intended for the bar,[21] an inclination to the practice of the civil or the common law; the former of these required a long course of academical institution, and how to succeed in the latter, he had not learned; but his father's inability to support him checked these wishes, and left him to seek the means of a future subsistence. If nature could be said to have pointed out a profession for him, that of the bar seems to have been it: in that faculty, his acuteness and penetration, and above all, his nervous and manly elocution, could scarcely have failed to distinguish him, and to have raised him to the highest honours of that lucrative profession; but, whatever nature might have intended for him, fortune seems to have been the arbiter of his destiny, and by shutting up the avenues to wealth and civil honours, to have left him to display his talents in the several characters of a moralist, a philosopher, and a poet.

The time of his continuance at Oxford is divisible into two periods, the former whereof commenced on the 31st day of October, 1728, and determined in December, 1729, when, as appears by a note in his diary in these words, '1729 Dec. S. J. Oxonio rediit,' he left that place, the reason whereof, was a failure of pecuniary supplies from his father; but meeting with another source, the bounty, as it is supposed, of some one or more of the members of the cathedral, he returned, and made up the whole of his residence in the university, about three years, during all which time his academical studies, though not orderly, were to an astonishing degree intense.[22] Whoever has perused Mr. Spence's life of Antonio Magliabechi, may discern a near resemblance in their manner of reading, between that person and Johnson: the former, says his author,

seems never to have applied himself to any particular study. A passion for reading was his ruling passion, and a prodigious memory his great talent: he read every book almost indifferently, as they happened to come into his hands: he read them with a surprising quickness, and yet retained, not only the sense of what he read, but, often, all the words and the very manner of spelling them, if there was anything peculiar of that kind in any author.

A like propensity to reading, and an equal celerity in the practice thereof, were observable in Johnson: it was wonderful to see, when he took up a book, with what eagerness he perused, and with what haste his eye, for it has been related, that he had the use of only one, travelled over it: he has been known to read a volume, and that not a small one, at a sitting; nor was he inferior in the power of memory to him with whom he is compared: whatever he read, became his own forever, with all the advantages that a penetrating judgment and deep reflection could add to it. I have heard him repeat, with scarce a mistake of a word, passages from favourite authors, of three or four octavo pages in length. One instance of the greatness of his retentive faculty himself has thought fit to give, in his life of the Earl of Rochester, where may be seen a Latin poem upon Nothing, written by Passerat; for the insertion whereof he had, as it is said, no other aid than his own recollection. How far he approved that method of reading, which he is above said to have pursued, and what value he set on the powers of memory, may be inferred from his character of the former of those persons in his lives of the poets, of whom he thus speaks:

He was remarkable for the power of reading with great rapidity, and of retaining with great fidelity what he so easily collected. He, therefore, always knew what the present question required; and when his friends expressed their wonder at his acquisitions, made in a state of apparent negligence and drunkenness, he never discovered his hours of reading or method of study, but involved himself in affected silence, and fed his own vanity with their admiration and conjectures.

It is little less than certain, that his own indigence, and the inability of his father to help him, called Johnson from the university sooner than he meant to quit it: his father, either during his continuance there, or possibly before, had been by misfortunes rendered insolvent, if not, as Johnson told me, an actual bankrupt. The non-attainment of a degree, which after a certain standing is conferred almost of course, he regretted not: it is true, he soon felt the want of one; but ample amends were afterwards made him, by the voluntary grant of the highest academical honours that two of the most learned seminaries in Europe could bestow.

The advantages he derived from an university education, small as they may hitherto seem, went a great way towards fixing, as well his moral as his literary character: the order and discipline of a college life, the reading the best authors, the attendance on public exercises, the early calls to prayer, the frequent instructions from the pulpit, with all the other means of religious and moral improvement, had their proper effect; and though they left his natural temper much as they found it, they begat in his mind those sentiments of piety which were the rule of his conduct throughout his future life, and made so conspicuous a part of his character.

He could not, at this early period of his life, divest himself of an opinion, that poverty was disgraceful; and was very severe in his censures of that economy in both our universities, which exacted at meals the attendance of poor scholars, under the several denominations of servitors in the one, and sizars in the other: [23] he thought that the scholar's, like the Christian life, levelled all distinctions of rank and worldly pre-eminence; but in this he was mistaken: civil policy had, long before his coming into the world, reduced the several classes of men to a regular subordination, and given servitude its sanction.[24]

Upon his leaving the university, he went home to the house of his father, which he found so nearly filled with relations, that is to say, the maiden sisters of his mother and cousin Cornelius

Ford, whom his father, on the decease of their brother in the summer of 1731, had taken in to board, that it would scarce receive him.[25]

He brought with him a deep sense of religion, a due reverence for the national church, and a respect for its ministers; and these he retained, though he had been a witness to the profligacy of his cousin Ford, which was nearly enough to have effaced all such impressions from a young mind. Having not then seen, as we now do, ecclesiastical benefices advertised for sale, and considered by the purchasers as lay-fees; nor beheld many of the beneficed clergy abandoning the duties of the clerical function to the lowest of their order, themselves becoming gentlemen at large, mixing in all public recreations and amusements, neglecting their studies for cards, preaching the sermons of others, and affecting, in many particulars of their dress, the garb of the laity, in disobedience to the canon which enjoins decency of apparel to ministers: I say, not having been a witness to these late refinements in manners, he, notwithstanding the ferocity of his temper, reverenced the clergy as a body of men, who have been the greatest improvers of learning, and to whom mankind have the highest obligations; but lamented that the race was nearly extinct.

As Johnson's stay at the university was not long enough for him to complete his studies, it is natural to suppose, that at his return to Lichfield, he devoted his time to the improvement of them, and that having no call from thence, he continued there till the death of his father, which, as he has noted it, was in the month of December, 1731.[26]

Being thus bereft of the little support his father was able to afford him, and having not only a profession, but the means of subsistence to seek, he, in the month of March, 1732, accepted of an invitation to the office of under-master or usher of a free grammar school, at Market Bosworth in Leicestershire, founded and endowed by Sir Wolfstan Dixie, Lord Mayor of London in 1586, the upper master whereof had been the Reverend Anthony Blackwall, the author of a well known book on the sacred classics, but was now a Mr. Crompton, a man of far inferior abilities.[27] The patron of this seminary was Sir Wolfstan Dixie, baronet, a descendant of the original founder; and the endowment being

very small, Johnson's residence was in the mansion-house of Sir
Wolfstan adjacent thereto; but the treatment he received from this
person, who, in the pride of wealth, showed no regard for learning or parts, nor respected any man for his mental endowments,
was such that, preferring the chance of the wide world to his patronage, Johnson, in the month of July, in the same year in which
he went to Bosworth, resigned his office, and took leave of a place,
which he could never after speak of but in terms of the utmost
dislike, and even of abhorrence.

By the middle of June, in the year 1732, he was able to estimate
that slender pittance which devolved to him upon the decease
of his father, the amount whereof I find ascertained by a memo-
randum in his diary, which, as it is descriptive of his circumstances
at the time, I here translate.*

1732, June 15, I laid by eleven guineas; on which day I received all
of my father's effects which I can hope for till the death of my mother,
(which I pray may be late), that is to say, twenty pounds; so that I have
my fortune to make, and care must be taken, that in the meantime, the
powers of my mind may not grow languid through poverty, nor want
drive me into wickedness.[28]

In the month of June in the following year, 1733, I find him
resident in the house of a person named Jarvis, at Birmingham,
where, as he has noted in his diary, he rendered into English from
the French, A *Voyage to Abyssinia*, which has since appeared to
be that of Padre Jerome Lobo, a Portuguese Jesuit, with the additions of Mons. l'Abbé Le Grand, very curious and entertaining,
of which the following is a character:

It contains a narration of the endeavours of a company of mis-
sionaries of the author's country to unite the Abyssins to the
church of Rome. It was translated from the original Portugese
into French by l'Abbé Le Grand, who, as Lobo had extended it
no farther than his own concern in the mission, continued it down
to the time when the Jesuits were finally driven out of Ethiopia,
with the addition of fifteen dissertations on subjects relating to
the history, antiquities, government, religion, manners, and nat-

* Here, as elsewhere, the asterisk indicates the omission of a brief passage.

ural history of Abyssinia, and other countries mentioned by the original author.

The preface, which bears stronger marks of Johnson's hand than any part of the work, is calculated to attract attention and credit: it commends the unaffected simplicity of the original narrative, and the learning of M. Le Grand; it acknowledges the omissions and deviations which the translator thought it prudent to make, and it apologizes for any defects that may be discovered. Johnson's disquisitive propensity just dawns in an observation on the erroneous method of the Roman church, in making converts; but there is nothing striking in the composition.

Were we to rest our judgment on internal evidence, Johnson's claim to the title of translator of this work would be disputable; it has scarce a feature resembling him: the language is as simple and unornamented as John Bunyan's; the style is far from elegant, and sometimes it is not even correct. These circumstances, together with frequent mistakes and various orthography, would almost stagger our belief, but that we have the authority of Johnson himself to rely on, who often acknowledged it for his own.[29]

Having completed this translation, which I conjecture he was paid for by some bookseller of Birmingham,[30] who published it in an octavo volume, Johnson, in February, 1733-4, left that place, and returned to Lichfield, from whence, in the month of August following, he issued a proposal, soliciting a subscription to an edition of Politian's poems.[31] The book was to be contained and printed in thirty octavo sheets, and delivered at the price of five shillings; but not meeting with sufficient encouragement, Johnson dropped the design.

From the above particulars it evidently appears, that he had entertained a resolution to depend for a livelihood upon what he should be able, either in the way of original composition, or translation, or in editing the works of celebrated authors, to procure by his studies, and, in short, to become an author by profession; an occupation, which, though it may, in some views of it, be deemed mercenary, as adapting itself to particular occasions and conjunctures, nay, to the interests, passions and prejudices, and even humours of mankind, has yet some illustrious examples, at least in our times, to justify it. It is true, that many persons distinguish between those writings which are the effect of a natural impulse of genius, and those other that owe their existence to interested motives, and, being the offspring of another parent, may, in some sense, be said to be illegitimate; but, Johnson knew of no such distinction, and would never acquiesce in it when made by others: on the contrary, I have, more than once, heard him assert, that he knew of no genuine motive for writing, other than necessity.

In the prosecution of this design, he, in the year 1734, made a tender of assistance to Cave, the editor, printer, and publisher of the *Gentleman's Magazine;* a man of whom I shall hereafter have frequent occasion to speak. The letter of Johnson to Cave, on this occasion, is yet extant, and is here given as a literary curiosity:

Nov. 25, 1734

Sir,

As you appear no less sensible than your readers, of the defects [32] of your poetical article, you will not be displeased, if, in order to the improvement of it, I communicate to you the sentiments of a person, who will undertake, on reasonable terms, sometimes to fill a column.

His opinion is, that the public would not give you a bad reception, if, beside the current wit of the month, which a critical examination would generally reduce to a narrow compass, you admitted, not only poems, inscriptions, &c. never printed before, which he will sometimes supply you with, but likewise short literary dissertations in Latin or English, critical remarks on authors ancient or modern, forgotten poems that deserve revival, or loose pieces, like Floyer's, worth preserving.[33] By this method, your Literary Article, for so it might be called, will, he thinks, be better recommended to the public, than by low jests, awkward buffoonery, or the dull scurrilities of either party.

If such a correspondence will be agreeable to you, be pleased to inform me, in two posts, what the conditions are on which you shall expect it. Your late offer [34] gives me no reason to distrust your generosity. If you engage in any literary projects besides this paper, I have other designs to impart, if I could be secure from having others reap the advantage of what I should hint.

Your letter, by being directed to S. Smith, to be left at the Castle in Birmingham, Warwickshire, will reach

Your humble servant.[35]

To this letter Cave returned an answer, dated 2d December following, wherein he accepted the services of Johnson, and retained him as a correspondent and a contributor to his magazine. This correspondence exhibits a view of the *Gentleman's Magazine* in its rudiments, and may excite a curiosity in the patrons thereof, to trace back to its origin the publication of a miscellany, the fame whereof has extended itself to the most remote parts of the literary world. Histories of the learned men of modern times, and short abridgments of their works, as also such pieces as for their brevity required some vehicle to convey them to posterity, it has been the practice of foreign countries, in their memoirs, and of universities and academies, in their acts and transactions, to give. The historical and memorable diurnal events of the passing times, have also been recorded in publications variously denominated, particularly, in a work, entitled the *Political State of Great Britain*, beginning with the year 1711, and compiled by the well known Abel Boyer. In this are contained debates and speeches in parliament; and also, abstracts of political pamphlets; but of a work that should comprehend intelligence of both these kinds, we know of no exemplar in this country, earlier than the year 1716, when an essay towards such a one was made in the publication of a book, entitled *The Historical Register*, containing, an impartial relation of all transactions foreign and domestic, by a body of men, from whom few would have expected anything of the kind. In short, the editors of the *Historical Register*, were the members of a society, associated about the year above-mentioned, for the purpose of insurance from fire, which, from the badge assumed by them, obtained the denomination of the Sun Fire Office, and is still subsisting in a flourishing state. One of the managing persons in this society, was, if my information misleads me not, a man of the name of Povey, who, by the way, was a great improver of that useful project, the Penny Post, and died within my memory. Having a scheming head, a plausible tongue, and a ready pen, he prevailed on his fellow members to undertake the above publication, foreign as it was to the nature of their institution. In Strype's continuation of Stow's *Survey*,[36] I find the following article respecting this society: 'All persons taking out policies for insurance, must pay two shillings and sixpence per quarter; and, besides their insurance, shall have a book, called the *Historical Register*, left every quarter at their house.'

The *Historical Register* gave also an account of the proceedings of parliament: the first volume contains the speeches in both houses, on the debate on the Septennial Bill; but, so great is the caution observed in drawing them up, that none of those in the House of Lords are appropriated, otherwise, than by such words as these: 'A noble Duke stood up, and said,' 'This speech was answered by a Northern Peer,' and other such vague designations. In those in the House of Commons, the names of the speakers, Mr. Shippen, Mr. Hampden, Sir Richard Steele, and others are given, without any artifices of concealment.

This publication was continued to the year 1737, inclusive, and may be supposed to have been superseded by the *Gentleman's Magazine*, which was then rising very fast in its reputation.

From the *Historical Register* the hint was taken, of a publication, entitled the *Grub-street Journal*, which, besides a brief account of public occurrences, contained criticisms and censures of dull and profane or immoral books and pamphlets, as also, original essays and letters to the editors. The chief conductors of it, were, Dr. John Martyn, then a young physician, afterwards professor of botany in the university of Cambridge, and Dr. Russel, also a physician; the former assumed the name Bavius, and the latter Mævius. Its first publication was in January, 1730, and it meeting with encouragement, Cave projected an improvement thereon in a pamphlet of his own, and in the following year gave to the world the first number of the *Gentleman's Magazine*, with a notification that the same would be continued monthly, incurring thereby a charge of plagiarism, which, as he is said to have confessed it, we may suppose he did not look upon as criminal.

Johnson had not by his letter, herein before inserted, so attached himself to Cave, as not to be at liberty to enter into a closer engagement with any other person: he, therefore, in 1736, made overtures to the Rev. Mr. Budworth, then master of the grammar school at Brerewood, in Staffordshire, and who had been bred under Mr. Blackwall, at Market Bosworth, to become his assistant; but Mr. Budworth thought himself under a necessity of declining them, from an apprehension, that those convulsive motions to which Johnson through life was subject, might render him an object of imitation, and possibly of ridicule, with his pupils.

It may be remembered that in a preceding page, Johnson is said to have resided for some months, in the year 1733,[37] in the house of a person named Jarvis, at Birmingham. To this circumstance, by a conjecture not improbable, may be referred an important event of his life. At that time there dwelt at Birmingham a widow, the relict of Mr. Porter a mercer, who dying, left her, if not well jointured, so provided for, as made a match with her to a man in Johnson's circumstances desirable: report says, she was rather advanced in years; it is certain that she had a son and daughter grown up; the former was in the last war a captain in the navy, and his sister, lately dead, inherited from him a handsome fortune, acquired in the course of a long service. Of her personal charms little can now be remembered: Johnson has celebrated them in an inscription on her tomb at Bromley; but, considering his infirmity, and admitting the truth of a confession, said to have been made by him, that he never saw 'the human face divine,' it may be questioned, whether himself was ever an eye-witness to them. The inscription further declares her to have been of the family of Jarvis, and gives colour to a supposition that she was either a sister or other relation of the Jarvis above-mentioned.[38]

With this person he married, his age being then about twenty-seven. Her fortune, which is conjectured to have been about eight hundred pounds, placed him in a state of affluence, to which before he had been a stranger. He was not so imprudent as to think it an inexhaustible mine; on the contrary, he reflected on the means of improving it. His acquisitions at school and at the university, and the improvement he had made of his talents in the study of the French and Italian languages, qualified him, in an eminent degree, for an instructor of youth in classical literature; and the reputation of his father, and the connections he had formed in and about Lichfield, pointed out to him a fair prospect of succeeding in that useful profession.

There dwelt in the above-mentioned city, a very respectable gentleman, Mr. Gilbert Walmsley, register of the ecclesiastical court of the bishop thereof, to whose house, in his school and also in his university vacations, Johnson was a welcome guest: the same person was also a friend of Captain Garrick, who had for some time been resident at Lichfield, and, by consequence, of Mr. David Garrick, his son. His character is so well portrayed by Johnson, and represents in such lively colours his friendship for him, that it would be injustice to omit the insertion of it, as given in the life of Edmund Smith:—

Of Gilbert Walmsley, thus presented to my mind, let me indulge myself in the remembrance. I knew him very early; he was one of the first friends that literature procured me; and, I hope that, at least, my gratitude made me worthy of his notice.

He was of an advanced age, and I was only not a boy; yet, he never received my notions with contempt. He was a whig, with all the virulence and malevolence of his party; yet difference of opinion did not keep us apart: I honoured him, and he endured me.

He had mingled with the gay world, without exemption from its vices or its follies, but had never neglected the cultivation of his mind; his belief of revelation was unshaken; his learning preserved his principles; he grew first regular, and then pious.

His studies had been so various, that I am not able to name a man of equal knowledge. His acquaintance with books was great, and what he did not immediately know, he could at least tell where to find. Such was his amplitude of learning, and such his copiousness of communication, that it may be doubted whether a day now passes, in which I have not some advantage from his friendship.

At this man's table I enjoyed many cheerful and instructive hours, with companions, such as are not often found; with one who has lengthened, and one who has gladdened life; with Dr. James, whose skill in physic will be long remembered; and with David Garrick, whom I hoped to have gratified with this character of our common friend: but what are the hopes of man! I am disappointed by that stroke of death, which has eclipsed the gaiety of nations, and impoverished the public stock of harmless pleasure.

The benevolent person, so gratefully remembered in the above encomium, knowing the abilities of Johnson, encouraged him in his design of becoming a teacher of literature: he suggested to him the taking a large house, situate in a place adjacent to Lichfield; which, however the name of it be spelled, the common people call Edjal: thither Johnson went, and with him young Garrick, who, though he had been educated in Lichfield school, and was then near eighteen years old, having been diverted in the course of his studies by a call to Lisbon, stood in need of improvement in the Latin and French languages.

The placing Garrick under the tuition of Johnson, was an act of Mr. Walmsley's, and resembles that politic device of country housewives, the placing one egg in the nest of a hen to induce her to lay more: it succeeded so far, as to draw from the families of the neighbouring gentry a few pupils, and among the rest, a son of Mr. Offley, of Staffordshire; a name, that for centuries past, may be traced in the history and records of that county.[39] But, so adverse were his fortunes in this early period, that this well-planned scheme of a settlement disappointed the hopes of Johnson and his friends; for, neither his own abilities, nor the patronage of Mr. Walmsley, nor the exertions of Mrs. Johnson and her relations, succeeded farther than to produce an accession of about five or six pupils; so that his number, at no time, exceeded eight, and of those not all were boarders.

After waiting a reasonable time in hopes of more pupils, Johnson, finding they came in but slowly, had recourse to the usual method of raising a school. In the year 1736, he advertised the instructing young gentlemen in the Greek and Latin languages, by himself, at his house, describing it near Lichfield.[40] That this notification failed of its end, we can scarce wonder, if we reflect, that he was little more than twenty-seven years of age when he published it, and that he had not the vanity to profess teaching all sciences, nor the effrontery of those, who, in these more modern times, undertake, in private boarding schools to qualify young men for holy orders.

By means of a paper which I have now before me, I am able to furnish, what I take to have been his method or plan of institution; and, as it may be deemed a curiosity, and may serve the purpose of future instructors of youth, I here insert it:

When the introduction or formation of nouns and verbs is perfectly mastered, the pupils learn

Corderius, by Mr. Clarke; beginning at the same time to translate out of his introduction. They then proceed to Erasmus, reading him with Clarke's translation. These books form the first class.

Class II. Read Eutropius and Cornelius Nepos, or Justin with the translation. The first class to repeat by memory, in the morning, the rules they had learned before; and, in the afternoon, the Latin rules of the nouns and verbs. They are also, on Thursdays and Saturdays to be examined in the rules they have learned.

The second class does the same while in Eutropius; afterwards, they are to get and repeat the irregular nouns and verbs; and also, the rules for making and scanning verses, in which they are to be examined as the first class.

Class III. Read Ovid's *Metamorphoses* in the morning, and Caesar's *Commentaries* in the afternoon. Continue the Latin rules till they are perfect in them. Proceed then to Leeds's *Greek Grammar*, and are examined as before.

They then proceed to Virgil, beginning at the same time to compose themes and verses, and learn Greek, and from thence pass on to Horace, Terence, and Sallust. The Greek authors afterwards read are, first, those in the Attic dialect, which are Cebes, Aelian, Lucian by Leeds, and Xenophon: next Homer in the Ionic, Theocritus Doric, Euripides Attic and Doric.

From two letters, first inserted in the *Gentleman's Magazine,* and since in sundry other publications, from Mr. Walmsley to his friend the Reverend Mr. Colson, a mathematician, and, in his later years, Lucasian Professor at Cambridge, little is to be learned respecting the history of Johnson and Garrick, at this period: the one wants the date of the month, the other that of the year; and though, in the order of their publication, the one immediately follows the other, there must have been some interval between the times of writing the first and the last. The first is dated in 1737, and as it contains a recommendation of Garrick to Mr. Colson, for instruction in mathematics, philosophy, and human learning, leads us to suppose, that before the time of writing it, Johnson's scheme of taking in boarders had proved abortive. The latter, written in what year we know not, and inserted below, recommends both Johnson and Garrick to his notice, the former as a good scholar and one that gave hopes of turning out a fine tragedy writer; and, we are from good authority assured, that in March, in the year last above-mentioned, they, on horseback, arrived in town together.

Lichfield, March 2.

Dear Sir,

I had the favour of yours, and am extremely obliged to you; but cannot say, I had a greater affection for you upon it, than I had before, being long since so much endeared to you, as well by an early friendship, as by your many excellent and valuable qualifications. And, had I a son of my own, it would be my ambition, instead of sending him to the university, to dispose of him as this young gentleman is.

He and another neighbour of mine, one Mr. S. Johnson, set out this morning for London together. Davy Garrick is to be with you early the next week, and Mr. Johnson to try his fate with a tragedy, and to see to get himself employed in some translation either from the Latin or the French. Johnson is a very good scholar and a poet, and, I have great hopes, will turn out a fine tragedy writer. If it should any ways lay in your way, doubt not but you would be ready to recommend and assist your countryman.

G. Walmsley.[41]

The hope suggested in this letter is grounded on a circumstance which will lead us back to about the year before he quitted his school at Edial. It must be imagined, the instruction of so small a number of scholars as were under his care, left him at leisure to pursue his private studies and amusements, which, for the most part, consisted in desultory reading. Let it not excite wonder in any that shall peruse these memoirs, to be told, that Burton on Melancholy was a book that he frequently resorted to for the purpose of exhilaration, or that, at times, he should find entertainment in turning over Knolles's voluminous and neglected history of the Turks.[42] In the many hours of leisure which he may be said rather to have endured than enjoyed, we must suppose some employed in the contemplation of his fortunes, the means of improving them, and of resisting the adverse accidents to which human life is exposed, and of which he had already had some experience. The stage holds forth temptations to men of genius, which many have been glad to embrace: the profits arising from a tragedy, including the representation and printing of it, and the connections it sometimes enables the author to form, were in Johnson's idea inestimable; and, it is not impossible, but that Garrick, who, before this time, had manifested a propensity towards the stage, had suggested to him the thought of writing one: certain it is, that during his residence at Edial, and under the eye of his friend Mr. Walmsley, he planned and completed that poem which gave this gentleman occasion to say, he was likely to become a fine tragedy writer.[43]

1737-1739

T NOWHERE appears that, in this journey to London, Mrs. Johnson was one of the company; it is rather to be conjectured, that her husband, having abandoned the hope of succeeding in his attempt to raise a school, left to her the care of the house, and the management of the small part of her fortune, which, after the fitting up and furnishing the same, together with two years' expenditure, must be supposed to be left; and, that this could be no other than small, may be inferred from her natural temper, which it is said was as little disposed to parsimony as that of her husband.

It is not my intention to pursue the history of Mr. Garrick's progress in life, both because I have not taken upon me to be his biographer, and, because the principal events of it occur in the memoirs of him, written with great candour and, I dare say, truth, by Mr. Thomas Davies, and by him published in two volumes, octavo; but the course of this narration requires me occasionally to mention such particulars concerning him, as in any manner connect him with the subject I am engaged in; and this leads me to mention a fact concerning them both, that I had from a person now living, who was a witness to it, and of whose veracity the least doubt cannot be entertained. They had been but a short time in London before the stock of money that each set out with, was nearly exhausted; and, though they had not, like the prodigal son, 'wasted their substance in riotous living,' they

began, like him, 'to be in want.' In this extremity, Garrick suggested the thought of obtaining credit from a tradesman, whom
he had a slight knowledge of, Mr. Wilcox, a bookseller, in the
Strand: to him they applied, and representing themselves to him,
as they really were, two young men, friends, and travellers from
the same place, and just arrived with a view to settle here, he
was so moved with their artless tale, that, on their joint note, he
advanced them all that their modesty would permit them to ask,
(five pounds), which was, soon after, punctually repaid.

It has been before related, that Johnson had engaged his pen
in the service of Cave; as it seems, under some fictitious name,
perhaps, that common one of Smith, which he directs Cave to
address him by, in his letter of 25th Nov., 1734. Being now come
to town, and determined, or rather constrained, to rely on the
labour of his brain for support, he, to improve the correspondence
he had formed, thought proper to discover himself, and in his
real name to communicate to Cave a project which he had
formed, and which the following letter will explain:

> Greenwich, next door to the Golden Heart,
> Church Street, July 12, 1737.
>
> Sir,
> Having observed in your papers very uncommon offers of encourage-
> ment to men of letters, I have chosen, being a stranger in London,
> to communicate to you the following design, which, I hope, if you join
> in it, will be of advantage to both of us.
> The history of the Council of Trent, having been lately translated
> into French, and published with large notes by Dr. Le Courayer, the
> reputation of that book is so much revived in England, that, it is
> presumed, a new translation of it from the Italian, together with Le
> Courayer's notes from the French, could not fail of a favourable re-
> ception.
> If it be answered that the history is already in English, it must be
> remembered that there was the same objection against Le Courayer's
> undertaking, with this disadvantage, that the French had a version by
> one of their best translators, whereas you cannot read three pages of
> the English history without discovering that the style is capable of
> great improvements; but whether those improvements are to be ex-
> pected from this attempt, you must judge from the specimen, which,
> if you approve the proposal, I shall submit to your examination.

Suppose the merit of the versions equal, we may hope that the addition of the notes will turn the balance in our favour, considering the reputation of the annotator.

Be pleased to favour me with a speedy answer, if you are not willing to engage in this scheme; and appoint me a day to wait on you, if you are.

I am, Sir, your humble servant,
Sam. Johnson.

Cave's acquiescence, in the above proposal, drew Johnson into a close intimacy with him: he was much at St. John's Gate, and taught Garrick the way thither. Cave had no great relish for mirth, but he could bear it; and having been told by Johnson, that his friend had talents for the theatre, and was come to London with a view to the profession of an actor, expressed a wish to see him in some comic character: Garrick readily complied; and, as Cave himself told me, with a little preparation of the room over the great arch of St. John's Gate, and, with the assistance of a few journeymen printers, who were called together for the purpose of reading the other parts, represented, with all the graces of comic humour, the principal character in Fielding's farce of *The Mock-Doctor*.

Cave's temper was phlegmatic: though he assumed, as the publisher of the magazine, the name of Sylvanus Urban, he had few of those qualities that constitute the character of urbanity. Judge of his want of them by this question, which he once put to an author: [1] 'Mr. ――――, I hear you have just published a pamphlet, and am told there is a very good paragraph in it, upon the subject of music: did you write that yourself?' His discernment was also slow; and as he had already at his command some writers of prose and verse, who, in the language of booksellers are called good hands,[2] he was the backwarder in making advances, or courting an intimacy with Johnson. Upon the first approach of a stranger, his practice was to continue sitting, a posture in which he was ever to be found, and, for a few minutes, to continue silent: if at any time he was inclined to begin the discourse, it was generally by putting a leaf of the magazine, then in the press, into the hand of his visitor, and asking his opinion of it. I remember that, calling in on him once, he gave me to read the beautiful poem of Collins, written for Shakespeare's *Cymbeline*, 'To fair Fidele's grassy

tomb,' which, though adapted to a particular circumstance in the
play, Cave was for inserting in his magazine, without any reference to the subject: I told him it would lose of its beauty if it
were so published: this he could not see; nor could he be convinced of the propriety of the name Fidele: he thought Pastora a
better, and so printed it.[3]

He was so incompetent a judge of Johnson's abilities, that,
meaning at one time to dazzle him with the splendour of some
of those luminaries in literature who favoured him with their
correspondence, he told him that, if he would, in the evening, be
at a certain alehouse in the neighbourhood of Clerkenwell, he
might have a chance of seeing Mr. Browne and another or two
of the persons mentioned in the preceding note: Johnson accepted
the invitation; and being introduced by Cave, dressed in a loose
horseman's coat, and such a great bushy uncombed wig as he
constantly wore, to the sight of Mr. Browne, whom he found
sitting at the upper end of a long table, in a cloud of tobacco
smoke, had his curiosity gratified.

Johnson saw very clearly those offensive particulars that made
a part of Cave's character; but, as he was one of the most quick-
sighted men I ever knew in discovering the good and amiable
qualities of others, a faculty which he has displayed, as well in
the life of Cave, as in that of Savage, printed among his works, so
was he ever inclined to palliate their defects; and, though he was
above courting the patronage of a man, whom, in respect of his
mental endowments he considered as his inferior, he disdained
not to accept it, when tendered with any degree of complacency.

And this was the general tenor of Johnson's behaviour; for,
though his character through life was marked with a roughness
that approached to ferocity, it was in the power of almost everyone to charm him into mildness, and to render him gentle and
placid, and even courteous, by such a patient and respectful attention as is due to everyone, who, in his discourse, signifies a
desire either to instruct or delight. Bred to no profession, without
relations, friends, or interest, Johnson was an adventurer in the
wide world, and had his fortunes to make: the arts of insinuation
and address were, in his opinion, too slow in their operation to
answer his purpose; and, he rather chose to display his parts to

all the world, at the risk of being thought arrogant, than to wait for the assistance of such friends as he could make, or the patronage of some individual that had power or influence, and who might have the kindness to take him by the hand, and lift him into notice. With all that asperity of manners with which he has been charged, and which kept at a distance many, who, to my knowledge, would have been glad of an intimacy with him, he possessed the affections of pity and compassion in a most eminent degree. In a mixed company, of which I was one, the conversation turned on the pestilence which raged in London, in the year 1665, and gave occasion to Johnson to speak of Dr. Nathanael Hodges, who, in the height of that calamity, continued in the city, and was almost the only one of his profession that had the courage to oppose the endeavours of his art to the spreading of the contagion. It was the hard fate of this person, a short time after, to die a prisoner for debt, in Ludgate: Johnson related this circumstance to us, with the tears ready to start from his eyes; and, with great energy said, 'Such a man would not have been suffered to perish in these times.'

It seems by the event of this first expedition, that Johnson came to London for little else than to look about him: it afforded him no opportunity of forming connections, either valuable in themselves, or available to any future purpose of his life. Mr. Pope had seen and commended his translation of the *Messiah;* but Johnson had not the means of access to him; and, being a stranger to his person, his spirit would not permit him to solicit so great a favour from one, who must be supposed to have been troubled with such kind of applications. With one person, however, he commenced an intimacy, the motives to which, at first view, may probably seem harder to be accounted for, than any one particular in his life. This person was Mr. Richard Savage, whose misfortunes, together with his vices, had driven him to St. John's Gate, and thereby introduced him to the acquaintance of Johnson, which, founded on his part in compassion, soon improved into friendship and a mutual communication of sentiments and counsels. The history of this man is well known by the life of him written by Johnson; which, if in no other respect valuable, is curious, in that it gives to view a character self-formed, as owing nothing to parental nurture, and scarce anything to moral tuition, and describes a mind, in which, as in a neglected garden, weeds, without the least obstruction, were suffered to grow into luxu-riance: nature had endowed him with fine parts, and those he cultivated as well as he was able; but his mind had received no moral culture; and for want thereof, we find him to have been a stranger to humility, gratitude, and those other virtues that tend to conciliate the affections of men, and insure the continuance of friendship.

It may be conjectured that Johnson was captivated by the ad-dress and demeanour of Savage, at his first approach; for it must be noted of him, that, though he was always an admirer of genteel manners, he at this time had not been accustomed to the conversa-tion of gentlemen; and Savage, as to his exterior, was, to a re-markable degree, accomplished: he was a handsome, well-made man, and very courteous in the modes of salutation. I have been told, that in the taking off his hat and disposing it under his arm, and in his bow, he displayed as much grace as those actions were capable of; and that he understood the exercise of a gentleman's weapon, may be inferred from the use he made of it in that rash encounter which is related in his life, and to which his greatest misfortunes were owing.[4] These accomplishments, and the ease and pleasantry of his conversation, were, probably, the charms that wrought on Johnson, and hid from his view those baser qualities of Savage, with which, as his historian, he has neverthe-less been necessitated to mark his character. The similarity of their circumstances might farther conduce to beget an unreserved con-fidence in each other; they had both felt the pangs of poverty and the want of patronage: Savage had let loose his resentment against the possessors of wealth, in a collection of poems printed about the year 1727, and Johnson was ripe for an avowal of the same sentiments: they seemed both to agree in the vulgar opinion, that the world is divided into two classes, of men of merit without riches, and men of wealth without merit; never considering the possibility that both might concenter in the same person, just as when, in the comparison of women, we say, that virtue is of more value than beauty, we forget that many are possessed of both.

In speculations of this kind, and a mutual condolence of their fortunes, they passed many a melancholy hour, and those at a time when, it might be supposed, the reflection on them had made repose desirable: on the contrary, that very reflection is known to have interrupted it. Johnson has told me, that whole nights have been spent by him and Savage in conversations of this kind, not under the hospitable roof of a tavern, where warmth might have invigorated their spirits, and wine dispelled their care; but in a perambulation round the squares of Westminster, St. James's in particular, when all the money they could both raise was less than sufficient to purchase for them the shelter and sordid comforts of a night cellar.

Of the result of their conversation little can now be known, save, that they gave rise to those principles of patriotism, that both, for some years after, avowed; they both with the same eye saw, or believed they saw, that the then minister [5] meditated the ruin of this country; that excise laws, standing armies, and penal statutes, were the means by which he meant to effect it; and, at the risk of their liberty, they were bent to oppose his measures; they might possibly have been encouraged by the success of Swift in his endeavours to obstruct the circulation of Wood's halfpence, who was prompted by his patriotism to say, 'Give me pen, ink, and paper, and ensure me against prosecution, and I will engage to write down any ministry whatever.' But Savage's spirit was broken by the sense of his indigence, and the pressure of those misfortunes which his imprudence had brought on him, and Johnson was left alone to maintain the contest.

The character and manners of Savage were such, as leave us little room to think, that Johnson could profit by his conversation: whatever were his parts and accomplishments, he had no reading, and could furnish no intelligence to such a mind as Johnson's: his vagrant course of life had made him acquainted with the town and its vices; and though I am not warranted to say, that Johnson was infected with them, I have reason to think, that he reflected with as little approbation on the hours he spent with Savage as on any period of his life.

Doubtless there is in the demeanour and conversation of some men a power that fascinates, and suspends the operation of our

own will: to this power in Savage, which consisted in the gentle-
ness of his manners, the elegance of his discourse, and the vivacity
of his imagination, we must attribute the ascendant which he
maintained over the affections of Johnson, and the inability of
the latter to pursue the suggestions of his own superior understanding.[6]

The intimacy between Savage and Johnson continued till the
beginning of the year 1738, when the distresses of the former, and
the cessation, by the death of Queen Caroline, of a pension,
which, for some years, she had directed to be paid him, moved
some of his friends to a subscription for his support, in a place so
far distant from the metropolis, as to be out of the reach of its
temptations; where he might beget new habits, and indulge himself in those exercises of his imagination, which had been the
employment of his happiest hours. The place fixed on for his
residence was Swansea in Wales; but as it was some time before
the subscription could be completed, his retirement thither was
retarded.

In this suspense of Savage's fortunes, Johnson seems to have
confirmed himself in a resolution of quarreling with the administration of public affairs, and becoming a satirist on the manners of
the times; and because he thought he saw a resemblance between
his own and those of Rome in its decline, he chose to express his
sense of modern depravity by an imitation of the third satire of
Juvenal, in which, with great judgment, and no less asperity, he
drew a parallel between the corruptions of each, and exemplified
it by characters then subsisting. In it he anticipated the departure
of his friend Thales, i.e. Savage, whom he describes as

> _____resolv'd, from vice and London far,
> To breathe, in distant fields, a purer air;
> And, fix'd on [7] Cambria's solitary shore,
> Give to St. David one true Briton more.

To this exercise of his talent he was, probably, excited by the
success of Mr. Pope, who had done the same by some of the
satires of Horace, and had vindicated, by the example of Dr.

Donne, a divine, that species of writing, even in Christian times, from the imputation of malevolence and the want of that charity 'which is not easily provoked, and endureth all things.'

The poem was finished, as appears by a manuscript note of the author in his own corrected copy, in 1738. While he was writing it, he lodged in an upper room of a house in Exeter Street, behind Exeter 'change, inhabited by one Norris, a staymaker; [8] a particular which would have been hardly worth noticing, but that it, in some measure, bespeaks his circumstances at the time, and accounts for his having, more than once, mentioned in the poem, and that with seeming abhorrence, the dungeons of the Strand. It is not unlikely that his aversion to such an abode was increased by the reflection on that distress, which by this time had brought his wife to town, and obliged her to participate in the inconveniences of a dwelling too obscure to invite resort, and to be a witness of the difficulties with which he was struggling.

Having completed his poem, he looked round for a bookseller, to whom, with a likelihood of obtaining the value of it, he might treat for the sale of it. His friend Cave, in respect of publications, was a haberdasher of small wares; the greatest of his undertakings being a translation of Du Halde's *History of China*, which was never completed.

Johnson thinking him a man for his purpose, made him an offer of his poem, in a letter in which, with great art, but without the least violation of truth, he conceals that himself was the author of it. The letter I here insert, as also another of his on the same subject.

Sir,

When I took the liberty of writing to you a few days ago, I did not expect a repetition of the same pleasure so soon, for a pleasure I shall always think it to converse in any manner with an ingenious and candid man; but having the enclosed poem in my hands to dispose of for the benefit of the author (of whose abilities I shall say nothing since I send you his performance,) I believed I could not procure more advantageous terms from any person than from you, who have so much distinguished yourself by your generous encouragement of poetry, and whose judgment of that art, nothing but your commendation of my trifle [9] can give me any occasion to call in question. I do not doubt but you will look over this poem with another eye, and reward it in a different manner from a mercenary bookseller, who counts the lines he is to purchase, and considers nothing but the bulk. I cannot help taking notice that, besides what the author may hope for on account of his abilities, he has likewise another claim to your regard, as he lies at present under very disadvantageous circumstances of fortune. I beg, therefore, that you will favour me with a letter tomorrow, that I may know what you can afford to allow him, that he may either part with it to you, or find out (which I do not expect) some other way more to his satisfaction.

I have only to add, that I am sensible I have transcribed it very coarsely, which, after having altered it, I was obliged to do. I will, if you please to transmit the sheets from the press, correct it for you, and will take the trouble of altering any stroke of satire which you may dislike.

By exerting on this occasion your usual generosity, you will not only encourage learning and relieve distress, but (though it be in comparison of the other motives of very small account) oblige in a very sensible manner, Sir,

Your very humble servant,
Sam. Johnson.

Monday, No. 6, Castle Street.

Sir,

I am to return you thanks for the present you were so kind to send me, and to entreat that you will be pleased to inform me, by the Penny-Post, whether you resolve to print the poem. If you please to send it me by the post, with a note to Dodsley,[10] I will go and read the lines to him, that we may have his consent to put his name in the title page. As to the printing, if it can be set immediately about, I will be so much the author's friend, as not to content myself with mere solicitations in his favour. I propose, if my calculation be near the truth, to engage for the reimbursement of all that you shall lose by an impression of 500, provided, as you very generously propose, that the profit, if any, be set aside for the author's use, excepting the present you made, which, if he be a gainer, it is fit he should repay. I beg you will let one of your servants write an exact account of the expense of such an impression, and send it with the poem, that I may know what I engage for. I am very sensible, from your generosity on this occasion, of your regard to learning, even in its unhappiest state; and cannot but think such a temper deserving of the gratitude of those, who suffer so often from a contrary disposition.

I am, Sir,

Your most humble servant,

Sam. Johnson.

Johnson and Dodsley were soon agreed; the price asked by the one and assented to by the other, was, as I have been informed, fifty pounds; [11] a reward for his labour and ingenuity, that induced Johnson ever after to call Dodsley his patron. It came abroad in the year above-mentioned with the name of Cave as the printer, though without that of the author. Lord Lyttelton, the instant it was published, carried it in rapture to Mr. Pope, who, having read it, commended it highly, and was very importunate with Dodsley to know the author's name; but, that being a secret the latter was bound not to reveal, Pope assured him that he could not long be unknown, recollecting, perhaps, a passage recorded of Milton, who, seeing a beautiful young lady pass him whom he had never seen before, turned to look at her, and said, 'Whoever thou art, thou canst not long be concealed.'

The topics of this spirited poem, so far as it respects this country, or the time when it was written, are evidently drawn from those weekly publications, which, to answer the view of a malevolent faction, first created, and for some years supported, a distinction between the interests of the government and the people, under the several denominations of the court and the country parties: these publications were carried on under the direction of men, professing themselves to be Whigs and friends of the people, in a paper entitled, *The Country Journal or the Craftsman*, now deservedly forgotten, the end whereof was, to blow the flame of national discontent, to delude the honest and well-meaning people of this country into a belief that the minister was its greatest enemy, and that his opponents, only, meant its welfare. To this end it was necessary to furnish them with subjects of complaint, and these were plentifully disseminated among them; the chief of them were, that science was unrewarded, and the arts neglected; that the objects of our politics were peace and the extension of commerce; that the wealth of the nation was unequally divided, for that, while some were poor, others were able to raise palaces and purchase manors; that restraints were laid on the stage; that the land was plundered, and the nation cheated; our senators hirelings, and our nobility venal; and, lastly, that in his visits to his native country, the king drained this of its wealth.

That Johnson has adopted these vulgar complaints, his poem must witness. I shall not take upon me to demonstrate the fallacy of most of the charges contained in it, nor animadvert on the wickedness of those, who, to effect their own ambitious designs, scruple not to oppose the best endeavours of the person in power, nor shall I mark the folly of those who suffer themselves to be so deluded: the succession of knave to knave, and fool to fool, is hereditary and interminable: our fathers were deceived by the pretensions of false patriots; the delusion stopped not with their children nor will it with ours.

The publication of this poem was of little advantage to Johnson, other than the relief of his immediate wants: it procured him fame but no patronage. He was therefore disposed to embrace any other prospect of advantage that might offer; for, a short time after, viz. in August, 1738,[12] hearing that the mastership of Appleby School in Leicestershire was become vacant, he, by the advice of Sir Thomas Griesly a Derbyshire baronet, and other friends, went to Appleby, and offered himself as a candidate for that employment; but the statutes of the school requiring, that the person chosen should be a Master of Arts, his application was checked. To get over this difficulty, he found means to obtain from the late Lord Gower, a letter to a friend of his, soliciting his interest with Dean Swift towards procuring him a master's degree from the university of Dublin: the letter has appeared in print, but with a mistaken date of the year, viz. 1737; for it mentions Johnson's being the author of the poem of *London*, which, as I have above fixed it, was written in 1738. It is as follows: [13]

Sir,

Mr. Samuel Johnson, (author of *London* a satire, and some other poetical pieces,) is a native of this country, and much respected by some worthy gentlemen in his neighbourhood, who are trustees of a charity school now vacant, the certain salary of which is 60£. per year, of which they are desirous to make him master; but, unfortunately, he is not capable of receiving their bounty, which would make him happy for life, by not being a Master of Arts, which, by the statutes of this school, the master of it must be.

Now these gentlemen do me the honour to think, that I have interest enough in you to prevail upon you to write to Dean Swift, to persuade the university of Dublin to send a diploma to me, constituting this poor man Master of Arts in their university. They highly extol the man's learning and probity, and will not be persuaded that the university will make any difficulty of conferring such a favour upon a stranger, if he is recommended by the Dean. They say he is not afraid of the strictest examination, though he is of so long a journey, and will venture it if the Dean thinks it necessary, choosing rather to die upon the road, than to be starved to death in translating for booksellers, which has been his only subsistence for some time past.

I fear there is more difficulty in this affair than these good natured gentlemen apprehend, especially, as their election cannot be delayed longer than the 11th of next month. If you see this matter in the same light that it appears to me, I hope you will burn this and pardon me for giving you so much trouble about an impracticable thing; but if you think there is a probability of obtaining the favour asked, I am sure your humanity and propensity to relieve merit in distress, will incline you to serve the poor man, without my adding any more to the trouble I have already given you, than assuring you that I am, with great truth,

Sir,
Your faithful humble servant,

Trentham, August 1, 1737.   Gower.

If ever Johnson had reason to lament the shortness of his stay at the university, it was now. The want of an honour, which, after a short efflux of years, is conferred almost of course, was, at this crisis, his greatest misfortune: it stood between him and the acquisition of an income of 60£. a year, in a country and at a time that made it equivalent to a much larger sum at present.

The letter of Lord Gower failing of its effect, Johnson returned to London, resolving on a vigorous effort to supply his wants: this was a translation into English of Father Paul's *History of the Council of Trent*: the former by Sir Nathaniel Brent, though a faithful one, being, in the judgment of some persons, rather obsolete. Johnson was well enough skilled in the Italian language for the undertaking, and was encouraged to it by many of his friends; as namely, Mr. Walmsley, Mr. Caslon the letter-founder, Mr. [afterwards Dr.] Birch, and others; but he chose to make it a joint project, and take Cave into the adventure, who, as the work proceeded, advanced him small sums, at two or three guineas a week, amounting together to near fifty pounds.[14]

It happened at this time that another person of the same Christian and surname,[15] the then keeper of Dr. Tenison's library in St. Martin's Parish, had engaged in the like design, and was supported therein by Dr. Zachary Pearce, and also by most of the bishops, and by many of the dignified clergy, which being the case, the solicitations in behalf of the two versions crossed each other, and rendered both abortive. Twelve quarto sheets of Johnson's were printed off; but what became of the other is not known. This disappointment, however mortifying, did not hinder Johnson from prosecuting a part of his original design, and writing the life of the author, which, with the assistance of a life of him, written by an Italian nobleman, whose name I could never learn, and published in a closely printed duodecimo, he was enabled to complete, and in an abridgment to insert in Cave's magazine.[16]

Various other projects about this time did he form of publications on literary subjects, which, in a subsequent page,[17] by the help of a list in his own handwriting, I have enumerated, but they were either blasted by other publications of a similar nature, or abandoned for want of encouragement.

However, that he might not be totally unemployed, Cave engaged him to undertake a translation of an *Examen* of Pope's *Essay on Man*, written by Mr. Crousaz, a professor in Switzerland, who had acquired some eminence by a treatise on logic of his writing, and also, by his *Examen de Pyrrhonisme*; and of whom Johnson, after observing that he was no mean antagonist, has given this character:—

His mind was one of those in which philosophy and piety are happily united. He was accustomed to argument and disquisition, and perhaps was grown too desirous of detecting faults, but his intention was always right, his opinions were solid, and his religion pure. His incessant vigilance for the promotion of piety disposed him to look with distrust upon all metaphysical systems of theology, and all schemes of virtue and happiness purely rational; and therefore, it was not long before he was persuaded that the positions of Pope, as they terminated for the most part in natural religion, were intended to draw mankind away from Revelation, and to represent the whole course of things as a necessary concatenation of indissoluble fatality; and it is undeniable, that in many passages, a religious eye may easily discover expressions not very favourable to morals or to liberty.

The reputation of the *Essay on Man* soon after its publication invited a translation of it into French, which was undertaken and completed by the Abbé Resnel, and falling into the hands of Crousaz, drew from him first a general censure of the principles maintained in the poem, and afterwards, a commentary thereon containing particular remarks on every paragraph. The former of these it was that Johnson translated,[18] as appears by the following letter of his to Cave, which is rendered somewhat remarkable by his styling himself *Impransus*.[19]

Dear Sir,
I am pretty much of your opinion, that the *Commentary* cannot be prosecuted with any appearance of success; for, as the names of the authors concerned are of more weight in the performance than its own intrinsic merit, the public will be soon satisfied with it. And I think the *Examen* should be pushed forward with the utmost expedition. Thus, 'This day, &c. An Examen of Mr. Pope's essay, &c. containing a succinct account of the philosophy of Mr. Leibnitz on the system of the Fatalists, with a confutation of their opinions, and an illustration of the doctrine of Free-will,' with what else you think proper.

It will, above all, be necessary to take notice, that it is a thing distinct from the *Commentary*.

I was so far from imagining they [the compositors] stood still, that I conceived them to have a good deal beforehand, and therefore was less anxious in providing them more. But if ever they stand still on my account, it must doubtless be charged to me; and whatever else will be reasonable I shall not oppose; but beg a suspense of judgment till morning, when I must entreat you to send me a dozen proposals, and you shall then have copy to spare.

I am, Sir, yours, *impransus*,
Sam. Johnson.

Johnson's translation of the *Examen* was printed by Cave, and came abroad, but without a name, in November, 1738, bearing the title of, *An Examination of Mr. Pope's Essay on Man, Containing a Succinct View of the System of the Fatalists, and a Confutation of Their Opinions; with an Illustration of the Doctrine of Free Will, and an Enquiry What View Mr. Pope Might Have in Touching upon the Leibnitzian Philosophy and Fatalism. By Mr. Crousaz, Professor of Philosophy and Mathematics at Lausanne, &c.*

All the world knows that the *Essay on Man* was composed from the dictamen of Lord Bolingbroke, and it is little less notorious that Pope was but meanly skilled in that sort of learning to which the subject of his poem related: he had not been conversant with the writings or opinions of the different sects of philosophers of whom some maintained and others denied the freedom of the will, and knew little more of the arguments for and against human liberty in opposition to what is called Necessity, than he was able to gather from the controversy between Anthony Collins and his opponents, or that between Dr. Clarke and Leibnitz. He was therefore unable to defend what he had written, and stood a dead mark for his adversaries to shoot at. Fortunate for him it was, that at this crisis there was living such a person as Mr. Warburton; and Pope had for all the remainder of his life reason to reflect with pleasure on the circumstances that brought them acquainted.[20]

The means by which this connection was formed were these: Warburton had distinguished himself as a man of parts and an original thinker by the publication of the *Divine Legation of Moses*, and being acquainted with Jacob Robinson, a bookseller in Ludgate Street, who by a monthly pamphlet containing extracts from and observations on the works of the learned, gave rise to the publications now called reviews, made his use of him. This man held a correspondence with Mr. Pope, which Warburton knowing, he solicited Robinson to bring them together, and Robinson undertook the office, but found it a business of some difficulty, Mr. Pope being at first shy of the proposal; at length, however, he yielded to it, and Warburton testified his thanks in a letter to Robinson for his mediation.

This transaction may be considered as a remarkable epoch in the life of Warburton, and was the leading circumstance to an acquaintance with Mr. Allen of Bath, a marriage with his niece, the subsequent possession of a fair estate, and his promotion to a bishopric.

The fruit of this interview and of the subsequent communications of the parties was, the publication, in November, 1739, of a pamphlet with this title, A Vindication of Mr. Pope's Essay on Man. By the Author of the Divine Legation of Moses. Printed for J. Robinson.

Whether or not Crousaz ever replied to this vindication, I am not at leisure to inquire. I incline to think he did not, and that the controversy rested on the foot of the Examen and the Commentary on the one part, and the Vindication on the other. In the year 1743, Johnson took it into his head to review the argument, and became a moderator in a dispute which, on the side of Warburton, had been conducted with a great degree of that indignation and contempt of his adversary, which is visible in most of his writings. This he did in two letters severally published in the Gentleman's Magazine for the months of March and November in the above year, with a promise of more, but proceeded no farther than to state the sentiments of Mr. Crousaz respecting the poem, from a seeming conviction that he was discussing an uninteresting question.

Johnson had already tried his hand at political satire, and had succeeded in it; and though no new occasion offered, he was either urged by distress or prompted by that clamour against the minister which in the year 1739 was become very loud, to join in the popular cry, and as it were, to carry war into his own quarters. This he did in a pamphlet, entitled, Marmor Norfolciense, or an Essay on an Ancient Prophetical Inscription, in Monkish Rhyme, Lately Discovered near Lynn in Norfolk, by Probus Britannicus.[21]

The inscription mentioned in the title page of the Marmor Norfolciense, as also the relation of the manner of finding it, are, as will be readily supposed, equally fictitious, as the sole end of writing and publishing it was to give occasion for a comment, which should concentrate all the topics of popular discontent: accordingly it is insinuated, because an act of parliament had then lately passed, by which it was enacted that all law proceedings should be in English, that therefore few lawyers understood Latin; and the people are taught to look on the descendants of the Princess Sophia [22] as intruders of yesterday, receiving an estate by voluntary grant, and erecting thereon a claim of hereditary right. The explanation of the prophecy, which is all ironical, resolves itself into an invective against a standing army, a ridicule of the balance of power, complaints of the inactivity of the British lion, and that the Hanover horse was suffered to suck his blood.

A publication so inflammatory as this, could hardly escape the notice of any government, under which the legal idea of a libel might be supposed to exist. The principles it contained were such as the Jacobites of the time openly avowed; and warrants were issued and messengers employed to apprehend the author, who, though he had forborne to subscribe his name to the pamphlet, the vigilance of those in pursuit of him had discovered. To elude the search after him, he, together with his wife, took an obscure lodging in a house in Lambeth Marsh, and lay there concealed till the scent after him was grown cold.[23]

In the same year, 1739, an event arose that gave occasion to Johnson again to exercise his talent of satire; viz. the refusal of a licence for acting a tragedy entitled, *Gustavus Vasa, or the De-liverer of his Country*, written by Henry Brooke, to account for which seeming injury, some previous information, such as I am now about to give, appears necessary.[24]

The places for theatrical representations in this country were anciently the king's palace, and the mansions of the nobility; but as the love of them increased, taverns and other public houses in different parts of the city and suburbs, were fitted up for the purpose, and called playhouses. The usurpation and the principles of the times put a stop to stage entertainments: at the Restoration they were revived, and the places for representation con-structed in the form of theatres: their number, at no time after that period, exceeded four, and in the year 1728, and long before, it was reduced to three, namely, Drury Lane, Lincoln's Inn Fields, and the French playhouse in the Haymarket. In that year, a man, of the name of Odell, took a throwster's shop in Ayliffe Street, Goodman's Fields, and collecting together a number of strolling players of both sexes, opened it as a theatre. Its contiguity to the city, soon made it a place of great resort, and what was apprehended from the advertisement of plays to be exhibited in that quarter of the town, soon followed: the adjacent houses became taverns, in name, but in truth they were houses of lewd resort; and the former occupiers of them, useful manufacturers and industrious artificers, were driven to seek elsewhere for a residence. In the course of the entertainments of this place, the manager ventured to exhibit some few new plays; among the rest a tragedy, entitled, *King Charles the First*, containing sentiments suited to the characters of republicans, sectaries and enthusiasts, and a scenical representation of the events of that prince's disastrous reign, better forgotten than remembered. Sober persons thought that the revival of the memory of past transactions of such a kind as these were, would serve no good purpose, but, on the contrary, perpetuate that enmity between the friends to and opponents of our ecclesiastical and civil establishment, which they had heretofore excited; and for suffering such representations as these, they execrated not so much the author as the manager. In this instance, the indignation of the public was ill-directed: the arguments arising from this supposed abuse of histrionical liberty were not local; they proved too much, and rather applied to stage entertainments in general than to the conduct of a particular manager.

But others looked on this new-erected theatre with an eye more penetrating: the merchants of London, then a grave sagacious body of men, found that it was a temptation to idleness and to pleasure that their clerks could not resist: they regretted to see the corruptions of Covent Garden extended, and the seats of industry hold forth allurements to vice and debauchery. The principal of these was Sir John Barnard, a wise and venerable man, and a good citizen: he, as a magistrate, had for some time been watching for such information as would bring the actors at Goodman's Fields playhouse within the reach of the vagrant laws; but none was laid before him that he could, with prudence, act upon. At length, however, an opportunity offered, which he not only embraced, but made an admirable use of: Mr. Henry Fielding, then a young barrister without practice, a dramatic poet, and a patriot, under the extreme pressure of necessity, had, in the year

1736, written a comedy, or a farce, we may call it either or both, entitled, *Pasquin*, a dramatic satire on the times, and brought it on the stage of the little playhouse in the Haymarket, which, being calculated to encourage popular clamour, and containing in it many reflections on the public councils, furnished reasons for bringing a bill into the House of Commons for prohibiting the acting of any interlude, tragedy, comedy, opera, play, farce, &c. without the authority of his Majesty's letters-patent or a licence from the lord chamberlain. In this bill a clause was inserted on the motion of Sir John Barnard, and a very judicious one it was, by which it was made penal, even with any such patent or licence, to act or represent any such interlude, &c. in any part of Great Britain, except in the city of Westminster and such other places as his Majesty, in person, should reside in.

The operation of this statute was twofold; it subjected theatrical representations to a licence, and suppressed a nuisance. And here let me observe, that although of plays it is said that they teach morality, and of the stage that it is the mirror of human life, these assertions are mere declamation, and have no foundation in truth or experience: on the contrary, a playhouse, and the regions about it, are the very hotbeds of vice: how else comes it to pass that no sooner is a playhouse opened in any part of the kingdom, than it becomes surrounded by an halo of brothels? Of this truth, the neighbourhood of the place I am now speaking of has had experience; one parish alone, adjacent thereto, having to my knowledge, expended the sum of 1300£. in prosecutions for the purpose of removing those inhabitants, whom, for instruction in the science of human life, the playhouse had drawn thither.

Mr. Brooke, the author above-mentioned, having with his eyes open, and the statute of the tenth of George the second staring him in the face, written a tragedy, in which, under pretence of a laudable zeal for the cause of liberty, he inculcates principles, not only anti-monarchical, but scarcely consistent with any system of civil subordination; what wonder is it, that, under a monarchical government, a licence for such a theatrical representation should be refused? or that such a refusal should be followed by a prohibition of the acting it?

This interposition of legal authority was looked upon by the author's friends, in which number were included all the Jacobites in the kingdom, as an infraction of a natural right, and as affecting the cause of liberty. To express their resentment of this injury, they advised him to send it to the press, and by a subscription to the publication, of near a thousand persons, encouraged others to the like attempts. By means of the printed copy anyone is enabled to judge of its general tendency, and, by reflecting on the sentiments inculcated in speeches therein to be found, to measure the injustice done him.

Upon occasion of this publication, Johnson was employed by one Corbet, a bookseller of small note, to take up the cause of this injured author, and he did it in a pamphlet, entitled, *A Compleat Vindication of the Licensers of the Stage, from the Malicious and Scandalous Aspersions of Mr. Brooke, Author of Gustavus Vasa.* 4to. 1739.

Criticism would be ill employed in a minute examination of the *Marmor Norfolciense*, and the *Vindication of the Licensers:* in general it may suffice to say that they are both ironical, that they display neither learning nor wit, and that in neither of them is there to be discovered a single ray of that brightness which beams so strongly in the author's moral and political essays. Did it become a man of his discernment, endowed with such powers of reasoning and eloquence as he possessed, to adopt vulgar prejudices, or, in the cant of the opposition, to clamor against place-men, and pensioners and standing armies? to ridicule the apprehension of that invasion in favour of the pretender, which himself, but a few years after became a witness to, or to compare the improbability of such an event with that of a general insurrection of all who were prohibited the use of gin?

Of all the modes of satire, I know none so feeble as that of uninterrupted irony. The reason of this seems to be, that in that kind of writing the author is compelled to advance positions which no reader can think he believes, and to put questions that can be answered in but one way, and that such an one as thwarts the sense of the propounder. Of this kind of interrogatories the pamphlet I am speaking of seems to be an example; 'Is the man without pension or place to suspect the impartiality or the judgment of those who are entrusted with the administration of public

affairs? Is he, when the law is not strictly observed in regard to
him, to think himself aggrieved, to tell his sentiments in print, to
assert his claim to better usage, and fly for redress to another
tribunal?'

Who does not see that to these several queries the answer must
be in the affirmative? and, if so, the point of the writer's wit is, in
this instance, blunted, and his argument baffled.

In the course of this mock vindication of power, Johnson has
taken a wide scope, and adopted all the vulgar topics of complaint
as they were vented weekly in the public papers, and in the
writings of Bolingbroke, flimsy and malignant as they are.[25]

Such was the conduct of opposition at this time, and by such
futile arguments as the above were the silly people of three kingdoms deluded into a belief, that their liberties were in danger, and
that nothing could save this country from impending ruin, and
that the most formidable of all the evils they had to dread, was
the continuance of the then administration, of which they had
nothing worse to say than that they hated it.

The truth is, that Johnson's political prejudices were a mist
that the eye of his judgment could not penetrate: in all the
measures of government he could see nothing right; nor could he
be convinced, in his invectives against a standing army, as the
Jacobites affected to call it, that the peasantry of a country was
not an adequate defence against an invasion of it by an armed
force. He almost asserted in terms, that the succession to the
crown had been illegally interrupted, and that from Whig politics
none of the benefits of government could be expected. He could
but just endure the opposition to the minister because conducted
on Whig principles; and I have heard him say, that during the
whole course of it, the two parties were bidding for the people.
At other times, and in the heat of his resentment, I have heard
him assert, that, since the death of Queen Anne, it had been the
policy of the administration to promote to ecclesiastical dignities
none but the most worthless and undeserving men: nor would he
then exclude from this bigoted censure those illustrious divines,
Wake, Gibson, Sherlock, Butler, Herring, Pearce, and least of all
Hoadly; in competition with whom he would set Hickes, Brett,
Leslie, and others of the nonjurors, whose names are scarcely now

remembered. From hence it appears, and to his honour be it said, that his principles co-operated with his necessities, and that the prostitution of his talents, taking the term in one and that its worst sense, could not, in justice, be imputed to him.

But there is another, and a less criminal sense of the word prostitution, in which, in common with all who are called authors by profession, he may be said to stand in need of an excuse. When Milton wrote the *Paradise Lost*, the sum he received for the copy was not his motive, but was an adventitious benefit that resulted from the exercise of his poetical faculty. In Johnson's case, as well in the instances above given as almost all the others that occurred during the course of his life, the impulse of genius was wanting: had that alone operated in his choice of subjects to write on, mankind would have been indebted to him for a variety of original, interesting and useful compositions; and translations of some, and new editions of others of the ancient authors. The truth of which assertion I think I may safely ground on a catalogue of publications projected by him at different periods, and now lying before me.* [26]

Under this notion of works written with a view to gain, and those that owe their existence to a more liberal motive, a distinction of literary productions arises which Johnson would never allow; on the contrary, to the astonishment of myself who have heard him, and many others, he has frequently declared, that the only true and genuine motive to the writing of books was the assurance of pecuniary profit. Notwithstanding the boldness of this assertion, there are but few that can be persuaded to yield to it; and, after all, the best apology for Johnson will be found to consist in his want of a profession, the pressure of his necessities, and the example of such men as Castalio, Gesner, and Salmasius, among foreigners; and Fuller, Howell, L'Estrange, Dryden, Chambers, and Hume, not to mention others now living, among ourselves.

The principle here noted was not only in the above instance avowed by Johnson, but seems to have been wrought by him into a habit. He was never greedy of money, but without money could not be stimulated to write. I have been told by a clergyman of some eminence with whom he had been long acquainted,[27] that, being to preach on a particular occasion, he applied, as others under a like necessity had frequently done, to Johnson for help. 'I will write a sermon for thee,' said Johnson, 'but thou must pay me for it.'

Yet he was not so indifferent to the subjects that he was requested to write on, as at any time to abandon either his religious or political principles. He would no more have put his name to an Arian or Socinian tract than to a defence of atheism. At the time when *Faction Detected* came out,[28] a pamphlet of which the late Lord Egmont is now generally understood to have been the author, Osborne the bookseller, held out to him a strong temptation to answer it, which he refused, being convinced, as he assured me, that the charge contained in it was made good, and that the argument grounded thereon was unanswerable.

Indeed whoever peruses that masterly performance must be convinced that a spirit similar to that which induced the Israelites, when under the conduct of their wise legislator, to cry out 'Ye take too much upon ye,' is the most frequent motive to opposition, and that whoever hopes to govern a free people by reason, is mistaken in his judgment of human nature. 'He,' says Hooker, 'that goeth about to persuade a people that they are not well governed, shall never want attentive and favourable hearers': and the same author speaking of legislation in general, delivers this as his sentiment:

Laws politic ordained for external order and regimen amongst men are never framed as they should be, unless presuming the will of man to be obstinate, rebellious and averse from all obedience unto the sacred laws of his nature: In a word, unless presuming man, in regard of his depraved mind, little better than a wild beast, they do accordingly provide, notwithstanding, so to frame his outward actions as that they be no hindrance unto the common good, for which societies were instituted. Unless they do this they are not perfect. (*Eccles. Pol.* Lib. I. Sect. 1. *Ibid.* Sect. 10).

That these were the sentiments of Johnson also, I am warranted to say, by frequent declarations to the same purpose, which I have heard him make; and to these I attribute it, that he ever after acquiesced in the measures of government through the succession of administrations.

It has already been mentioned in the account above given of Savage, that the friends of that ill-starred man had set on foot a subscription for his support, and that Swansea was the place they had fixed on for his residence: the same was completed at the end of the year 1739. Johnson at that time lodged at Greenwich, and there parted with that friend and companion of his midnight rambles, whom it was never his fortune again to see. The event is antedated in the poem of *London*; but in every particular, except the difference of a year, what is there said of the departure of Thales must be understood of Savage, and looked upon as true history.[29] In his life of Savage, Johnson has mentioned the circumstances that attended it, and deplored this separation as he would have done a greater misfortune than it proved: that it was, in reality, none, may be inferred from Savage's inability, arising from his circumstances, his course of life, and the laxity of his mind, to do good to anyone: it is rather to be suspected that his example was contagious, and tended to confirm Johnson in his indolence and those other evil habits which it was the labour of his life to conquer. They who were witnesses of Johnson's persevering temperance in the article of drinking, for, at least, the latter half of his life, will scarcely believe that, during part of the former, he was a lover of wine, that he not only indulged himself in the use of it when he could procure it, but, with a reflex delight, contemplated the act of drinking it, with all the circumstances that render it grateful to the palate or pleasing to the eye: in the language of Solomon 'he looked upon the wine when it was red, when it gave his colour in the cup, and when it moved itself aright.' [30] In contradiction to those, who, having a wife and children, prefer domestic enjoyments to those which a tavern affords, I have heard him assert, that a tavern chair was the throne of human felicity.—'As soon,' said he, 'as I enter the door of a tavern, I experience an oblivion of care, and a freedom from solicitude: when I am seated, I find the master courteous, and the servants obsequious to my call; anxious to know and ready to supply my wants: wine there exhilarates my spirits, and prompts me to free conversation and an interchange of discourse with those whom I most love: I dogmatize and am contradicted, and in this conflict of opinions and sentiments I find delight.'

How far his conversations with Savage might induce him thus to delight in tavern society, which is often a temptation to greater enormities than excessive drinking, cannot now be known, nor would it answer any good purpose to inquire. It may, nevertheless, be conjectured, that whatever habits he had contracted of idleness, neglect of his person, or indifference in the choice of his company, received no correction or check from such an example as Savage's conduct held forth; and farther it is conjectured, that he would have been less troubled with those reflections, which, in his latest hours, are known to have given him uneasiness, had he never become acquainted with one so loose in his morals, and so well acquainted with the vices of the town as this man appears to have been. We are to remember that Johnson was, at this time, a husband: can it therefore be supposed that the society of such a man as Savage had any tendency to improve him in the exercise of the domestic virtues? nay rather we must doubt it, and ascribe to an indifference in the discharge of them, arising from their nocturnal excursions, the incident of a temporary separation of Johnson from his wife, which soon took place, and that, while he was in a lodging in Fleet Street, she was harboured by a friend near the Tower. It is true that this separation continued but a short time, and that if indeed his affection, at that instant, was alienated from her, it soon returned; for his attachment to her appears, by a variety of notes and memorandums concerning her in books that she was accustomed to read in, now in my custody, to have been equal to what it ought to be: nay Garrick would often risk offending them both, by mimicking his mode of gallantry and his uxorious behaviour towards her.

The little profit, or indeed reputation, that accrued to Johnson by the writing of political pamphlets, led him to think of other exercises for his pen. He had, so early as 1734, solicited employment of Cave; but Cave's correspondents were so numerous that he had little for him till the beginning of the year 1738, when Johnson conceived a thought of enriching the magazine with a biographical article, and wrote for it the "Life of Father Paul,"

an abridgment, as it seems to be, of that life of him which Johnson intended to have prefixed to his translation of the *History of
the Council of Trent.* The motive to this and other exertions of
the same talent in the lives of Boerhaave, Blake, Barretier, and
other eminent persons, was his wants, which at one time were so
pressing as to induce him in a letter to Cave, hereinbefore inserted, to intimate to him that he wanted a dinner.

Johnson who was never deficient in gratitude, for the assistance
which he received from Cave became his friend; and, what was
more in Cave's estimation than any personal attachment whatever, a friend to his magazine, for he being at this time engaged in
a controversy with a knot of booksellers the proprietors of a rival
publication, the *London Magazine,* Johnson wrote and addressed
to him the following Ode:

AD URBANUM

> Urbane, nullis fesse laboribus,
> Urbane, nullis victe calumniis,
>   Cui fronte sertum in erudita
>   Perpetuo viret et virebit.
>
> Quid moliatur gens imitantium,
> Quid et minetur, sollicitus parum,
>   Vacare solis perge musis
>   Juxta animo studiisque felix.
>
> Linguae procacis plumbea spicula,
> Fidens, superbo frange silentio;
>   Victrix per obstantes catervas
>   Sedulitas animosa tendet.[31]

.   .   .   .   .   .

It was published in the magazine for March, 1738, and imitated
in the following stanzas in that for the month of May following:

> Hail Urban! indefatigable man,
> Unwearied yet by all thy useful toil!
>   Whom num'rous slanderers assault in vain;

Whom no base calumny can put to foil.
But still the laurel on thy learned brow
Flourishes fair, and shall for ever grow.

What mean the servile imitating crew,
What their vain blust'ring, and their empty noise,
  Ne'er seek: but still thy noble ends pursue,
Unconquer'd by the rabble's venal voice.
  Still to the muse thy studious mind apply,
  Happy in temper as in industry.

The senseless sneerings of an haughty tongue,
Unworthy thy attention to engage,
  Unheeded pass: and tho' they mean thee wrong,
By manly silence disappoint their rage.
  Assiduous diligence confounds its foes,
  Resistless, tho' malicious crowds oppose.

.   .   .   .

May 22, 1738.   Briton.

The provocation that gave rise to this furious contest, as it will
presently appear to have been, was the increasing demand for
Cave's publication, and the check it gave to the sale of its rival,
which at one time was so great as to throw back no fewer than
seventy thousand copies on the hands of the proprietors. To
revenge this injury, the confederate booksellers gave out, that
Sylvanus Urban, whom, for no conceivable reason, they dignified
with the appellation of Doctor, was become mad, assigning as the
cause of his insanity, his publication in the magazine of sundry
mathematical problems, essays and questions on abstruse subjects,
sent him by many of his learned correspondents. Cave who for
some months had been rebutting the calumnies of his adversaries,
and that with such success as provoked them to the outrage above-
mentioned, now felt that he had them at mercy. With that
sagacity which we frequently observe, but wonder at in men of
slow parts, he seemed to anticipate the advice contained in the
second and third stanzas of Johnson's ode, and forbore a reply,
though not his revenge, which he gratified in such a manner as

seems to absolve him from the guilt imputable in most cases to that passion; this he did by inserting as an article of public intelligence in his Historical Chronicle for the month of February, 1738, the following paragraph:

Monday 20. About 8 o'clock the famous Dr. Urban, having some time past been possessed with a violent frenzy, broke loose from his nurse, and run all through the streets of London and Westminster distributing quack bills, swearing he would go visit his beautiful *Garden of Eden*; raving against *Common Sense*, and the London Magazine, and singing a mad song set to music by Peter the Wild Youth; but being at last secured, was conveyed to his lodgings in Moorfields, where he continues uttering horrid imprecations against several booksellers and printers. 'Tis thought this *poor* man's misfortune is owing to his having lately perplexed himself with *biblical questions, mathematical problems, astronomical equations, and* methods to find the longitude.—*This silly paragraph, and such like buffoonery, inserted in the newspapers at the charge of the proprietors of the* London Magazine, *is all the answer given to the remarks on their inimitable preface, some passages of which are quoted in the beginning of this magazine.*

The publication in the manner above-mentioned of this senseless and malignant fiction, and the care and attention of Cave in the compilation of his magazine, together with the assistance he received from a variety of ingenious and learned correspondents, enabled him in a short time to triumph over his rivals, and increased the sale thereof to a number that no other could ever equal.

1740-1744

T WAS no part of Cave's original design to give the debates in either house of parliament, but the opposition to the minister, and the spirit that conducted it, had excited in the people a great eagerness to know what was going forward in both, and he knew that to gratify that desire was to increase the demand for his pamphlet. Indeed the experiment had already been made, for the speeches in parliament had for some time been given in the *Political State of Great Britain,* a publication above spoken of, and though drawn up by persons no way equal to such an undertaking, were well received. These for the most part were taken by stealth, and were compiled from the information of listeners and the under-officers and doorkeepers of either house; but Cave had an interest with some of the members of both, arising from an employment he held in the post office, that of inspector of the franks, which not only gave him the privilege of sending his letters free of postage, but an acquaintance with, and occasions of access to many of them.

Of this advantage he was too good a judge of his own interest not to avail himself. He therefore determined to gratify his readers with as much of this kind of intelligence as he could procure and it was safe to communicate: his resolution was to frequent the two houses whenever an important debate was likely to come on, and from such expressions and particulars in the course thereof as could be collected and retained in memory, to give the arguments on either side. This resolution he put into practice in July, 1736. His method of proceeding is variously reported; but I have been informed by some who were much about him, that taking with him a friend or two, he found means to procure for them and himself admission into the gallery of the House of Commons, or to some concealed station in the other, and that then they privately took down notes of the several speeches, and the general tendency and substance of the arguments. Thus furnished, Cave and his associates would adjourn to a neighbouring tavern, and compare and adjust their notes, by means whereof and the help of their memories, they became enabled to fix at least the substance of what they had so lately heard and remarked.

The reducing this crude matter into form, was the work of a future day, and of an abler hand, viz. Guthrie, the historian, a writer for the booksellers, whom Cave retained for the purpose: the speeches thus composed were given monthly to the public, and perused and read with great eagerness; those who contemplated them thought they discovered in them not merely the political principles, but the style and manner of the speaker; the fact is, that there was little discrimination of the latter between the speeches of the best and the worst orators in either assembly, and in most instances the persons to whom they were ascribed were here made to speak with more eloquence and even propriety of diction, than, in the place of debate they were able to do: Sir John Barnard, for instance, a man of no learning or reading, and who by the way had been bred a Quaker, had a style little better than an ordinary mechanic, and which abounded with such phrases as, if so be—set case—and—nobody more so—and other such vulgarisms, yet was he made in the magazine to debate in language as correct and polished as that of Sir William Wyndham or Mr. Pulteney; though it must be confessed that so weighty was his matter on subjects of commerce, that Sir Robert Walpole, as I have been credibly informed, was used to say, that when he had answered Sir John Barnard, he looked upon that day's business in the House of Commons to be as good as over.

The vigorous opposition to the minister, and the motion in both houses of the thirteenth of February, 1740-1, to remove him, were a new era in politics; and, as the debates on that occasion were warmer than had ever then been known, the drawing them up required, in Cave's opinion, the pen of a more nervous writer than he who had hitherto conducted them. Johnson, who, in his former publications in prose, had given no very favourable specimens of style, had by this time, by the study of the best of our old English writers, such as Sir Thomas More, Ascham, Hooker, Spenser, Archbishop Sandys, Jewel, Chillingworth, Hales of Eton, and others, formed a new one, consisting in original phrases and new combinations of the integral parts of sentences, which, with the infusion of words derived from the Latin and accommodated to our idiom, were such an improvement of the language as greatly tended to enrich it: Cave therefore thought him a fit person to conduct this part of his monthly publication, and, dismissing Guthrie, committed the care of it to Johnson.

Before this change of hands, Cave had been checked by some intimations from the clerks of the House of Commons, that his printing the debates had given offence to the speaker, and might subject him to censure; this he, for some time, regarded but little, relying possibly upon the indulgence that had been shown as well to the publishers of the *Political State of Great Britain*, who were the first that ventured on this practice, as to himself; but a resolution of the house at length gave him to understand, that it would be prudence in him to desist from it. The thought of putting his readers on short allowance was very unpleasing to him, and this, with the apprehension that the sale of his magazine might be affected by the omission of a kind of intelligence which they had been accustomed to, drove him to many contrivances to evade the prohibition, out of which he chose one that scarce any man but himself would have thought of: it was the giving to the public the debates in the British senate under a fictitious designation. Every one, he knew, was acquainted with *Gulliver's Travels;* he therefore, in his magazine for June, 1738, begins the month by feigning, that the debates in the senate of Magna Lilliputia were then extant; and referring to the resolution of the House of Commons, above-mentioned, whereby he was forbidden to insert any account of the proceedings of the British parliament, he pretends to doubt not but his readers will be pleased with the insertion of what he calls the appendix to Captain Gulliver's account of Lilliput, in their room. A change of fictitious for real names of persons, countries, and provinces, was absolutely necessary for the carrying on this design, and accordingly, by transposing the letters, and otherwise anagrammatizing proper names, he has, through the medium of nonsense, given light to that which he would be thought to conceal.[1]

The proprietors of the *London Magazine*, who also gave the debates, but from documents less authentic than those of Cave, compelled by the same necessity that forced him to this artifice, took another course: they feigned to give the debates in the Roman senate, and by adapting Roman names to the several speeches, rendered them more plausible than they appear under Cave's management.

The artifice however succeeded in both instances: the resolution of the Commons was never enforced, and the debates were published with impunity. I will not disgrace my page by the insertion of any of those barbarous appellations which Cave had invented, and which, I dare say, were music to his ear; but content myself with saying, that Guthrie acquiesced in Cave's fiction and the nonsense which it involved, and as it was found to answer its end, Johnson scrupled not to adopt it.

The debates penned by Johnson were not only more methodical and better connected than those of Guthrie, but in all the ornaments of style superior: they were written at those seasons when he was able to raise his imagination to such a pitch of fervour as bordered upon enthusiasm, which, that he might the better do, his practice was to shut himself up in a room assigned him at St. John's Gate, to which he would not suffer any one to approach, except the compositor or Cave's boy for matter, which, as fast as he composed it, he tumbled out at the door.

Never were the force of reasoning or the powers of popular eloquence more evidently displayed, or the arts of sophistry more clearly detected than in these animated compositions. Nor are they more worthy of admiration for these their excellencies than for that peculiarity of language which discriminates the debates of each assembly from the other, and the various colouring which he has found the art of giving to particular speeches. The characteristic of the one assembly we know is Dignity; the privilege of the other Freedom of Expression. To speak of the first, when a member thereof endowed with wisdom, gravity, and experience, is made to rise, the style which Johnson gives him is nervous, his matter weighty, and his arguments convincing; and when a mere popular orator takes up a debate, his eloquence is by him represented in a glare of false rhetoric, specious reasoning, an affectation of wit, and a disposition to trifle with subjects the most interesting. With great judgment also does Johnson adopt the unrestrained oratory of the other house, and with equal facility imitate the deep-mouthed rancour of Pulteney, and the yelping pertinacity of Pitt.[2]

In the perusal of these debates, as written, we cannot but wonder at the powers that produced them. The author had never passed those gradations that lead to the knowledge of men and business: born to a narrow fortune, of no profession, conversant chiefly with books, and, if we believe some, so deficient in the formalities of discourse, and the practices of ceremony, as in conversation to be scarce tolerable; unacquainted with the style of any other than academical disputation, and so great a stranger to senatorial manners, that he never was within the walls of either house of parliament. That a man, under these disadvantages, should be able to frame a system of debate, to compose speeches of such excellence, both in matter and form, as scarcely to be equalled by those of the most able and experienced statesmen, is, I say, matter of astonishment, and a proof of talents that qualified him for a speaker in the most august assembly on earth.

Cave, who had no idea of the powers of eloquence over the human mind, became sensible of its effects in the profits it brought him: he had long thought that the success of his magazine proceeded from those parts of it that were conducted by himself, which were the abridgment of weekly papers written against the ministry, such as the *Craftsman, Fog's Journal, Common Sense,* the *Weekly Miscellany,* the *Westminster Journal,* and others, and also marshalling the pastorals, the elegies, and the songs, the epigrams, and the rebuses that were sent him by various correspondents, and was scarcely able to see the causes that at this time increased the sale of his pamphlet from ten to fifteen thousand copies a month. But if he saw not, he felt them, and manifested his good fortune by buying an old coach and a pair of older horses; and, that he might not incur the suspicion of pride in setting up an equipage, he disclosed to the world the source of his affluence, by a representation of St. John's Gate, instead of his arms, on the door panel. This he told me himself was the reason of distinguishing his carriage from others, by what some might think a whimsical device, and also for causing it to be engraven on all his plate.

Johnson had his reward, over and above the pecuniary recompense vouchsafed him by Cave, in the general applause of his labours, which the increased demand for the magazine implied; but this, as his performances fell short of his powers, gratified him but little; on the contrary, he disapproved the deceit he was compelled to practise; his notions of morality were so strict, that he would scarcely allow the violation of truth in the most trivial instances, and saw, in falsehood of all kinds, a turpitude that he would never be thoroughly reconciled to: and though the fraud was perhaps not greater than the fictitious relations in Sir Thomas More's *Utopia*, Lord Bacon's *Nova Atlantis*, and Bishop Hall's *Mundus Alter et Idem*, Johnson was not easy till he had disclosed the deception.

In the meantime it was curious to observe how the deceit operated. It has above been remarked, that Johnson had the art to give different colours to the several speeches, so that some appear to be declamatory and energetic, resembling the orations of Demosthenes; others like those of Cicero, calm, persuasive; others, more particularly those attributed to such country gentlemen, merchants, and seamen as had seats in parliament, bear the characteristic of plainness, bluntness, and an affected honesty as opposed to the plausibility of such as were understood or suspected to be courtiers: the artifice had its effect; Voltaire was betrayed by it into a declaration, that the eloquence of ancient Greece and Rome was revived in the British senate, and a speech of the late Earl of Chatham when Mr. Pitt, in opposition to one of Mr. Horatio Walpole, received the highest applause, and was by all that read it taken for genuine; [3] and we are further told of a person in a high office under the government, who being at breakfast at a gentleman's chambers in Gray's Inn, Johnson being also there, declared, that by the style alone of the speeches in the debates, he could severally assign them to the persons by whom they were delivered. Johnson upon hearing this, could not refrain from undeceiving him, by confessing that himself was the author of them all.

It must be owned, that with respect to the general principles avowed in the speeches, and the sentiments therein contained, they agree with the characters of the persons to whom they are ascribed. Thus, to instance in those of the upper house, the speeches of the Duke of Newcastle, the lords Carteret and Ilay, are calm, temperate and persuasive; those of the Duke of Argyle and Lord Talbot, furious and declamatory, and Lord Chesterfield's and Lord Hervey's florid but flimsy. In the other house the speeches may be thus characterized; the minister's mild and conciliatory, Mr. Pulteney's nervous, methodical and weighty, Mr. Shippen's blunt and dogmatical, Sir John Barnard's clear, especially on commercial subjects, Lyttelton's stiff and imitative of the Roman oratory, and Pitt's void of argument but rhapsodically and diffusively eloquent. In other particulars the debates of Johnson are liable to the same objections, but in a greater degree, as those of Guthrie; the language of them is too good, and the style such as none of the persons to whom the speeches are assigned were able to discourse in.

The confession of Johnson above-mentioned, was the first that revealed the secret that the debates inserted in the *Gentleman's Magazine* were fictitious, and composed by himself. After that, he was free, and indeed industrious, in the communication of it, for being informed that Dr. Smollet was writing a history of England, and had brought it down to the last reign, he cautioned him not to rely on the debates as given in the magazine, for that they were not authentic, but, excepting as to their general import, the work of his own imagination.[4]

As I shall have but little occasion to say more of the debates in parliament as they appear in the magazine, I shall close the account above given of them with saying, that Johnson continued to write them till the passing the bill for restraining the sale of spirituous liquors, which was about the end of the year 1743.[5] After that they were written by Dr. Hawkesworth, and by him continued to about 1760, within which period the plan of the magazine was enlarged by a review of new publications. In this, Mr. Owen Ruffhead was first employed, but he being, in about two years, invited to superintend a re-publication of the Statutes at large, the office of reviewer dropped into the hands of Dr. Hawkesworth, who, though he was thought to exercise it with some asperity, continued in it till about the year 1772, when he was employed to digest the papers of sundry late navigators, and to become the editor of that collection of voyages which in the catalogues of booksellers is distinguished by his name.

About this time Johnson was solicited to undertake an employment of a kind very different from any he had ever been accustomed to: it was to compile a catalogue of books; a task, which at first view, seems to be not above the capacity of almost the lowest of literary artificers, but on a nearer was found to require the abilities of one of the highest. Osborne the bookseller, had ventured on the purchase of the Earl of Oxford's library of printed books, at the price of 13,000£. and meaning to dispose of them by sale at his shop in the ordinary way, projected a catalogue thereof distributed into commonplaces, in five octavo volumes, which being sold for five shillings each, would pay itself, and circulate throughout the kingdom and also abroad.

It is probable that Osborne had consulted Maittaire, then one of the masters of Westminster School, and who had formerly assisted in making out the *Catalogus Librorum Manuscriptorum Angliae & Hiberniae*, on the subject of his intended catalogue, and that Maittaire might have furnished the general heads or classes under which the several books are arranged, a work of some labour, and that required no small stock of erudition. This at least is certain, that he drew up a Latin dedication of the whole to Lord Carteret, then Secretary of State, and subscribed it with his name; but the under-workmen were, as I conjecture, first Oldys, and afterwards Johnson, who while he was engaged in so servile an employment resembled a lion in harness. The former of these persons was a natural son of Dr. Oldys, a civilian of some eminence, and subsisted by writing for the booksellers. Having a general knowledge of books, he had been long retained in the service of Edward Earl of Oxford, and was therefore by Osborne thought a fit person for his purpose; but whether they disagreed, or that Oldys was hindered by the restraint of his person in the Fleet, a misfortune that he laboured under some time about that period, he desisted, after having proceeded to the end of the second volume. The third and fourth I conceive to be the work of Johnson: [6] the fifth is nothing more than a catalogue of Osborne's old stock.

The catalogue of the Harleian printed books, for of the manuscripts there is another in being, drawn up by an able hand, is of that kind which philologists call Bibliothèque Raisonée, in which besides the title, and the colophon containing the place and year of publication, a description of each article is given, serving to show both its intrinsic and extrinsic worth, the hands through which it has passed, and various other particulars that tend to recommend it.[7]

The catalogue having passed the press, turned out to be very voluminous, and being of a singular kind, Osborne hoped to be able to make the public pay for it; to this end it was, that he directed Johnson to draw up the preface, giving an account of the contents of the library, and containing a variety of arguments to vindicate a solicitation for a subscription, that is to say, a demand of five shillings for each volume of the catalogue, to defray the expense of printing it; the volume or volumes so purchased, to be taken in exchange for any book rated at the same value. This paper was, as I conjecture, a precursor to the catalogue, and was with great industry circulated throughout the kingdom. It answered its end; the catalogue was printed in five octavo volumes, the collectors and lovers of books bought it, and Osborne was reimbursed.

While the catalogue was compiling, Johnson was further employed by Osborne to select from the many thousand volumes of which the library consisted, all such small tracts and fugitive pieces as were of greatest value or were most scarce, with a view to the reprinting and publishing them under the title of the *Harleian Miscellany*. To recommend a subscription for printing the collection, proposals were published containing an account of the undertaking, and an enumeration of its contents, penned by Johnson with great art.[8]

We may well conclude that the proposal met with all due encouragement, as the pieces recommended in it were in the year 1749, published in eight quarto volumes. To the first of them was prefixed, as an introduction, an essay on the origin and importance of small tracts and fugitive pieces.

Osborne was an opulent tradesman, as may be judged from his ability to make so large a purchase as that above-mentioned; he was used to boast that he was worth forty thousand pounds, but of booksellers he was one of the most ignorant: of title pages or editions he had no knowledge or remembrance, but in all the tricks and arts of his trade he was most expert. Johnson, in his life of Pope says, that he was entirely destitute of shame, without sense of any disgrace, but that of poverty. He purchased a number of unsold copies of Mr. Pope's *Iliad*, of the folio size, printed on an inferior paper, and without cuts, and cutting off the top and bottom margins, which were very large, had the impudence to call them the subscription books, and to vend them as such. His insolence to his customers was also frequently past bearing. If one came for a book in his catalogue, he would endeavour to force on him some new publication of his own, and, if he refused, would affront him.

I mention the above particulars of this worthless fellow as an introduction to a fact respecting his behaviour to Johnson, which I have often heard related, and which himself confessed to be true. Johnson, while employed in selecting pieces for the *Harleian Miscellany*, was necessitated, not only to peruse the title page of each article, but frequently to examine its contents, in order to form a judgment of its worth and importance, in the doing whereof, it must be supposed, curiosity might sometimes detain him too long, and whenever it did, Osborne was offended. Seeing Johnson one day deeply engaged in perusing a book, and the work being for the instant at a stand, he reproached him with inattention and delay, in such coarse language as few men would use, and still fewer could brook: the other in his justification asserted somewhat, which Osborne answered by giving him the lie; Johnson's anger at so foul a charge, was not so great as to make him forget that he had weapons at hand: he seized a folio that lay near him, and with it felled his adversary to the ground, with some exclamation, which, as it is differently related, I will not venture to repeat.[9]

This transaction, which has been seldom urged with any other view than to show that Johnson was of an irascible temper, is generally related as an entertaining story: with me it has always been a subject of melancholy reflection. In our estimation of the enjoyments of this life, we place wisdom, virtue, and learning in the first class, and riches and other adventitious gifts of fortune in the last. The natural subordination of the one to the other we see and approve, and when that is disturbed we are sorry. How then must it affect a sensible mind to contemplate that misfortune, which could subject a man endued with a capacity for the highest offices, a philosopher, a poet, an orator, and, if fortune had so ordered, a chancellor, a prelate, a statesman, to the insolence of a mean, worthless, ignorant fellow, who had nothing to justify the superiority he exercised over a man so endowed, but those advantages which Providence indiscriminately dispenses to the worthy and the worthless! to see such a man, for the supply of food and raiment, submitting to the commands of his inferior, and, as a hireling, looking up to him for the reward of his work, and receiving it accompanied with reproach and contumely, this, I say, is a subject of melancholy reflection.

Having completed the Harleian catalogue and miscellany, and thereby disengaged himself from Osborne, Johnson was at liberty to pursue some scheme of profit, less irksome than that in which he had so lately been employed. Biography was a kind of writing that he delighted in; it called forth his powers of reflection, and gave him occasion to contemplate human life and manners. He had made some essays of his talent in the lives of Barretier and Boerhaave, men unknown to him, and was now prompted to give to the world that of a friend with whom he had been closely intimate, whose singular character and adverse fortunes afforded ample scope for discussion, and furnished matter for many admirable lessons of morality.

This friend was Savage, of whom it has above been related, that his friends had undertaken to raise an annual subscription for his support at Swansea in Wales, but that his departure for that place was retarded by some difficulties that occurred in the

course of their endeavours to raise it: these, however, were overcome, and Savage, in July, 1739, took leave of London, and also
of Johnson, who, as himself tells us, parted from him with tears
in his eyes. His subsequent history is, that taking his way through
Bristol, he was for some time detained there by an embargo on
the shipping. After some stay he was enabled to depart, and he
reached Swansea; but not liking the place, and resenting the
treatment of his contributors, who seem to have been slack in
the performance of their engagements to support him, he returned to Bristol with an intent to come to London, a purpose
he was hindered from effecting by an arrest of his person, on the
10th of January, 1742–3, for the small sum of eight pounds, and
carried to Newgate in that city, where, not being able to extricate
himself from his confinement, he, on the 31st day of July, in the
same year, died.

This event, and the affection which he had long entertained
for the man, called forth Johnson to an exercise of his pen, which,
as it is said, employed it only thirty-six hours, in a narrative of
events so singular as could scarcely fail to gratify the curiosity of
every one who wished to be instructed in the science of human
life. The subject was such an one as is seldom exhibited to view;
a man dropped into the world as from a cloud, committed to the
care of those who had little interest in his preservation, and none
in the forming his temper, or the infusing into him those little
precepts of morality, which might germinate in his mind, and be
productive of habitual virtue; these are advantages which children of the lowest birth enjoy, in some degree, in common with
those of a higher; but of these he never participated. All the knowledge he attained to, from his infancy upwards, was self-acquired,
and, bating that he was born in a city where the refinements of
civil life presented to his view a rule of moral conduct, he may
be said to have been little less a miracle than Hai Ebn Yokdhan
is feigned to be.[10]

It has been observed of those children who owe their nurture
and education to a certain benevolent institution in this metropolis,[11] that being by their misfortune strangers to those charities
that arise from the relations of father, son, and brother, their
characters assume a complexion that marks their conduct through

life. The same may be said of Savage, and will perhaps account for that want of gratitude to his benefactors, and other defects in his temper, with which he seems to have been justly chargeable.

The manner in which Johnson has written this life is very judicious: it afforded no great actions to celebrate, no improvements in science to record, nor any variety of events to remark on. It was a succession of disappointments, and a complication of miseries; and as it was an uniform contradiction to the axiom that human life is chequered with good and evil accidents, was alone singular. The virtues and vices which like flowers and weeds sprang up together, and perhaps with an equal degree of vigour, in the mind of this unfortunate man, afforded, it is true, a subject of speculation, and Johnson has not failed to avail himself of so extraordinary a moral phenomenon as that of a mind exalted to a high degree of improvement without the aid of culture.

But if the events of Savage's life are few, the reflections thereon are many, so that the work may as well be deemed a series of economical precepts as a narrative of facts. In it is contained a character, which may he said to be *sui generis*; a woman who had proclaimed her crimes,[12] and solicited reproach, disowning from the instant of his birth, and procuring to be illegitimated by parliament, her own son, dooming him to poverty and obscurity, and launching him upon the ocean of life, only that he might be swallowed by its quicksands, or dashed upon its rocks, and lastly, endeavouring to rid herself from the danger of being at any time made known to him, by secretly sending him to the American plantations.

It farther exhibits to view, a man of genius destitute of relations and friends, and with no one to direct his pursuits, becoming an author by necessity, and a writer for the stage, and forming such connections as that profession leads to, sometimes improving, and at others slighting them, but at all times acting with a spirit that better became his birth than his circumstances; for who that knew how to distinguish between one and the other, would, like Savage, have solicited assistance, and spurned at the offer of it? or repaid reiterated kindnesses with neglect or oblivious taciturnity?

Interspersed in the course of the narrative are a great variety of

moral sentiments, prudential maxims, and miscellaneous observations on men and things; but the sentiment that seems to per-
vade the whole is, that idleness, whether voluntary or necessitated,
is productive of the greatest evils that human nature is exposed
to; and this the author exemplifies in an enumeration of the ca-
lamities that a man is subjected to by the want of a profession,
and by showing how far less happy such an one must be than
he who has only a mere manual occupation to depend on for
his support.

The concluding paragraph of the book explains the author's
intention in writing it, and points out the use that may be made
of it in such pointed terms, that I shall need, as I trust, no excuse
for inserting so fine a specimen of style and sentiment.

This relation will not be wholly without its use, if those who lan-
guish under any part of his sufferings shall be enabled to fortify their
patience by reflecting, that they feel only those afflictions from which
the abilities of Savage did not exempt him; or if those who in confidence of superior capacities or attainments, disregard the common
maxims of life, shall be reminded, that nothing will supply the want
of prudence, and that negligence and irregularity long continued, will
make knowledge useless, wit ridiculous, and genius contemptible.

This celebrated essay in biography was published in the month
of February, 1744, and gave occasion to Henry Fielding, the author of a periodical paper entitled *The Champion*, to commend
it in these words:

This pamphlet is, without flattery to its author, as just and well
written a piece as, of its kind, I ever saw; so that, at the same time
that it highly deserves, it stands certainly very little in need of this
recommendation.—As to the history of the unfortunate person whose
memoirs compose this work, it is certainly penned with equal accuracy and spirit, of which I am so much the better judge, as I knew
many of the facts mentioned in it to be strictly true, and very fairly
related. Besides, it is not only the story of Mr. Savage, but innumerable incidents relating to other persons and other affairs, which
render this a very amusing, and withal, a very instructive and valuable
performance. The author's observations are short, significant and

just, as his narrative is remarkably smooth and well disposed: his reflections open to us all the recesses of the human heart, and, in a word, a more just or pleasant, a more engaging or a more improving treatise on the excellencies and defects of human nature, is scarce to be found in our own or perhaps in any other language.

4

1745-1750

THE LIFE I am now writing seems to divide itself into two periods; the first marked by a series of afflictions, the last by some cheering rays of comfort and comparative affluence. Johnson, at this time, had passed nearly the half of his days: here, therefore, let me make a stand, and having hitherto represented him in his literary, endeavour to exhibit him in his religious, moral, and economical character, adverting first to such particulars respecting the course of life he had chosen, and the evils to which it exposed him, as seem properly to belong to the first member of the above division.

As the narrowness of his father's circumstances had shut him out of those professions for which an university education is a necessary qualification, and his project of an academy had failed, he had, as to his course of life, no choice but idleness or the exercise of his talents in a way that might afford him subsistence, and provide for the day that was passing over him, so that the profession of an author was the only one in his power to adopt. That it was far from an eligible one, he had in some degree experienced, and his aversion to labour magnified the evils of it, by bringing to his recollection the examples of Amhurst, of Savage, of Boyse, and many others, from which he inferred, that slavery and indigence were its inseparable concomitants, and reflecting on the lives and conduct of these men, might fear that it had a necessary tendency to corrupt the mind, and render the followers of it, with respect to religion, to politics, and even to morality, altogether indifferent. Nor could he be ignorant of that mortifying dependence which the profession itself exposes men to, a profession that leads to no preferment, and for its most laborious exertions confers no greater a reward than a supply of natural wants.

Ralph, a writer of this class, and who had formed some such connections as would have flattered the hopes of any man, was the tool of that party of which the late Lord Melcombe laboured to be the head. To serve the interest of it, he wrote a periodical paper, and a voluminous history of England, fraught with such principles as he was required to disseminate. This man, in a pamphlet entitled *The Case of Authors by Profession*, has enumerated all the evils that attend it, and shown it to be the last that a liberal mind would choose.

All this Johnson knew and had duly weighed: the lesser evils of an author's profession, such as a dependence on booksellers, and a precarious income, he was able to endure, and the greater, that is to say, the prostitution of his talents, he averted; for, whatever sacrifices of their principles such men as Waller, Dryden, and others, have made in their writings, or to whatever lengths they may have gone in panegyrics or adulatory addresses, his integrity was not to be warped: his religious and political opinions he retained and cherished; and in a sullen confidence in the strength of his mental powers, disdained to solicit patronage by any of the arts in common use with writers of almost every denomination. That this firmness was not affected, will appear by a retrospect to the methods he took for the attainment of knowledge, and the settling his notions as to the great duties of life.

His course of study at the university was irregular and desultory, and scarcely determined as to its object. Mathematics and physics he had but little relish for, from whence it may be inferred, that his natural powers had received comparatively but small improvement from an academical education. An habitual disposition to thought and reflection enabled him however upon his leaving it, to attain to that degree of improvement which, in many minds, is not effected without intense application and labour; and the sentiments of piety which he had imbibed in his youth, directed him to those studies, which, without attending to secular rewards, he thought of greatest importance to his future happiness. In conformity to this motive, he applied himself to the study of the Holy Scriptures, and the evidences of religion, to the writings of the fathers and of the Greek moralists, to ecclesiastical and civil history, and to classical literature and philology.

The result of these his mental exercises was a thorough conviction of the truth of the Christian religion, an adherence to the doctrine and discipline of our established church, and to that form of civil government which we number among the blessings derived to us from the wisdom and bravery of our ancestors, with this farther advantage, that they rooted in his mind those principles of religion, morality, and, I will add, loyalty, that influenced his conduct during the remainder of his life.

To speak of the first, his religion, it had a tincture of enthusiasm, arising, as is conjectured, from the fervour of his imagination, and the perusal of St. Augustine and other of the fathers, and the writings of Kempis and the ascetics, which prompted him to the employment of composing meditations and devotional exercises. It farther produced in him an habitual reverence for the name of God, which he was never known to utter but on proper occasions and with due respect, and operated on those that were admitted to his conversation as a powerful restraint of all profane discourse, and idle discussions of theological questions; and, lastly, it inspired him with that charity, meaning thereby a general concern for the welfare of all mankind, without which we are told that all pretensions to religion are vain.

To enable him at times to review his progress in life, and to estimate his improvement in religion, he, in the year 1734, began to note down the transactions of each day, recollecting, as well as he was able, those of his youth, and interspersing such reflections and resolutions as, under particular circumstances, he was induced to make. This register, which he entitled 'Annales,' does not form an entire volume, but is contained in a variety of little books folded and stitched together by himself, and which were found mixed with his papers. Some specimens of these notanda have been lately printed with his prayers; but to warrant what I have said, respecting his religious character, I have selected from

the 'Annales,' and insert in the margin below, an earlier extract
than any contained in that collection.†

His moral character displayed itself in the sincerity of his friendships, his love of justice and of truth, and his placability; of all
which qualities, the testimonies in his favour are innumerable.
But as the character here proposed to be given him is not intended to palliate his errors in behaviour, truth obliges me to
say, that his outward deportment was in many instances a just
subject of censure. Before his arrival in town, he was but little
accustomed to free conversation with his superiors, so that that
kind of submission he had been used to pay them he seemed to
exact from others, and when it was refused him he was petulant,
captious, and dogged. His discourse, which through life was of
the didactic kind, was replete with original sentiments expressed
in the strongest and most correct terms, and in such language,
that whoever could have heard and not seen him, would have
thought him reading. For the pleasure he communicated to his
hearers, he expected not the tribute of silence: on the contrary, he
encouraged others, particularly young men, to speak, and paid
a due attention to what they said; but his prejudices were so strong
and deeply rooted, more especially against Scotchmen and Whigs,
that whoever thwarted him ran the risk of a severe rebuke, or at
best became entangled in an unpleasant altercation.

He was scarce settled in town before this dogmatical behaviour,
and his impatience of contradiction, became a part of his character, and deterred many persons of learning, who wished to enjoy the delight of his conversation, from seeking his acquaintance.
There were not wanting those among his friends who would sometimes hint to him, that the conditions of free conversation imply
an equality among those engaged in it, which are violated when-

† Friday, August 27th. (1736) [1] 10 at night. This day I have trifled away,
except that I have attended the school in the morning. I read tonight in
Rogers's sermons. Tonight I began the breakfast law anew.

Sept. 7th, 1736. I have this day entered upon my 28th year. Mayest thou,
O God, enable me for Jesus Christ's sake, to spend this in such a manner that
I may receive comfort from it at the hour of death, and in the day of judg-
ment. Amen.

I intend tomorrow to review the rules I have at any time laid down, in
order to practise them.

ever superiority is assumed: their reproofs he took kindly, and would in excuse for what they called the pride of learning, say, that it was of the defensive kind. The repetition of these had, however, a great effect on him; they abated his prejudices, and produced a change in his temper and manners that rendered him at length a desirable companion in the most polite circles.

In the lesser duties of morality he was remiss: he slept when he should have studied, and watched when he should have been at rest: his habits were slovenly, and the neglect of his person and garb so great as to render his appearance disgusting. He was an ill husband of his time, and so regardless of the hours of refection, that at two he might be found at breakfast, and at dinner at eight. In his studies, and I may add, in his devotional exercises, he was both intense and remiss, and in the prosecution of his literary employments, dilatory and hasty, unwilling, as himself confessed,[2] to work, and working with vigour and haste.

His indolence, or rather the delight he took in reading and reflection, rendered him averse to bodily exertions. He was ill made for riding, and took so little pleasure in it, that, as he once told me, he has fallen asleep on his horse. Walking he seldom practised, perhaps for no better reason, than that it required the previous labour of dressing. In a word, mental occupation was his sole pleasure, and the knowledge he acquired in the pursuit of it he was ever ready to communicate: in which faculty he was not only excellent but expert; for, as it is related of Lord Bacon by one who knew him,[3] that 'in all companies he appeared a good proficient, if not a master, in those arts entertained for the subject of everyone's discourse,' and that 'his most casual talk deserved to be written,' so it may be said of Johnson, that his conversation was ever suited to the profession, condition, and capacity of those with whom he talked.

Of a mind thus stored it is surely not too much to say, that it qualified the possessor of it for many more important employments than the instruction of non-adults in the elements of literature; yet so humbly did he seem to think of himself when he published the advertisement of his little academy at Edial, that to be able to establish it, was the utmost of his ambition; but that hope failing, his necessities drove him to London, and placed him in the station of life in which we are now to contemplate him.

It has been mentioned in a preceding page, that in the course of his studies he had formed a list of literary undertakings, on which, when time should serve or occasion invite, he meant to exercise his pen: but such was the versatility of his temper, that of forty-nine articles which he had fixed on, not one appears to have engaged his future attention. Among the rest he had purposed to give a history of the revival of learning in Europe, and also a comparison of philosophical and Christian morality, by sentences collected from the moralists and fathers. The former of these, as it required the labour of deep research, and the perusal of a great variety of authors, was a work that we may suppose he was deterred from by frequent reflections on the pains it would cost him; but that he should abandon a work so easy in the execution, and so much to the credit of the religion he professed, as the latter, is not less to be wondered at than lamented.

These projects of Johnson were most of them resolved on in his early days, but it is not improbable that he was induced to give them up by the prospect of the gain that might arise from the publication of a new edition of Shakespeare, which it is certain he meditated, about the year 1745. To an undertaking of this kind the temptations were very strong, for, besides that the former editors had fallen short in their endeavours to explain and settle the text, he had great reason to hope it would be well received, for at that time it was observable, that the taste of the public was refining, and that the lovers of stage entertainments and dramatic literature had begun to nauseate the tragedies and comedies of the last age, which were formed after French models, and to discern the beauties and excellencies of this author.

That this hope was not ill-grounded, may reasonably be inferred from the success of those many editions of this author that have appeared since the above time, of one whereof above eleven thousand copies have been sold, and next, from the effects of Mr. Garrick's acting, which had revived the exhibition of Shakespeare's plays, and excited readers of every class to the perusal of them.

But, perhaps, the greatest of Johnson's temptations to this undertaking, saving at all times his necessities, was, a desire to display his skill in English literature and rational criticism in their widest extent, in both which requisites the deficiencies of the former editions were obvious. Of those of the players and others, down to the year 1685, little in favour can be said: the first that made any pretensions to correctness was that of Rowe in 1709, and next to that, Mr. Pope's in 4to, 1723. Whatever other were the merits of these two persons, it is certain that neither of them was sufficiently qualified for the task he had undertaken; not that they wanted the power of discerning the excellencies of their author, or clearing his page of many corruptions that had long obscured his sense, but that they were deficient in that lower kind of literature, without which all endeavours to fix or explain the text of an old writer will ever be found to be vain.

To this kind of knowledge, as far as may be judged from the course of his studies, and indeed from the preface to his edition, Rowe had not the least pretension. Nor does it appear that Pope was at all conversant with, or that he understood the phraseology of the writers contemporary with his author. So little was he used to that kind of reading, that, as himself confessed, he had never heard of the *Virgidemiarum* of Bishop Hall, a collection of the wittiest and most pointed satires in our language, till it was shown to him, and that so late in his life, that he could only express his approbation of it by a wish that he had seen it sooner. That vernacular erudition, contemptible as it has been represented, is an indispensable qualification for the restoring or explaining the sense of corrupted or obsolete authors, and even of those more recent, is most clearly evidenced in one case by the later editions of our great dramatic poet, and in the other by Dr. Grey's edition of *Hudibras*, without the assistance whereof, the many allusions to facts, circumstances, and situations therein contained, must for ever have remained unintelligible. Theobald was the first of this class of editors. For the purpose of publishing Shakespeare, he, in the preface to his first edition, asserts, that he had read no fewer than eight hundred old English plays, besides histories and novels to a great amount; and the same kind of study has, with different degrees of assiduity, been pursued by others, even to the last of his successors.

With these inducements, and the aid of two valuable editions then extant, Theobald's and that of Sir Thomas Hanmer, Johnson projected a new one, and, as a specimen of his abilities for the undertaking, published in the year 1745, *Miscellaneous Observations on the Tragedy of Macbeth, with Remarks on Sir Thomas Hanmer's Edition of Shakespeare,* with proposals for one by himself. These observations, as they go rather to adjust the various readings, and settle the text by conjectural notes, than explain allusions, did not enough attract the notice of the public to induce him actually to engage in the work; they were however evidences of great sagacity, and drew from Dr. Warburton a testimony that set him above all other competitors; for thus does he speak of Johnson: [4] 'As to all those things which have been published under the titles of Essays, Remarks, Observations, &c. on Shakespeare, (if you except some critical notes on *Macbeth*, given as a specimen of a projected edition, and written as appears by a man of parts and genius) the rest are absolutely below a serious notice'; and Johnson, who never forgot a kindness, remembered it by mentioning Warburton in terms of great respect, as occasion offered, in his edition of Shakespeare, which he published many years after.

By this and other of Johnson's writings, his reputation as a scholar and a philologist was so well established, that the booksellers of greatest opulence in the city, who had long meditated the publication of a dictionary, after the model of those of France and the Accademia della Crusca, looked upon him as a fit person to be employed in such an undertaking. He was at that time in the vigour of his life, and by the offer of a liberal reward from men of such known worth as those were who made it, was tempted to engage with them, and accordingly set himself to compile that work, which, he living to complete it, does him and all concerned in it great honour.

Nor can we suppose but that he was in a great measure incited to the prosecution of this laborious work, by a reflection on the state of our language at this time, from the imperfection of all English dictionaries then extant, and the great distance in point of improvement in this kind of literature between us and some of our neighbours. And here let me take occasion, by an enumeration of the several authors that had gone before him, to point out the sources of that intelligence which Johnson's voluminous work contains.

Of Latin dictionaries and such as give the significations of

English appellatives with a view only to illustrate the Latin, he must be supposed to have made some use, and of these the earliest is Sir Thomas Elyot's *Bibliotheca Eliotae*, published in 1541. This was improved by Cooper after many years' labour, by the addition of 33,000 words, and published in 1565 in a large folio, and was a reason with Queen Elizabeth for promoting him to the bishopric of Lincoln.

In 1572 was published an Alvearie or quadruple dictionary of four sundry tongues, namely, English, Latin, Greek and French, by John Baret of Cambridge, compiled with the assistance of his pupils, but arranged and methodized by himself.*

To Baret's succeeded John Minsheu's *Guide into the Tongues*, first published in 1617 in eleven, and in 1627 in nine languages, but with a considerable increase in the number of radical words. In this the author undertakes to give the etymologies or derivations of the greater part of the words therein contained, but as they amount at the most to no more than 14,713, the work must be deemed not sufficiently copious.

In 1656, Thomas Blount, a lawyer of the Inner Temple, published a small volume, entitled *Glossographia, or a Dictionary Interpreting Such Hard Words, whether Hebrew, Greek, Latin, Italian, &c. That Are Now Used in Our Refined English Tongue, &c.* in which the articles though few are well explained. This book, as far as it went, was of singular use to Edward Philips, a nephew and pupil of Milton, in the compilation of a dictionary by him published in folio, 1657, entitled *The New World of Words*, which, as it is much more copious than that of Blount, and comprehends a great quantity of matter, must be looked on as the basis of English lexicography.

Of technical as also of etymological dictionaries, many have long been extant, namely, *The Interpreter* or Law Dictionary of Dr. Cowell a civilian, a Common-Law Dictionary of the above Thomas Blount, the *Etymologicum* of Junius, and another of Skinner, both well known and frequently referred to, and of these did Johnson avail himself.

The dictionary of Nathan Bailey, a schoolmaster, was first published in a thick octavo volume, so well disposed with respect to the character and method of printing, as to contain more matter than could otherwise have been comprised in a volume of that size. After it had passed many editions with improvements by the author himself, he meditated an enlargement of it, and being assisted in the mathematical part by Mr. Gordon, in the botanical by the famous gardener Philip Miller, and in the etymological by Mr. Lediard, a professor of the modern languages, it was published in a folio size. The last improvement of it was by Dr. Joseph Nicoll Scott, who, of a dissenting teacher had become a physician and a writer for the booksellers.

Johnson, who before this time, together with his wife, had lived in obscurity, lodging at different houses in the courts and alleys in and about the Strand and Fleet Street, had, for the purpose of carrying on this arduous work, and being near the printers employed in it, taken a handsome house on Gough Square, and fitted up a room in it with desks and other accommodations for amanuenses, who, to the number of five or six, he kept constantly under his eye. An interleaved copy of Bailey's dictionary in folio he made the repository of the several articles, and these he collected by incessant reading the best authors in our language, in the practice whereof, his method was to score with a black-lead pencil the words by him selected, and give them over to his assistants to insert in their places. The books he used for this purpose were what he had in his own collection, a copious but a miserably ragged one, and all such as he could borrow; which latter, if ever they came back to those that lent them, were so defaced as to be scarce worth owning, and yet, some of his friends were glad to receive and entertain them as curiosities.

It seems that Johnson had made a considerable progress in his work when he was informed, that the Earl of Chesterfield had heard and spoken favourably of his design. He had never till this time experienced the patronage of any other than booksellers, and though he had but an indistinct idea of that of a nobleman, a reputed wit, and an accomplished courtier, and doubted whether he was to rate it among the happy incidents of his life, it might mean a liberal present or an handsome pension to encourage him in the prosecution of the work; he therefore resolved not to reject it by a supercilious comparison of his own talents with those of his lordship, or to slight a favour which he was not able to estimate. Accordingly, he in the year 1747, drew up and dedicated to Lord Chesterfield, then a secretary of state, a plan of his dictionary, the manuscript whereof he delivered to Mr. Whitehead the late laureate, who undertook to convey it to his lordship, but he having communicated it first to another person, it passed through other hands before it reached that to which it was immediately directed: the result was an invitation from Lord Chesterfield to the author.[5]

Never could there be a stronger contrast of characters than this interview produced: a scholar and a courtier, the one ignorant of the forms and modes of address, the other, to an affected degree, accomplished in both: the one in a manly and sententious style directing his discourse to a weighty subject; the other dreading to incur the imputation of pedantry, and by the interposition of compliments and the introduction of new topics as artfully endeavouring to evade it. The acquaintance thus commenced was never improved into friendship. What his lordship thought of Johnson we may learn from his letters to an illegitimate son, now extant.[6] Johnson was so little pleased with his once supposed patron, that he forbore not ever after to speak of him in terms of the greatest contempt.

How far Johnson was right in his opinion of this popular nobleman, or whether he is to be suspected of having resented more than he ought to have done, the coldness of his reception, or the disappointment of his hopes, will best appear by a survey of his character, as it arises out of the memoirs of his life prefixed to his miscellaneous works, and the sentiments and principles which, for the instruction of his son, he, in a course of letters to him, from time to time communicated, and with the utmost solicitude laboured to inculcate and enforce.

After about two years stay at the university,[7] Lord Stanhope, for that was then his only title, went abroad to travel, and at that enchanting place the Hague, began to be acquainted with the world. The college rust, which, if we may believe his panegyrist, he contracted in the university during so long a residence there, he found means to rub off, and exchanged for the polish of gaming, which rendered him the dupe of knaves and sharpers almost throughout his life, and this not from any real propensity to this

pernicious vice, but to acquire, what throughout his life he seems
to have above all things been desirous of, the insipid character
of a man of fashion.

Nature, it must be owned, had endowed him with fine parts,
and these he cultivated with all the industry usually practised by
such as prefer the semblance of what is really fit, just, lovely,
honourable, to the qualities themselves; thus he had eloquence
without learning, complaisance without friendship, and gallantry
without love.

His dissimulation, deep and refined as it was, did not lead him
to profess any sincere regard to virtue or religion: the grosser
immoralities he affects to speak of with abhorrence; but such as
might be practised without the loss of health and reputation he
seemed to think there was no law against. He was therefore, if
secret, vain in his amours, and though, setting aside his mien,
his person had little to recommend it, for he was low of stature,
had coarse features, and a cadaverous complexion, his confidence
in the prosecution of them was such as exposed him to greater
risks of personal safety than most men would choose to run; and
of this I shall now produce an instance.

A lady of high quality, and a relation of one who had the story
from her own mouth and told it me, having been married some
few years but never having brought her lord a child, was surprised
one morning by a visit from Lord Chesterfield, whom she had
frequently seen and conversed with at court. After the usual compliments had passed, his lordship in that easy gay style which he
so strongly recommends to his son, gave her to understand, that
he should be happy to form such a connection with her ladyship,
as it was more than probable might give being to an heir to the
honours and possessions of that noble family into which she had
matched. I will not attempt to describe the indignation which the
lady felt at such an unexampled instance of impudence as the
proposal indicated. She rose from her chair, and with all the dignity of insulted modesty, commanded this well-bred lover, this
minion of the graces, to quit her house, with this menace, 'Think
yourself well off, my lord, that for this affront I do not order my
servants to push you headlong out of doors.'

It is a refinement in modern gallantry, but an affront to human policy, to recognize in public, by the unqualified appellation of son, those to whom the laws of most civilized countries deny not only that but the privilege of heirs; yet this has this slave to forms and usages done in a series of letters to a young gentleman begotten by him out of wedlock, and in the lifetime of one to whom we must suppose he once tendered himself, his honours, his possessions, and his heart. With a solicitude for his welfare, commendable it must be said in its general intention, he takes on himself to mold his person, to form his manners, and to furnish his mind. In the first of these particulars his lordship had great difficulties to encounter: the clay he had chosen to work upon was stiff, and resisted the plastic touch: the boy was encumbered with flesh, and nature had so carelessly compacted his limbs as scarcely to leave them the power of flexure. In a word, in infancy he was shapeless, and in youth a looby. Never did a she-bear with more anxious assiduity labour to lick her cub into shape than this fond parent did to correct the errors of nature in the formation of this his darling: the head, the shoulders and the hands, were, by turns, the objects of his care; but the legs and feet seem to have engaged most of his attention: these upon his being sent abroad, were committed to the care of a dancing master at Paris, whose instructions he estimates at a higher rate than the precepts of Aristotle.

The hopeful documents contained in this institute of politeness, Lord Chesterfield's letters to his son, failed in a great measure of their end. His lordship's interest with the ministry, founded on a seat in parliament, which, though a great declaimer against corruption, he bought as he would have done a horse, procured him the appointment of an envoy-extraordinary to the court of Dresden. We find not that the young man had any female attachments, but that on the contrary he had more grace than his father. He married a woman, who becoming a widow, and provoked by real or imaginary ill treatment of Lord Chesterfield, published those letters, which, had he been living, he would have given almost anything to have suppressed, as they show him to have been a man devoted to pleasure, and actuated by vanity, without religious, moral, or political principles, a smatterer in learning, and in manners a coxcomb.

Such was the person whom Johnson in the simplicity of his heart chose for a patron, and was betrayed to celebrate as the Maecenas of the age; and such was the opinion he had conceived of his skill in literature, his love of eloquence, and his zeal for the interests of learning, that he approached him with the utmost respect, and that he might not err in his manner of expressing it, the style and language of that address which his plan includes are little less than adulatory. With a view farther to secure his patronage, he waited on him in person, and was honoured by him with conversations on the subject of literature, in which he found him so deficient as gave him occasion to repent the choice he had made, and to say, that the labour he had bestowed in his address to Lord Chesterfield resembled that of gilding a rotten post, that he was a wit among lords and a lord among wits, and that his accomplishments were only those of a dancing master.

It is pretty well understood that, as Johnson had chosen this nobleman for his patron, he meant to have dedicated to him his work, and he might possibly have done so, even after he had discovered that he was unworthy of that honour; but the earl's behaviour in a particular instance prevented him. Johnson one day made him a morning visit, and being admitted into an antechamber, was told, that his lordship was engaged with a gentleman, but would see him as soon as the gentleman went. It was not till after an hour's waiting that Johnson discovered that this gentleman was Colley Cibber, which he had no sooner done, than he rushed out of the house with a resolution never to enter it more.[8]

Johnson was, by this time, able to determine on a fact which, in his address to this nobleman, he expresses a doubt of, viz. whether the unexpected distinction his lordship had shown him, was to be rated among the happy incidents of his life: he was now convinced that it was not, and that, far from everything like encouragement or assistance, or what else is included in the idea of patronage, his lordship's approbation of his plan was to be the only recompense for the labour of drawing it out and reducing it to form. Besides declaring, whenever occasion required it, his mistake in supposing that Lord Chesterfield was either a judge of or a friend to literature, he expressed in a letter to his lordship himself his resentment of the affront he had received at his last visit, and concluded it with a formal renunciation forever of his lordship's patronage.[9]

If Johnson had reflected a moment on the little effect likely to be produced by a letter in which he professed to reject that which he could not retain, he would never have wrote it. Those evils which cannot be remedied must be borne with patience, and to resent injuries when we cannot enforce redress, is to give our adversaries an occasion of triumph: Lord Chesterfield knew this, and made no reply: when the dictionary was completed and about to be published, he wrote two essays in a periodical paper, entitled *The World*, that contain some forced compliments of the author, which being mentioned to Johnson he rejected with scorn.

Further to appease him, his lordship sent two persons, the one a specious but empty man, Sir Thomas Robinson, more distinguished by the tallness of his person than for any estimable qualities; the other an eminent painter now living.[10] These were instructed to apologize for his lordship's treatment of him, and to make him tenders of his future friendship and patronage. Sir Thomas, whose talent was flattery, was profuse in his commendations of Johnson and his writings, and declared that were his circumstances other than they were, himself would settle five hundred pounds a year on him. 'And who are you,' asked Johnson, 'that talk thus liberally?' 'I am,' said the other, 'Sir Thomas Robinson, a Yorkshire baronet.' 'Sir,' replied Johnson, 'if the first peer of the realm were to make me such an offer, I would show him the way downstairs.'

No one will commend this manner of declining an intentional kindness, even where the sincerity of the intention might be doubtful, but the rejecting it with a menace was both unnecessary and insolent. The pride of independence was most strong in Johnson at those periods of his life when his wants were greatest, and though at other times he would subject himself to great obligations, he was uniform, except only in one instance, in an opinion that an offer of pecuniary assistance was an insult, and not seldom rejected it with such indignation, that were I to characterize it more particularly, I should do it by an allusion to the following apologue: A gardener's dog had fallen into a well and was unable to get out: his master passing by, and seeing his distress, put down his arm to save him: the dog bit his hand, and the gardener left him to drown.

The uneasiness which Johnson felt, at the time when he wrote the above-mentioned letter, gave way to a call of his friend Garrick, who in the same year, 1747, was, by a series of occurrences, become master of Drury Lane Theatre. I was never much conversant with the history of the stage, and therefore can give but a slight account of an event, which, at that time, interested many, and was deemed a very important one. Mr. Fleetwood's extravagance had reduced him to the necessity of seeking out for some one or more persons to whom, for an adequate consideration, he might relinquish his interest in the patent. At that time a man of the name of Lacy had attracted the notice of the town by a competition with Orator Henley, which he began at the great room in York buildings, with a satirical discourse of great licence, which he advertised by the name of Peter's Visitation. The liberties he had taken with the clergy and the principal officers of state in this ludicrous discourse gave great offence: he was seized, dealt with as a vagrant, and, in short, silenced. This man had lived among players, and was supposed to understand stage-management, and had some friends. Mr. Garrick had many, and those opulent men: three of them, Mr. Draper the partner of Mr. Tonson the bookseller, Mr. Clutterbuck a mercer, and Mr. Samuel Sharp one of the surgeons of Guy's hospital, negotiated a partnership between those two persons, and by purchasing of them and assisting them to dispose of what are called renters' shares, enabled them to buy out Fleetwood, and before the commencement of the acting season, they were become joint-patentees of the theatre above-mentioned.

Mr. Garrick's province in the management was to appoint the plays and to cast the parts; Lacy's was to superintend the workmen and servants, to order the scenery, and, with the assistance of artists, to adjust the ornaments and decorations. It was their resolution to banish from their stage, pantomimes and all grotesque representations, and to exhibit such only as a rational and judicious audience might be supposed inclined to approve.

To notify this their intention to the town, it seemed to them that a prologue was necessary: Johnson was easily prevailed upon by Mr. Garrick to write one, and at the opening of the theatre in 1747, it was spoken by the latter in a manner that did equal honour to the author and himself.

Prologues are addresses from the stage to the people, and either respect merely the drama that is to follow, or are of more general import setting forth to the audience the views and designs of managers, their anxiety to please, and the methods by which they hope to obtain the favour of the public: these latter are for the most part occasional, and adapted to such circumstances as the opening a new theatre, a change of management, or any other of those great theatrical revolutions in which the players affect to think all men as much interested as themselves. In the addresses of this kind the powers of wit seem to have been nearly exhausted: sometimes the audience has been cajoled, at others, betrayed into good humour; and by the help of allegory, the stage has been made to resemble everything unlike it. One poet feigns that the town is a sea, the playhouse a ship, the manager the captain, the players sailors, and the orange-girls powder-monkies; and Mr. Garrick, in one of his prologues, would make his audience believe, that his theatre is a tavern, himself the master, the players waiters, and his entertainment wines suited to all palates: one of his liquors, in particular, he strongly recommends, and calls Shakespeare, which that he may be constantly able to supply, he says it is

_____his wish, his plan,
To lose no drop of that immortal man.[11]

And, to be more particular, that

_____to delight ye,
Bardolph is gin, and Pistol aqua-vitae.[12]

Johnson's prologue is of a very different cast. It is a sober, rational, and manly appeal to the good sense and candour of the audience, and contains a brief history of theatric representations from the time of Shakespeare and Jonson to their decline, when, as he says, the writers of pantomime and song had confirmed the sway of folly. It states the hardships which those lie under, whose business it is to furnish entertainment for the public, in being obliged to watch the wild vicissitudes of taste, and exhorts the hearers to patronize virtue and reviving sense.[13]

This masterly and spirited address failed in a great measure of its effect; the town, it is true, submitted to the revival of Shakespeare's plays, recommended as they were by the exquisite acting of Mr. Garrick; but in a few winters they discovered an impatience for pantomimes and ballad-farces, and were indulged with them. From that time Mr. Garrick gave up the hope of correcting the public taste, and at length became so indifferent about it, that he once told me, that if the town required him to exhibit the *Pilgrim's Progress* in a drama, he would do it.

Two years after, the management of Drury Lane Theatre being in the hands of his friends, Johnson bethought himself of bringing his tragedy on the stage. It was not only a juvenile composition, but was written before he had become conversant with Shakespeare, indeed before he had ever read *Othello*, and having now, for more than ten years, lain by him, in which time his judgment had been growing to maturity, he set himself to revise and polish it, taking to his assistance Mr. Garrick, whose experience of stage decorum, and the mechanic operation of incidents and sentiments on the judgment and passions of an audience, was, by long attention, become very great. With these advantages and all those others which Mr. Garrick's zeal prompted him to supply, such as magnificent scenery, splendid and well chosen dresses, and a distribution of the principal parts, himself taking a very active one, to the best performers then living, namely, Barry, Mrs. Cibber and Mrs. Pritchard; it was, in the winter of the year 1749, presented to a polite, a numerous, and an unprejudiced audience. Never was there such a display of eastern magnificence as this spectacle exhibited, nor ever were fine moral sentiments more strongly enforced by correct and energetic utterance and just action, than in the representation of this laboured tragedy; but the diction of the piece was cold and philosophical; it came from the head of the writer, and reached not the hearts of the hearers.

The consequence whereof was, that it was received with cold applause, and having reached to a ninth night's performance, was laid by. During the representation Johnson was behind the scenes, and thinking his character of an author required upon the occasion some distinction of dress, he appeared in a gold-laced waistcoat.

The truth of the above assertion, as to the language of this tragedy, is to be judged of by the perusal of it; for, notwithstanding its ill success as a dramatic representation, Johnson found his account in giving it to the world as a poem. Of the fable, the characters, and the sentiments, it is beside my purpose to speak; they are also now open to examination. It is nevertheless worthy of a remark, that the author has shown great judgment in deviating from historical verity, as will appear by a comparison of the drama with the story as related by Knolles *; for whereas the historian describes Irene as endowed with the perfections as well of the mind as of the body, and relates that she was an innocent victim to the ferocity of a tyrant, Johnson thought that such a catastrophe was too shocking for representation, and has varied the narrative by making the lady renounce her religion, and subjecting her to the suspicion of being a joint conspirator in a plot to assassinate the Sultan; but of which he is afterwards convinced she is innocent.

In thus altering the story, it must however be confessed, that much of its beauty is destroyed, and the character of Mahomet represented with none of those terrible graces that dignify the narrative: his public love and command over himself are annihilated, and he is exhibited as a tyrant and a voluptuary.

The world soon formed an opinion of the merit of *Irene*, which has never fluctuated: a representation during nine nights, was as much as a tragedy which excited no passion could claim; for, however excellent its precepts, and however correct its language, that it wants those indispensable qualities in the drama, interest and pathos, cannot be denied. We read it, admit every position it advances, commend it, lay it by, and forget it: our attention is not awakened by any eminent beauties, for its merit is uniform throughout: all the personages, good or bad, are philosophers: those who execute and those who issue the orders talk the same

language: the characters cause no anxiety, for the virtuous are
superior to all mortal calamity, and the vicious beneath our care:
the fate of Irene, though deplorable, is just; notwithstanding she
suffers by a false accusation, her apostasy and treachery to her
friend deserve punishment: the morality, it is needless to say of
Johnson's spontaneous productions, is excellent; but how were un-
impassioned precepts to make their way alone, where variety,
business and plot are always expected? where lively nonsense
and pathetic imbecility often succeed against the conviction
of reason? Or how could it be hoped that frigid virtue could
attract those who suffer their pity to be easily moved either by
the hero or the villain, if he has the address first to engage their
passions?

Of the expectations that Johnson had entertained of the success of his tragedy, no conjecture can now be formed. If they are
to be judged of by his outward demeanour after the town had
consigned it to oblivion, they were not very sanguine; indeed the
receipt of three nights must have afforded him some consolation; [14] and we must suppose that he increased the emolument
thence arising, by the sale of the copy. We are therefore not to
impute it to the disappointment of a hope that the play would be
better received than it was, that in the winter of the same year
he published another imitation of Juvenal, viz. of his tenth satire,
with the title of *The Vanity of Human Wishes*; [15] the subject
whereof, as it is an enumeration of the evils to which mankind are
exposed, could not, at any period of his life, have been other than
a tempting one. Pursuing the track of his author, he expatiates on
the miseries that await empire, grandeur, wealth, and power, and
the disappointments that frustrate the hopes of ambition, learning, eloquence, and beauty; in all which instances he has been able
to point out examples the most striking and apposite.

The poem concludes with an answer to an inquiry that must
necessarily result from the perusal of the foregoing part of it, viz.
what are the consolations that human life affords? or, in other
words, in whom or on what is a virtuous man to rest his hope?
the resolution of this question is contained in the following lines,
which for dignity of sentiment, for pious instruction, and purity
of style, are hardly to be equalled by any in our language.

Where then shall hope and fear their objects find?
Must dull suspense corrupt the stagnant mind?
Must helpless man, in ignorance sedate,
Roll darkling down the torrent of his fate?
Must no dislike alarm, no wishes rise,
No cries invoke the genius of the skies?
Enquirer, cease, petitions yet remain,
Which Heav'n may hear, nor deem religion vain,
Still raise for good the supplicating voice,
But leave to Heav'n the measure and the choice,
Safe in his pow'r, whose eyes discern afar
The secret ambush of a specious pray'r;
Implore his aid, in his decisions rest,
Secure, whate'er he gives, he gives the best.
Yet when the sense of sacred presence fires,
And strong devotion to the skies aspires,
Pour forth thy fervours for a healthful mind,
Obedient passions, and a will resign'd;
For love, which scarce collective man can fill;
For patience, sov'reign o'er transmuted ill;
For faith, that panting for a happier seat,
Counts death kind nature's signal of retreat.
These goods for man, the laws of Heav'n ordain;
These goods he grants, who grants the pow'r to gain;
With these celestial wisdom calms the mind,
And makes the happiness she does not find.

In the following year, it having been discovered, that a grand-daughter of Milton was living,[16] Mr. Garrick was prevailed on to permit the representation of the masque of *Comus* at his theatre, for her benefit. Upon this occasion, Johnson, forgetting the enmity which he had always borne towards Milton, wrote a prologue, wherein he calls the attention of the audience to his memory, and without imputing to his descendant any other merit than industrious poverty and conjugal fidelity, implores them to crown desert beyond the grave.

Johnson's beneficence was of the most diffusive kind: Distress was the general motive, and merit, whether in the object or any to whom he claimed relation, the particular incentive to it. There was living at this time, a man of the name of DeGroot, a painter

by profession, and no contemptible artist, who, after having
travelled over England, and at low prices painted as many persons
as could be persuaded to sit to him, settled in London, and became reduced to poverty: him Oldys, or someone other of his
friends, introduced to Johnson, who found out by his conversation
that he was a descendant of Grotius; and thereupon exerting his
interest in his behalf, he procured for him an admission into the
Charterhouse, in which comfortable retreat he died.

 OHNSON WAS all this while working at the dictionary, having to assist him a number of young persons whose employment it was to distribute the articles with sufficient spaces for the definitions, which it is easy to discern are of his own composition.

Of these his assistants, some were young men of parts, others mere drudges. Among the former was one of the name of Shiells, a Scotchman, the author of a poem in blank verse, entitled *Beauty*, and also of a collection of the lives of the poets, in four volumes, which for a gratuity of ten guineas, Theophilus Cibber suffered to be printed with his name, a book of no authority other than what it derives from Winstanley, Langbaine, and Jacob, and in other respects of little worth; but concerning which it is fit that the following fact should be made known: Cibber at the time of making this bargain, was under confinement for debt in the King's Bench Prison, and with a view to deceive the public into a belief that the book was of his father's writing, it was concerted between the negotiators of it and himself to suppress his Christian name, and that it should be printed as a work of Mr. Cibber.[1]

The intense application with which he was obliged to pursue his work, deprived Johnson of many of the pleasures he most delighted in, as namely, reading in his desultory manner, and the conversation of his friends. It also increased his constitutional melancholy, and at times excited in him a loathing of that employment to which he could not but look upon himself as doomed by his necessities. The sum for which he had stipulated with the booksellers, was by the terms of the agreement, to be paid as the work went on, and was indeed his only support. Being thus compelled to spend every day like the past, he looked on himself as in a state of mental bondage, and reflecting that while he was thus employed, his best faculties lay dormant, was unwillingly willing to work.

And here we cannot but reflect on that inertness and laxity of mind which the neglect of order and regularity in living, and the observance of stated hours, in short, the waste of time, is apt to lead men to: this was the source of Johnson's misery throughout his life; all he did was by fits and starts, and he had no genuine impulse to action, either corporal or mental. That the compilation of such a work as he was engaged in, was necessarily productive of that languor, which, in the prosecution of it he manifested, is by no means clear: all employments, all occupations whatever, are intrinsically indifferent, and excite neither pain nor pleasure, but as the mind is disposed towards them. Fame, mere posthumous fame has engaged men to similar undertakings, and they have pursued them with zeal and even delight. Canne, the editor of a bible printed in 1664, spent many years in collecting parallel passages in the Old and New Testament, to such a number as to crowd the margin of the book, and in the preface thereto he declares that it was the most delightful employment of his life; and what but a real pleasure in that kind of labour, and the consideration of its benefit to mankind, could be the inducement with such a man as Hoffman to compile a lexicon more than twice as voluminous as that of Johnson?

And, to speak more at large, viz. of men who have benefited the world by their literary labours, avowing as their motive the desire of gain, we find not all infected with that disease, which as it affected Johnson, may almost be said to have converted all his mental nutriment to poison: on the contrary, there have been many who mixed with the world, and by a good use of their time, were capable of great application and enjoying the benefits of society; and of these I shall mention three persons, his contemporaries, men of very different characters from each other;

all authors by profession, and of great eminence in literature.[2] The first was the Reverend Dr. Thomas Birch, a divine of the Church of England, but originally a Quaker. Having had the happiness of a recommendation to Sir Philip Yorke, then attorney general, and being honoured with his favour and patronage, he, in 1730, entered into holy orders, and was presented to a rectory and also to a vicarage in Gloucestershire. Soon after this, in conjunction with the Reverend Mr. Bernard, the well known Mr. John Lockman, and Mr. George Sale the translator of the Koran, he compiled a general biographical dictionary in ten volumes in folio, including therein a translation of that of Bayle, and collected and published Thurloe's state papers, in seven folio volumes, and was the editor of Lord Bacon's, Mr. Boyle's, and Archbishop Tillotson's works, as also of the prose writings of Milton, and the miscellaneous pieces of Sir Walter Raleigh, and the works of Mrs. Catharine Cockburn.[3] The above is but a partial enumeration of his publications, for he wrote the lives of Henry Prince of Wales, of Bacon, Boyle, Milton, and Tillotson, and other persons, and many tracts not here noticed. In the midst of all this employment, Dr. Birch was to be seen, at home, at the Royal and Antiquarian societies, at Sion College, at the Academy of Ancient Music, which had long subsisted at the Crown and Anchor in the Strand, at Tom's coffee house in Devereux Court; in short, in all places where a clergyman might with propriety appear. Nor was this all; he found time for the exercise of walking, before many people were stirring. I have been with him at nine in a winter's morning, and have found him just returned from an excursion of some miles.[4] He held a conversation on Sunday evenings with his friends, who were men of the first eminence for learning and intelligence, at his house in Norfolk Street in the Strand, in which all, particularly the library, was neat and elegant, without litter or disorder.

The mental endowments of Dr. Birch were singular; he had a great eagerness after knowledge, and a memory very retentive of facts; but his learning, properly so called, bore no proportion to his reading; for he was in truth neither a mathematician, a natural philosopher, a classical scholar, nor a divine; but, in a small degree, all, and though lively in conversation, he was but a dull writer.

Johnson was used to speak of him in this manner: 'Tom is a lively
rogue; he remembers a great deal, and can tell many pleasant
stories; but a pen is to Tom a torpedo, the touch of it benumbs
his hand and his brain: Tom can talk; but he is no writer.'

Dr. John Campbell was an eminent writer, and a labourer in a
voluminous work undertaken at the expense and risk of the booksellers, the *Universal History*. Besides many other books, he wrote
the lives of the English admirals in four octavo volumes. He had
a considerable hand in the *Biographia Britannica*, and was the
author of a valuable work in two quarto volumes entitled, *A
Political Survey of Britain*. By the exercise of his pen alone, and
a good use of his time, he was for many years enabled to support
himself, and enjoy the comforts of domestic life in the society of
an excellent wife and a numerous offspring. In 1765, he was appointed his majesty's agent for the province of Georgia in North
America, and was thereby raised to a state of comparative affluence. His residence for some years before his death, was the
large new-built house situate at the northwest corner of Queen
Square, Bloomsbury, whither, particularly on a Sunday evening,
great numbers of persons of the first eminence for science and
literature were accustomed to resort for the enjoyment of conversation.[5]

Dr. John Hill was originally an apothecary and a student in
botany; but finding that an unprofitable pursuit, he made two or
three attempts as a writer for the stage: a failure in them drove
him back to his former study. His first publication was a translation from the Greek of a small tract, Theophrastus on gems,
which being printed by subscription, produced him some money,
and such a reputation as induced the booksellers to engage him in
writing a general natural history in two volumes in folio, and soon
after, a supplement to Chambers's dictionary. He had received no
academical education; but his ambition prompting him to be a
graduate, he obtained, from one of those universities which would
scarce refuse a degree to an apothecary's horse, a diploma for
that of doctor of physic.[6] After this, he engaged in a variety of
works; and though his character was never in such estimation
with the booksellers as to entitle him to an extraordinary price for
his writings, he has been known by such works as those above-

mentioned, by novels, pamphlets, and a periodical paper called *The Inspector*, the labour of his own head and hand, to have earned, in one year, the sum of 1500£. He was vain, conceited, and in his writings disposed to satire and licentious scurrility, which he indulged without any regard to truth, and thereby became engaged in frequent disputes and quarrels that always terminated in his own disgrace. For some abuse in his *Inspector*, of a gentleman of the name of Brown, he had his head broke in the circus of Ranelagh gardens. He insulted Woodward the player in the face of an audience, and engaged with him in a pamphlet-war, in which he was foiled. In the midst of all this employment, he found time and means to drive about the town in his chariot, and to appear abroad and at all public places, at Batson's coffee house, at masquerades, and at the opera and play-houses, splendidly dressed, and as often as he could, in the front row of the boxes. Towards the end of his life, his reputation as an author was so sunk by the slovenliness of his compilations, and his disregard to truth in what he related, that he was forced to betake himself to the vending a few simple medicines, namely, essence of water-dock, tincture of Valerian, balsam of honey, and elixir of Bardana, and by pamphlets ascribing to them greater virtues than they had, imposed on the credulity of the public, and thereby got, though not an honest, a competent livelihood.

Besides these, there was another class of authors who lived by writing, that require to be noticed: the former were, in fact, pensioners of the booksellers: these vended their compositions when completed, to those of that trade who would give most for them. They were mostly books of mere entertainment that were the subjects of this kind of commerce, and were and still are distinguished by the corrupt appellation of novels and romances. Though fictitious, and the work of mere invention, they pretended to probability, to be founded in nature, and to delineate social manners. The first publication of the kind was the *Pamela* of Mr. Richardson,[7] which being read with great eagerness by the young people of the time, and recommended from the pulpit, begat such a craving for more of the same stuff, as tempted some men whose necessities and abilities were nearly commensurate, to try their success in this new kind of writing.

At the head of these we must, for many reasons, place Henry Fielding, one of the most motley of literary characters. This man was, in his early life, a writer of comedies and farces, very few of which are now remembered; after that, a practising barrister with scarce any business; then an anti-ministerial writer, and quickly after, a creature of the Duke of Newcastle, who gave him a nominal qualification of 100£. a year, and set him up as a trading-justice, in which disreputable station he died.[8] He was the author of a romance, entitled *The History of Joseph Andrews*, and of another, *The Foundling, or the History of Tom Jones*, a book seemingly intended to sap the foundation of that morality which it is the duty of parents and all public instructors to inculcate in the minds of young people, by teaching that virtue upon principle is imposture, that generous qualities alone constitute true worth, and that a young man may love and be loved, and at the same time associate with the loosest women. His morality, in respect that it resolves virtue into good affections, in contradiction to moral obligation and a sense of duty, is that of Lord Shaftesbury vulgarized, and is a system of excellent use in palliating the vices most injurious to society. He was the inventor of that cant phrase, goodness of heart, which is every day used as a substitute for probity, and means little more than the virtue of a horse or dog; in short, he has done more towards corrupting the rising generation than any writer we know of.

He afterwards wrote a book of the same kind, but of a less mischievous tendency, his *Amelia*. For each of these he was well paid by Andrew Millar the bookseller, and for the last he got six hundred pounds.

Dr. Tobias Smollet, another writer of familiar romance, and a dealer with the booksellers, was originally a surgeon's mate, and served at the siege of Carthagena. His first publication of this kind was *The Adventures of Roderick Random*, and his next those of Peregrine Pickle, in which is introduced the history of a well known woman of quality, written, as it is said, by herself, under the name of Lady Frail. These, and other compositions of the like kind, Smollet sold to the booksellers at such rates as enabled him to live without the exercise of his profession. He had a hand in *The Universal History* and translated *Gil Blas* and also *Telemachus*. The success of the former of these tempted him to translate *Don Quixote*, which, as he understood not the Spanish language, he could only do through the medium of the French and the former English versions, none of which do, as it is said, convey the humour of the original.

I might here speak of Richardson as a writer of fictitious history, but that he wrote for amusement, and that the profits of his writings, though very great, were accidental. He was a man of no learning nor reading, but had a vivid imagination, which he let loose in reflections on human life and manners, till it became so distended with sentiments, that for his own ease, he was necessitated to vent them on paper. In the original plan of his *Clarissa*, it was his design, as his bookseller once told me, to continue it to the extent of twenty-four volumes, but he was, with great difficulty, prevailed on to comprise it in six. The character of Richardson as a writer is to this day undecided, otherwise than by the avidity with which his publications are by some readers perused, and the sale of numerous editions. He has been celebrated as a writer similar in genius to Shakespeare, as being acquainted with the inmost recesses of the human heart, and having an absolute command of the passions, so as to be able to affect his readers as himself is affected, and to interest them in the successes and disappointments, the joys and sorrows of his characters. Others there are who think that neither his *Pamela*, his *Clarissa*, nor his *Sir Charles Grandison* are to be numbered among the books of rational and instructive amusement, that they are not just representations of human manners, that in them the turpitude of vice is not strongly enough marked, and that the allurements to it are represented in the gayest colours; that the texture of all his writings is flimsy and thin, and his style mean and feeble; that they have a general tendency to inflame the passions of young people, and to teach them that which they need not to be taught; and that though they pretend to a moral, it often turns out a bad one. The cant terms of him and his admirers are sentiment and sentimentality.

Johnson was inclined, as being personally acquainted with Richardson, to favour the former opinion of his writings, but he seemed not firm in it, and could at any time be talked into a

disapprobation of all fictitious relations, of which he would frequently say they took no hold of the mind.

I am tired of adducing instances of men who lived by the profession of writing and thought it an eligible one, and should now
proceed to relate the subsequent events of Dr. Johnson's life, and
mark the state of his mind at different periods, but that I find
myself detained by a character, which, as it were, obtrudes itself
to view, and is of importance enough to claim notice.

Laurence Sterne, a clergyman and a dignitary of the cathedral
church of York, was remarkable for a wild and eccentric genius,
resembling in many respects that of Rabelais. The work that
made him first known as a writer, was, *The Life and Opinions of
Tristram Shandy*, a whimsical rhapsody, but abounding in wit
and humour of the licentious kind. He too was a sentimentalist,
and wrote sentimental journeys and sentimental letters in abun-
dance, by which both he and the booksellers got considerably.[9]
Of the writers of this class or sect it may be observed, that being
in general men of loose principles, bad economists, living without
foresight, it is their endeavour to commute for their failings by
professions of greater love to mankind, more tender affections and
finer feelings than they will allow men of more regular lives, whom
they deem formalists, to possess. Their generous notions super-
sede all obligation: they are a law to themselves, and having good
hearts and abounding in the milk of human kindness, are above
those considerations that bind men to that rule of conduct which
is founded in a sense of duty. Of this new school of morality,
Fielding, Rousseau, and Sterne are the principal teachers, and
great is the mischief they have done by their documents.[10]

From the above enumeration of characters and particulars it
may be inferred, that Johnson's indolence and melancholy were
diseases of his mind, and not the necessary consequence of the
profession he had taken up, that he saw human life through a
false medium, and that he voluntarily renounced many comforts,
gratifications, and even pleasures, obviously in his power. One
effort however he made to soothe his mind and palliate the fatigue
of his labours, which I here relate.

The great delight of his life was conversation and mental intercourse. That he might be able to indulge himself in this, he had,

in the winter of 1749, formed a club that met weekly at the King's Head, a famous beefsteak house, in Ivy Lane near St. Paul's, every Tuesday evening. Thither he constantly resorted, and, with a disposition to please and be pleased, would pass those hours in a free and unrestrained interchange of sentiments, which otherwise had been spent at home in painful reflection. The persons who composed this little society were nine in number: I will mention their names, and, as well as I am able, give a slight sketch of the several characters of such of them as cannot now be affected by either praise or blame: they were, the Reverend Dr. Salter, father of the late master of the Charterhouse,—Dr. Hawkesworth,—Mr. Ryland, a merchant, a relation of his,—Mr. John Payne, then a bookseller, but now or very lately chief accountant of the bank,—Mr. Samuel Dyer, a learned young man intended for the dissenting ministry,—Dr. William M'Ghie, a Scots physician,—Dr. Edmund Barker, a young physician,—Dr. Richard Bathurst, also a young physician, and myself.

Dr. Samuel Salter was a Cambridge divine, whom some disagreement between him and his children had driven from his abode at Norwich, at the age of seventy, to settle in London. Being thus far advanced in years, he could carry his recollection back to the time when Dr. Samuel Clarke was yet a member of that university, and would frequently entertain us with particulars respecting him. He was a dignitary of the church, I think Archdeacon of Norfolk, a man of general reading, but no deep scholar: he was well bred, courteous, and affable, and enlivened conversation by the relation of a variety of curious facts, of which his memory was the only register.

Dr. Hawkesworth is a character well known in the literary world: I shall not attempt a delineation of it, as I find in the biographic dictionary an article for him.[11]

Mr. Samuel Dyer was the son of a jeweller of eminence in the city. He, as also his wife, were dissenters, and this their youngest son was educated by Professor Ward, at the time when he kept a private school in one of the alleys near Moorfields; and from thence, being intended by his father for the dissenting ministry, was removed to Dr. Dodderidge's academy at Northampton. After having finished his studies in this seminary, he was removed to

Glasgow, where, under Dr. Hutcheson, he was instructed in the writings of the Greek moralists, and went through several courses of ethics and metaphysics. To complete this plan of a learned education, the elder Mr. Dyer, by the advice of Dr. Chandler, sent his son to Leyden, with a view to his improvement in the Hebrew literature under Schultens, a celebrated professor in that university. After two years' stay abroad, Mr. Dyer returned, eminently qualified for the exercise of that profession to which his studies had been directed, and great were the hopes of his friends that he would become one of its ornaments. To speak of his attainments in knowledge, he was an excellent classical scholar, a great mathematician and natural philosopher, well versed in the Hebrew, and master of the Latin, French and Italian languages. Added to these endowments, he was of a temper so mild, and in his conversation and demeanour so modest and unassuming, that he engaged the attention and affection of all around him. In all questions of science, Johnson looked up to him, and in his life of Watts, among the poets, has cited an observation of his, that Watts had 'confounded the idea of space with that of empty space, and did not consider that though space might be without matter, yet matter being extended, could not be without space.'

It was now expected that Mr. Dyer would attach himself to the profession for which so liberal and expensive an education was intended to qualify him, and that he would, under all the discouragements that attended non-conformity, appear as a public teacher, and by preaching give a specimen of his talents; and this was the more wished, as he was a constant attendant on divine worship, and the whole of his behaviour suited to such a character. But being pressed by myself and other of his friends, he discovered an averseness to the undertaking, which we conceived to arise from modesty, but some time after found to have sprung from another cause.

Mr. Dyer commenced a man of the world, and with a sober and temperate deliberation resolved on a participation of its pleasures and enjoyments. His company, though he was rather a silent than a talkative man, was courted by many, and he had frequent invitations to dinners, to suppers, and card parties. By these means he became insensibly a votary of pleasure, and to justify this choice, had reasoned himself into a persuasion that, not only in the moral government of the world but in human manners, through all the changes and fluctuations of fashion and caprice, whatever is, is right. With this and other opinions equally tending to corrupt his mind, it must be supposed that he began to grow indifferent to the strict practice of religion, and the event showed itself in a gradual declination from the exercises of it, and his easy compliance with invitations to Sunday evening parties, in which mere conversation was not the chief amusement.

In his discourse he was exceedingly close and reserved: it was nevertheless to be remarked of him, that he looked upon the restraints on a life of pleasure with an unapproving eye. He had an exquisite palate, and had improved his relish for meats and drinks up to such a degree of refinement, that I once found him in a fit of melancholy occasioned by a discovery that he had lost his taste for olives!

He was a man of deep reflection, and very able in conversation on most topics; and after he had determined on his course of life, which was, to be of no profession, but to become a gentleman at large, living much at the houses of his friends, he seemed to adopt the sentiments of a man of fashion.

Dyer's support, in the idle way of life which he had made choice of, was the produce of a patrimony in the funds, that could not be great; his father, from whom he derived it, having left, besides himself, a widow, an elder son and a daughter. Johnson and myself, that he might be getting something, strongly pressed him to write the life of Erasmus; but he could not be induced to undertake it. A work of less labour, but less worthy of him, he was however prevailed on by Mr. Samuel Sharp, the surgeon, to engage in: this was a revision of the old translation of Plutarch's lives by several hands. He undertook, and, with heavy complaints of the labour of his task, completed it.

While he was a member of the club, Johnson suspected that his religious principles, for which at first he honoured him, were giving way, and it was whispered to me by one who seemed pleased that he was in the secret, that Mr. Dyer's religion was that of Socrates. What farther advances he made in Theism I could not learn, nor will I venture to assert, that which some expres-

sions that I have heard drop from him led me to fear, viz. that
he denied, in the philosophical sense of the term, the freedom of
the human will, and settled in materialism and its consequent
tenets.

Having admitted these principles into his mind, he settled into
a sober sensualist; in a perfect consistency with which character,
he was content to eat the bread of idleness, laying himself open
to the invitations of those that kept the best tables, and con-
tracting intimacies with men not only of opposite parties, but
with some who seemed to have abandoned all principle, whether
religious, political or moral. The houses of many such in succession were his home; and for the gratifications of a well spread
table, choice wines, variety of company, card parties, and a participation in all domestic amusements and recreations, the owners
thought themselves recompensed by his conversation and the
readiness with which he accommodated himself to all about him.
Nor was he ever at a loss for reasons to justify this abuse of his
parts or waste of his time: he looked upon the practice of the
world as the rule of life, and thought it did not become an individual to resist it.

I have been thus particular in the history of this accomplished
and hopeful young man, whom I once loved with the affection of
a brother, with a view to show the tendency of idleness, and to
point out at what avenues vice may gain admittance in minds
seemingly the most fortified. The assailable part of his was laxity
of principle: at this entered infidelity, which was followed by such
temptations to pleasure as he could see no reason to resist: these
led on desires after the means of gratification, and the pursuit of
them was his destruction.

M'Ghie was a Scotchman by birth, and educated, in one of the
universities of that country, for the profession of physic. In the rebellion in 1745, he, with a party of young men who, as volunteers,
had associated on the side of government, bore arms, and was engaged in the skirmish at Falkirk, which he ever spoke of as an ill-
conducted business. When matters were become pretty quiet in
Scotland, he took a doctor's degree, and came to London, where,
trusting to the friendship of his countrymen he hoped to succeed
in practice, but the town was overstocked with Scotch physicians,

and he met with small encouragement, though, by the favour of Dr. Benjamin Avery, the treasurer of Guy's Hospital, who had been a dissenting teacher, and at that time was at the head of that interest, he got to be elected one of the physicians of that charity. He was a learned, ingenious, and modest man; and one of those few of his country whom Johnson could endure. To say the truth, he treated him with great civility, and may almost be said to have loved him. He inherited a patrimony too small for his subsistence, and failing in his hope of getting forward in his profession, died of a broken heart, and was buried by a contribution of his friends.

Barker, being by education a dissenter, was sent to study physic at Leyden, from whence he returned about the time I am speaking of. He was introduced to us by Dyer, and had been a fellow student with him and with Akenside, Askew, Munckley, Mr. Dyson of the House of Commons, and others, few of whom are now living. From the conversation of these persons, he learned the principles of Lord Shaftesbury's philosophy, and became, as most of them were, a favourer of his notions, and an acute reasoner on the subject of ethics. He was an excellent classical scholar, a deep metaphysician, and had enriched his fancy by reading the Italian poets; but he was a thoughtless young man, and in all his habits of dress and appearance so slovenly as made him the jest of all his companions. Physicians in his time were used to be full dressed; and in his garb of a full suit, a brown tie-wig with a knot over one shoulder, and a long yellow-hilted sword, and his hat under his arm, he was a caricature. In his religious principles he professed himself an unitarian, for which Johnson so often snubbed him, that his visits to us became less and less frequent. After such a description as that above, it is needless to add that Barker succeeded ill in his profession. Upon his leaving us, he went to practise at Trowbridge in Wiltshire, but at the end of two years returned to London, and became librarian to the college of physicians, in the room of Edwards the ornithologist; but for some misbehaviour was displaced, and died in obscurity.

Dr. Richard Bathurst was a native of Jamaica, and the son of an eminent planter in that island, who coming to settle in England, placed his son in London, in order to qualify him for the practice of physic. In the course of his studies he became acquainted with Johnson, and was greatly beloved by him for the pregnancy of his parts and the elegance of his manners. Besides these he possessed the qualities that were most likely to recommend him in his profession; but, wanting friends, could make no way in it. He had just interest enough to be chosen physician to an hospital that was supported by precarious donations, and which yielded him little or no recompense for his attendance, which, as it was only a few hours on certain days in the week, left him, in a great measure, master of his time. Of this he was a good manager, employing it in the studies relative to his profession, and the improvement of himself in polite literature. In conjunction with Johnson, Hawkesworth, and others, he wrote *The Adventurer*, a periodical paper that will hereafter be spoken of, pursuing at the same time the most prudent and probable methods for acquiring reputation and advancing himself in his profession; but missing of success, he embraced the offer of an appointment of physician to the army that was sent on the expedition against the Havannah, where, soon after his arrival, he was seized with a fever that then raged among the troops, and which, before he could be a witness of the reduction of the place, put a period to an innocent and useful life.[12]

The Spaniards have a proverb, that he who intends to be pope must think of nothing else. Bathurst thought of becoming an eminent London physician, and omitted no means to attain that character: he studied hard, dressed well, and associated with those who were likely to bring him forward, but he failed in his endeavours, and shortly before his leaving England confessed to Johnson, that in the course of ten years' exercise of his faculty, he had never opened his hand to more than one guinea.

The failure of three such persons as those above-mentioned, in a profession in which very many ignorant men have been known to succeed, was matter of wonder to Johnson and all that knew them. He obeyed that precept of Scripture, which exhorts us to honour the physician, and would frequently say of those of his country, that they did more good to mankind, without a prospect of reward, than any profession of men whatever. Bathurst's want of encouragement affected him much: he often expressed to me his surprise, that a young man of his endowments and engaging manners, should succeed no better, and his disappointment drew from him a reflection, which he has inserted in his life of Akenside, that by an acute observer who had looked on the transactions of the medical world for half a century, a very curious book might be written on the fortune of physicians.[13] Such a book I should be glad to see; and if any person hereafter shall be induced to pursue Johnson's hint, he may possibly think the following remarks which have occurred to me in the course of a long intimacy with some of the most eminent of the profession, not altogether beneath his notice.[14]

Of the professors of medicine, in cities remote from London and in country towns, I know but little; but in the metropolis I am able to say, that in my time not only the track of a young physician was pretty plainly pointed out, and it is curious to follow it, but that the conduct of such an one was reducible to a system. Mead was the son of a nonconforming minister the teacher of a numerous congregation, who trusting to his influence over them, bred his son a physician, with what success is well known. He raised the medical character to such a height of dignity as was never seen in this or any other country. His example was an inducement with others of the dissenting ministers to make physicians of their sons. Oldfield, Clark, Nesbit, Lobb, and Munckley were the sons of dissenting teachers, and they generally succeeded. The hospital of St. Thomas, and that of Guy, in Southwark, were both under the government of dissenters and Whigs; and as soon as any one became physician of either, his fortune was looked upon as made.

The same advantage attended the election of a physician to the hospitals of Bethlehem and St. Bartholomew, which are of royal foundation, and have been under Tory government. By cultivating an interest with either of the two parties, the succession of a young physician was almost ensured. The frequenting Batson's or Child's was a declaration of the side he took, and his business was to be indiscriminately courteous and obsequious to all men, to appear much abroad and in public places, to increase his acquaintance and form good connections, in the doing whereof, a wife, if he were married, that could visit, play at cards, and tattle, was oftentimes very serviceable.[15] A candidate for practice, pursuing these methods and exercising the patience of a setting-dog for half a score years in the expectation of deaths, resignations, or other accidents that occasion vacancies, at the end thereof either found himself an hospital physician,[16] and if of Bethlehem a monopolist of one, and that a very lucrative branch of practice; or doomed to struggle with difficulties for the remainder of his life.

Political associations and religious sects are excellent nurses to young men of professions, especially of that of which I am speaking; Ratcliffe and Freind owed their fortunes to the support of the Tories and Jacobites; Mead and Hulse to the Whigs, and Schomberg to the Jews. The Quakers also, no contemptible body of men, had power and interest sufficient to introduce into great practice one of their own denomination; this was John Fothergill, a young man of parts and industry, who being bred an apothecary, and having obtained a Scotch degree, settled in London, and attached himself to Schomberg, taking him, in many parts of his conduct, for his exemplar: so that, upon Schomberg's decease, he slid into his practice, and became one of the most popular of the city physicians.

From these, and many other instances that might be produced, it is evident, that neither learning, parts, nor skill, nor even all these united, are sufficient to ensure success in the profession I am speaking of; and that, without the concurrence of adventitious circumstances, which no one can pretend to define, a physician of the greatest merit may be lost to the world.

To return from this digression, the club in Ivy Lane, composed of the persons above described, was a great relief to Johnson after the fatigue of study, and he generally came to it with both a corporal and mental appetite; for our conversation seldom began till after a supper, so very solid and substantial, as led us to think, that with him it was a dinner. By the help of this refection, and no other incentive to hilarity than lemonade, Johnson was, in a short time after our assembling, transformed into a new creature: his habitual melancholy and lassitude of spirit gave way; his countenance brightened; his mind was made to expand, and his wit to sparkle: he told excellent stories; and in his didactic style of conversation, both instructed and delighted us.

It required, however, on the part of us, who considered ourselves as his disciples, some degree of compliance with his political prejudices: the greater number of our company were Whigs, and I was not a Tory, and we all saw the prudence of avoiding to call the then late adventurer in Scotland, or his adherents, by those names which others hesitated not to give them, or to bring to remembrance what had passed, a few years before, on Tower Hill.[17] But the greatest of all our difficulties was, to keep alive in Johnson's mind a sense of the decorum due to the age, character, and profession of Dr. Salter, whom he took delight in contradicting, and bringing his learning, his judgment, and sometimes his veracity to the test. And here I must observe, that Johnson, though a high-churchman, and by consequence a friend to the clergy as a body of men, was, with respect to individuals, frequently, not to say wanting in civility, but to a very great degree splenetic and pertinacious. For this behaviour we could but one way account: He had been bred in an university, and must there have had in prospect those advantages, those stations in life, or perhaps those dignities, which an academic education leads to. Missing these by his adverse fortunes, he looked on every dignitary under a bishop, for to those of that order he was more than sufficiently respectful, and, to descend lower, on everyone that possessed the emoluments of his profession, as occupying a station to which himself had a better title, and, if his inferior in learning or mental endowments, treated him as little better than an usurper.

Dr. Salter was too much a man of the world to resent this behaviour: 'Study to be quiet' seemed to be his rule; and he might possibly think, that a victory over Johnson in any matter of dispute, could it have been obtained, would have been dearly purchased at the price of peace. It was nevertheless a temerarious act in him to venture into a society, of which such a man was the head. Dean Swift in his character of Corusodes,[18] has so developed the arts by which mere men of the world attain to ecclesiastical dignities and preferments, as should make such forever cautious

how they risk detection; and accordingly we see that many among
them are in general backward in forming connections and as-
sociating with scholars and the learned of the laity, at least with
men of Johnson's temper, who, where he had reason to expect
learning, never showed mercy to ignorance.

Hawkesworth was a man of fine parts, but no learning: his
reading had been irregular and desultory: the knowledge he had
acquired, he, by the help of a good memory retained, so that it
was ready at every call, but on no subject had he ever formed any
system. All of ethics that he knew, he had got from Pope's *Essay
on Man*, and *Epistles*; he had read the modern French writers,
and more particularly the poets, and * had attained such an insight into physics, as enabled him to talk on the subject. In the
more valuable branches of learning, he was deficient. His office of
curator of the magazine gave him great opportunities of improvement, by an extensive correspondence with men of all professions; it increased his little stock of literature, and furnished
him with more than a competent share of that intelligence which
is necessary to qualify a man for conversation. He had a good
share of wit, and a vein of humour. With all these talents,
Hawkesworth could be no other than an instructive and entertaining companion.

Of a far more valuable kind were the endowments of Dyer;
keen penetration and deep erudition were the qualities that so
distinguished his character, that, in some instances, Johnson
might almost be said to have looked up to him. As the purpose
of our meetings was the free communication of sentiments and
the enjoyment of social intercourse, our conversations were unrestrained, and the subjects thereof multifarious. Dyer was a
divine, a linguist, a mathematician, a metaphysician, a natural
philosopher, a classical scholar, and a critic; this Johnson saw and
felt, and never, but in defence of some fundamental and important truth, would he contradict him. The deference thus
shown by Johnson to Dyer, may be said to have been involuntary,
or respect extorted; for in their religious and political sentiments
their disagreement was so great, that less of it would, in some
minds, have engendered hatred. Of the fundamental and important truths above-mentioned, there was one, namely the

nature of moral obligation, of which Johnson was uniformly tenacious. Everyone, versed in studies of this kind, knows, that there are, among the moderns, three sects or classes of writers on morality, who, though perhaps deriving their respective tenets from the Socratic, the Academic and other ancient schools, are, in these times, considered, at least, as the guides of sects; these are the characteristic Lord Shaftesbury, Dr. Samuel Clarke, and Mr. Wollaston: the first of these makes virtue to consist in a course of action conformable to what is called the moral sense; Wollaston says it is acting, in all cases, according to truth, and treating things as they are; Dr. Clarke supposes all rational agents as under an obligation to act agreeably to the relations that subsist between such, or according to what he calls the fitness of things. Johnson was ever an admirer of Clarke, and agreed with him in this and most other of his opinions, excepting in that of the Trinity, in which he said, as Dr. Bentley, though no very sound believer, had done before, that Dr. Waterland had foiled him. He therefore fell in with the scheme of fitness, and thereby professed himself an adversary, in the mildest sense of the word, and an opponent of Dyer, who, having been a pupil of Hutcheson, favoured, notwithstanding his suspected infidelity, this and many other notions and opinions of Lord Shaftesbury.

To say of Lord Shaftesbury that he was but a suspected infidel, is surely treating him mildly, and I forbear to tax him with unbelief, only because in his *Letters to a Student at the University*, he has affected to speak of the Christian religion, as if half persuaded of its truth. Nevertheless, throughout his works it may be discerned, that he omits no opportunity of branding it with superstition and enthusiasm, and of representing the primitive professors of it as provoking, by their factious and turbulent behaviour, those persecutions from whence they derive the glory of martyrs. For these sentiments, as also for the invidious comparisons he is ever drawing between the philosophers Plato, Epictetus, Seneca and others, and the fathers, and his many contemptuous sneers at the writers on the side of Christianity, Johnson bore him no good will, neither did he seem at all to relish the cant of the Shaftesburian school, nor inclined to admit the pretensions of those who professed to be of it, to tastes and perceptions which are not common to all men; a taste in morals, in poetry, and prose-writing, in painting, in sculpture, in music, in architecture, and in government! a taste that censured every production, and induced them to reprobate every effort of genius that fell short of their own capricious standard.

Little as Johnson liked the notions of Lord Shaftesbury, he still less approved those of some later writers, who have pursued the same train of thinking and reasoning, namely, Hutcheson, Dr. Nettleton, and Mr. Harris of Salisbury, of which latter, for the many singularities of sentiment and style in his *Hermes*, he scrupled not to speak very lightly. There is a book extant, entitled, *Letters Concerning Mind*, written by a person of the same school, named Petvin, which, with an arrow taken from the quiver of their great master, a stroke of ridicule shot from one of the *Idlers*, Johnson may be fairly said to have transfixed. The passage is in a high degree ludicrous, and will, I am persuaded, justify the insertion of it here at length.

The author begins by declaring, that *the sorts of things are things that now are, have been, and shall be, and the things that strictly* ARE. In this position, except the last clause, in which he uses something of the scholastic language, there is nothing but what every man has heard, and imagines himself to know. But who would not believe that some wonderful novelty is presented to his intellect, when he is afterwards told, in the true *bugbear* style, that *the* ares, *in the former sense, are things that lie between the* have-beens *and* shall-bees. *The* have-beens *are things that are past; the* shall-bees *are things that are to come: and the things that* ARE, *in the latter sense, are things that have not been, nor shall be, nor stand in the midst of such as are before them, or shall be after them. The things that have been, and shall be, have respect to present, past, and future. Those likewise that now* ARE *have moreover place; that, for instance, which is here, that which is to the east, that which is to the west.*

All this, my dear reader, is very strange; but though it be strange, it is not new; survey these wonderful sentences again, and they will be found to contain nothing more than very plain truths, which, till this author arose, had always been delivered in plain language.[19]

The topics above-mentioned were, not infrequently, the subjects of altercation between Johnson and Dyer, in which it might be observed, as Johnson once did of two disputants, that the one had ball without powder, and the other powder without ball; for Dyer, though best skilled in the controversy, was inferior to his adversary in the power of reasoning, and Johnson, who was not always master of the question, was seldom at a loss for such sophistical arguments as the other was unable to answer.

In these disputations I had opportunities of observing what others have taken occasion to remark, viz. not only that in conversation Johnson made it a rule to talk his best, but that on many subjects he was not uniform in his opinions, contending as often for victory as for truth: at one time *good*, at another *evil* was predominant in the moral constitution of the world. Upon one occasion, he would deplore the non-observance of Good Friday, and on another deny, that among us of the present age there is any decline of public worship. He would sometimes contradict self-evident propositions, such as, that the luxury of this country has increased with its riches; and that the practice of card playing is more general than heretofore. At this versatility of temper, none, however, took offence; as Alexander and Caesar were born for conquest, so was Johnson for the office of a symposiarch, to preside in all conversations; and I never yet saw the man who would venture to contest his right.

Let it not, however, be imagined, that the members of this our club met together, with the temper of gladiators, or that there was wanting among us a disposition to yield to each other in all diversities of opinion; and indeed, disputation was not, as in many associations of this kind, the purpose of our meeting: nor were our conversations, like those of the Rota Club,[20] restrained to particular topics. On the contrary, it may be said, that with our gravest discourses was intermingled

> Mirth, that after no repenting draws,
> Milton.[21]

for not only in Johnson's melancholy there were lucid intervals, but he was a great contributor to the mirth of conversation, by the many witty sayings he uttered, and the many excellent stories which his memory had treasured up, and he would on occasion relate; so that those are greatly mistaken who infer, either from the general tendency of his writings, or that appearance of hebetude which marked his countenance when living, and is discernible in the pictures and prints of him, that he could only reason and discuss, dictate, and control.

In the talent of humour there hardly ever was his equal, except perhaps among the old comedians, such as Tarleton, and a few others mentioned by Cibber. By means of this he was enabled to give to any relation that required it, the graces and aids of expression, and to discriminate with the nicest exactness the characters of those whom it concerned. In aping this faculty I have seen Warburton disconcerted, and when he would fain have been thought a man of pleasantry, not a little out of countenance.

I have already mentioned, that Johnson's motive for the institution of this society was, his love of conversation, and the necessity he found himself under of seeking relief from the fatigue of compiling his dictionary: the same necessity operated still farther, and induced him to undertake, what most other men would have thought an additional fatigue, the publishing a periodical paper. The truth is, that not having now for a considerable space committed to writing aught but words and their significations, his mind was become tumid, and laboured to be delivered of those many and great conceptions, which for years it had been forming. The study of human life and manners, had been the chief employment of his thoughts, and to a knowledge of these, all his reading, all his conversation, and all his meditations tended. By these exercises, and the aid of an imagination that was ever teeming with new ideas, he accumulated a fund of moral science, that was more than sufficient for such an undertaking, and became in a very eminent degree qualified for the office of an instructor of mankind in their greatest and most important concerns.

1750-1755

I AM SENSIBLE of the contempt and ridicule with which those authors are treated by Lord Shaftesbury, who, differing from his favourites the ancients, have preferred to their method of writing in soliloquy and dialogue, the more authoritative and didactic form of essays; but who knows not that the ways by which intelligence and wisdom may be communicated are many and various, and that Johnson has followed the best exemplars? What are the sapiential books in the Scriptures, and all collections of precepts and counsels, but moral essays, lessons of economical prudence, and rules for the conduct of human life?

In a full persuasion of the utility of this mode of instruction, it undoubtedly was, that Montaigne, Lord Bacon, Osborne, Cowley, Sir William Temple, and others, in those excellent discourses, which they have not scrupled to term essays, have laid out their minds, and communicated to mankind that skill in worldly, and I will add, in heavenly prudence, which is scarcely attainable but by long experience, and an exercise both of the active and contemplative life; and to disseminate and recommend the principles and practice of religion and virtue; as also, to correct the lesser foibles in behaviour, and to render human intercourse easy and delightful, was the avowed design of those periodical essays, which, in the beginning of this century, contributed to form the manners of the then rising generation.

A long space had intervened since the publication of the

Tatlers, Guardians, and *Spectators:* it is true it had been filled up by *The Lover,* and *The Reader, The Theatre, The Lay Monastery, The Plain Dealer, The Freethinker, The Speculatist, The Censor,* and other productions of the like kind, but of some of these it may be said, that they were nearly stillborn, and of others, that they enjoyed a duration little more extended than that of the ephemeron: so that Johnson had no competitors for applause; his way was open, and he had the choice of many paths. Add to this, that a period of near forty years, in a country where commerce and its concomitant luxury had been increasing, had given rise to new modes of living, and even to characters that had scarcely before been known to exist. The clergyman was now become an amphibious being, that is to say, both an ecclesiastic and a laic; the stately stalking fop, whose gait, as Cibber describes it, resembled that of a peacock, was succeeded by a coxcomb of another species, a fidgeting, tripping animal, that for agility might be compared to a grasshopper; the shopkeeper was transformed into a merchant, and the parsimonious stockbroker into a man of gallantry; the apron, the badge of mechanic occupations, in all its varieties of stuff and colour, was laid aside; physicians and lawyers were no longer distinguishable by their garb; the former had laid aside the great wig, and the latter ceased to wear black, except in the actual exercise of their professions: in short, a few years of public tranquillity had transformed a whole nation into gentlemen.

In female life the refinements were also to be noted. In consequence of a better education than it had been usual to bestow on them, women were become proficients in literature, and a man might read a lady's letter without blushing at the spelling. The convenience of turnpike-roads had destroyed the distinction between town and country manners, and the maid of honour and the farmer's wife put on a cap of the latest form, almost at the same instant. I mention this, because it may have escaped the observation of many, that a new fashion pervades the whole of this our island almost as instantaneously as a spark of fire illuminates a mass of gunpowder.[1]

These, it may be said, were but foibles in the manners of the times; but there were certain notions and opinions, which having been disseminated subsequent to the publication of the last of the collections of essays above-mentioned, escaped their censure, and were now become principles that had misled many, and were likely to affect the moral conduct of the young and unthinking: these had for their authors and propagators such men as Collins, Mandeville,[2] Morgan and Tindal; the first pair deists, and the latter infidels. And to these I might add, though I would not brand them with so harsh an appellation as the last, Toland, Gordon, Trenchard, and others of that class of writers, men who having drunk the lees of the Bangorian Controversy,[3] were become so intoxicated in their notions of civil and religious liberty, as to talk of the majesty of the people! and showed themselves anxious that their zeal for religion might be estimated by their jealousy of all establishments for the support of it.

The flimsy arguments contained in Collins's discourse on freethinking,[4] had been refuted with great learning and pleasantry by Bentley, before which time, as I have been informed, a clergyman in his habit, walking the streets of London, was in danger of being affronted; but the poison of Mandeville had affected many. His favourite principle is, the title to the most noted of all his books, 'Private vices, public benefits,' throughout which he labours to inculcate, as a subordinate position, this other, that man is a selfish being, and that all that we call human beneficence is to be accounted for upon principles that exclude the love of any but ourselves.

Johnson has remarked, that malevolence to the clergy is seldom at a great distance from irreverence for religion. He saw the features of that malevolence in the writings of these men, and the point at which freethinking was likely to terminate; and taking up the defence of religion where Mr. Addison left it, he made it a part of his design as well to adduce new arguments for its support, and to enforce the practice of virtue, as to correct those errors in the smaller concerns and occupations of life, the ridiculing which rendered his paper an amusement.

In this situation and state of public manners Johnson formed the plan of his *Rambler*, and with what spirit he entered upon it may be inferred from the following solemn address, which he composed and offered up to the divine Being for a blessing on the undertaking:

Almighty God, the giver of all good things, without whose help all labour is ineffectual, and without whose grace all wisdom is folly; grant, I beseech Thee, that in this undertaking thy holy spirit may not be withheld from me, but that I may promote thy glory, and the salvation of myself and others; grant this, O Lord, for the sake of thy son Jesus Christ. Amen.

The work was undertaken without the communication of his design to any of his friends, and consequently without any desire of assistance from them; it was from the stores of his own mind alone that he hoped to be able to furnish that variety of matter which it would require; which, that it might at no time fail him, he kept up by noting in a commonplace book that he carried about him, such incidents, sentiments, and remarks on familiar life and manners as were for his purpose. This method of accumulating intelligence had been practised by Mr. Addison, and is humorously described in one of the *Spectators*,[5] wherein he feigns to have dropped his paper of Notanda, consisting of a diverting medley of broken sentences and loose hints, which he tells us he had collected, and had meant to make use of. Much of the same kind is Johnson's Adversaria.[6]

Being thus stored with matter, Johnson proceeded to publish his paper; and the first number came abroad on Tuesday the twentieth day of March, 1750.

It was the office of a censor of manners to curb the irregularities into which, in these new modes of living, the youthful of both sexes were apt to fall, and this he endeavoured to effect by gentle exhortation, by sober reproof, and, not seldom, by the powers of wit and ridicule; but with what success, others are as well able to tell as myself; however, if that is to be judged of by the sale of the paper, it was doubtless great, for though its reception was at first cool, and its progress slow, the world were too wise to suffer it to sink into oblivion: it was collected into volumes, and it would be too much for anyone to say, that ten impressions of twelve hundred and fifty each, of a book fraught with the soundest precepts of economical wisdom, have been disseminated in vain.

On the first publication of the *Rambler* it met with a few readers who objected to it for certain particularities in the style, which they had not been used to in papers of the like kind, new and original combinations of words, sentences of an unusual form, and words derived from other languages, though accommodated to the genius of our own; but for these such reasons are assigned in the close of the last paper, as not only are a defence of them, but show them to be improvements of our language.[7]

That Johnson owed his excellence as a writer to the divines and others of the last century, myself can attest, who have been the witness of his course of reading, and heard him declare his sentiments of their works. Hooker he admired for his logical precision, Sanderson for his acuteness, and Taylor for his amazing erudition; Sir Thomas Browne for his penetration, and Cowley for the ease and unaffected structure of his periods. The tinsel of Sprat disgusted him, and he could but just endure the smooth verbosity of Tillotson. Hammond and Barrow he thought involved, and of the latter that he was unnecessarily prolix.

It may perhaps be thought, as his literary acquaintance was extensive, and the toil of compiling his dictionary very great, that Johnson was helped in the publication of the *Rambler* by the communications of others; but this was not the fact, he forbore to solicit assistance, and few presumed to offer it, so that in the whole series of those papers, we know with certainty of only four that were not of his own writing. Of these, No. 30, was sent him by Mrs. Catherine Talbot, daughter of Mr. Edward Talbot; * No. 97, by Mr. Richardson, the author of *Clarissa*, and numbers 44 and 100, by Mrs. Elizabeth Carter of Deal, a lady to whose reputation for learning, and the most estimable qualities of her sex, no praise of mine can make any addition.[8] Hence arises that uniformity of subject and sentiment which distinguishes the *Rambler* from other papers of the like kind; but how great must its merit be, when wanting the charm of variety and that diversity of characters, which, by the writers of them, was thought necessary to keep attention awake, it could support itself to the end, and make instruction a substitute for amusement! Nor can this defect, if it be any, be deemed a deviation from Johnson's original purpose, which was not so much to instruct young persons of both sexes in the manners of the town, as in that more important science, the conduct of human life; it being certain, that he had it in his power as well to delight as to instruct his readers; and this he has in some instances done, not only by the introduction of fictitious characters and fancied portraits, but by ironical sarcasms and original strokes of wit and humour, that have, perhaps, excited more smiles than the writings of many, whose chief purpose it was, like that of L'Estrange and others, to make their readers merry.

And hence we may take occasion to observe, the error of those who distinguish so widely between men of study and reflection, and such as are hackneyed in the ways of the world, as to suppose the latter only qualified to instruct us in the offices of life. Lord Chesterfield, in his letters to his son, takes every occasion to express his hatred of an university education, to brand it with pedantry, and to declare that it unfits a man for social intercourse. Some have asserted, that travelling is the only means to attain a knowledge of mankind; and the captain in Swift, in a less extensive view of human life, swears that

> To give a young gentleman right education,
> The army's the very best school in the nation.[9]

To say the truth, there are numbers of men who contemn all knowledge derived from books, and prefer to it what they call turning over the great volume of the world. I had once a gardener that could not endure the mention of Miller's dictionary, and would contend with me, that 'practice was everything'; and innumerable are the instances of men who oppose mother-wit to acquired intelligence, and had rather grope their way through the world, than be indebted for instruction to the researches of others. Such men as these, in situations they have not been accustomed to, are ever awkward and diffident; and it is for a reason nearly akin to this, that few rakes are able to look a modest woman in the face. On the contrary, the attainments of Johnson were such as, notwithstanding his home-breeding, gave him confidence, and qualified him for the conversation of persons of all ranks, conditions, characters, and professions, so that no sooner had the *Rambler* recommended itself to the favour of the public, and the author was known to be of easy access, than his acquaintance was sought, and even courted, by persons, of whom many, with all the improvement of travel, and the refinements of court-manners, thought that somewhat worth knowing was to be learned from the conversation of a man, whose fortunes and course of life had precluded him from the like advantages.

Johnson's talent for criticism, both preceptive and corrective, is now known and justly celebrated; and had he not displayed it in its utmost lustre in his *Lives of the Poets*, we should have lamented that he was so sparing of it in the *Rambler*, which seemed to be a vehicle, of all others the most proper, for that kind of communication. An eulogium on Knolles's *History of the Turks*, and a severe censure on the *Samson Agonistes* of Milton are the only critical essays there to be found; [10] to the latter he seems to have been prompted by no better a motive, than that hatred of the author for his political principles which he is known to have entertained, and was ever ready to avow. What he has remarked of Milton in his *Lives of the Poets* is undoubtedly true: he was a political enthusiast, and, as is evident from his panegyric on Cromwell, a base and abject flatterer.[11] His style in controversy was sarcastic and bitter, and not consistent with Christian charity; nor does he seem in his private character to have possessed many of those qualities that most endear men to each other. His friends were few; and there is reason to suspect, from the sternness of his temper, and the rigid discipline of his family, that his domestic manners were far from amiable, and that he was neither a kind husband nor an indulgent parent. But neither these nor those other qualities that rendered him both a bitter enemy and a railing disputant, could justify the severity of Johnson's criticism on the above-mentioned poem, nor apologize for that harsh and groundless censure which closes the first of his discourses on it, that it is 'a tragedy which ignorance has admired, and bigotry applauded.'

The reflection on that enmity of Johnson towards Milton, which I have above remarked, leads me to mention another instance of it, which about this time fell under my observation. A man of the

name of Lauder, a native of Scotland, had conceived a hatred
against the memory of Milton, and formed a scheme to convict
him of plagiarism, by showing that he had inserted in the *Paradise
Lost* whole passages taken from the writings of sundry modern
Latin poets, namely, Masenius the Jesuit, Taubman, a German
professor, Staphorstius, a Dutch divine, and other writers less
known; and of this crime he attempted to prove him guilty, by
publishing instances in forged quotations, inserted from time to
time in the *Gentleman's Magazine,* which not being detected,
he made additions to, and again published in a volume entitled
*An Essay on Milton's Use of and Imitation of the Moderns in
His Paradise Lost,* 8vo. 1750. While the book was in the press,
the proof sheets were submitted to the inspection of our club,
by a member of it who had an interest in its publication,[12] and
I could all along observe that Johnson seemed to approve, not
only of the design but of the argument, and seemed to exult in
a persuasion, that the reputation of Milton was likely to suffer
by this discovery. That he was not privy to the imposture I am
well persuaded, but that he wished well to the argument must be
inferred from the preface, which indubitably was written by Johnson.

The charges of plagiarism contained in this production, Lauder
has attempted to make out by citations to a very great number.
For a time the world gave credit to them, and Milton's reputation
was sinking under them, till a clergyman of great worth, learning
and industry, Mr. now Dr. John Douglas, prompted at first by
mere curiosity, set himself to find out and compare the parallel
passages, in the doing whereof he discovered, that in a quotation
from Staphorstius, Lauder had interpolated eight lines taken from
a Latin translation of the *Paradise Lost,* by a man named Hogaeus
or Hog, and opposed them to the passage in the original, as evidence of Milton's plagiarism. Proofs of the like fraud in passages
cited from Taubman and many others are produced by Dr. Douglas; but a single instance of the kind would have been sufficient to
blast the credit of his adversary.

Having made these discoveries, Dr. Douglas communicated
them to the world in a pamphlet entitled, *Milton Vindicated from
the Charge of Plagiarism,* 8vo. 1750. Upon the publication thereof

his booksellers called on Lauder for a justification of themselves, and a confirmation of the charge; but he, with a degree of impudence not to be exceeded, acknowledged the interpolation of the books by him cited, and seemed to wonder at 'the folly of mankind in making such a rout about eighteen or twenty lines.' However, being a short time after convinced by Johnson and others, that it would be more for his interest to make an ample confession of his guilt, than to set mankind at defiance, and stigmatize them with folly; he did so in a letter addressed to Mr. Douglas, published in quarto, 1751.

Notwithstanding this humiliating and abject confession, which, though it was penned by Johnson, was subscribed by himself, Lauder had the impudence, in a postscript thereto, in effect to retract it, by pretending that the design of his essay was only to try how deeply the prepossession in favour of Milton was rooted in the minds of his admirers; and that the stratagem, as he calls it, was intended to impose only on a few obstinate persons; and, whether that was so criminal as it has been represented, he leaves the impartial mind to determine.

In 1756, Dr. Douglas published a new edition of his pamphlet, with the title of *Milton No Plagiary*: to this is an appendix, containing part of an apology of Lauder's booksellers, in which they give an account of their conduct, after the first discovery of his villainy, in the following words:

An immediate application to Lauder was necessary, as well to justify ourselves, as to remove or confirm the charge. Accordingly, we acquainted him, that if he did not instantly put into our hands the books from which he had taken the principal passages, we would publicly disclaim all connection with him, and expose his declining the only step left for his defence. This declaration brought him to us the following day, when, with great confidence, he acknowledged the interpolation of all the books; and seemed to wonder at mankind in making such a rout about eighteen or twenty lines. As this man then has been guilty of such a wicked imposition upon us, our friends, and the public, and is capable of so daring an avowal of it, we declare, that we will have no farther intercourse with him, and that we now sell his book only as a curiosity of fraud and interpolation, which all the ages of literature cannot parallel!

With a character thus blasted, it was next to impossible for this man to continue in England; he therefore left it, and went to settle at Barbadoes, proposing to set up a school there; but, upon his arrival on the island, he met with small encouragement, and is said to have died about the year 1771.

To return to Johnson, I have already said that he paid no regard to time or the stated hours of refection, or even rest; and of this his inattention I will here relate a notable instance. Mrs. Lenox, a lady now well known in the literary world, had written a novel entitled, *The Life of Harriot Stuart*, which in the spring of 1751, was ready for publication. One evening at the club, Johnson proposed to us the celebrating the birth of Mrs. Lenox's first literary child, as he called her book, by a whole night spent in festivity. Upon his mentioning it to me, I told him I had never sat up a whole night in my life; but he continuing to press me, and saying, that I should find great delight in it, I, as did all the rest of our company, consented. The place appointed was the Devil Tavern, and there, about the hour of eight, Mrs. Lenox and her husband, and a lady of her acquaintance, now living, as also the club, and friends to the number of near twenty, assembled. Our supper was elegant, and Johnson had directed that a magnificent hot apple pie should make a part of it, and this he would have stuck with bay leaves, because, forsooth, Mrs. Lenox was an authoress, and had written verses; and further, he had prepared for her a crown of laurel, with which, but not till he had invoked the muses by some ceremonies of his own invention, he encircled her brows. The night passed, as must be imagined, in pleasant conversation, and harmless mirth, intermingled at different periods with the refreshments of coffee and tea. About five, Johnson's face shone with meridian splendour, though his drink had been only lemonade; but the far greater part of us had deserted the colours of Bacchus, and were with difficulty rallied to partake of a second refreshment of coffee, which was scarcely ended when the day began to dawn. This phenomenon began to put us in mind of our reckoning; but the waiters were so overcome with sleep, that it was two hours before we could get a bill, and it was not till near eight that the creaking of the street door gave the signal for our departure.

My mirth had been considerably abated by a severe fit of the toothache, which had troubled me the greater part of the night, and which Bathurst endeavoured to alleviate by all the topical remedies and palliatives he could think of; and I well remember, at the instant of my going out of the tavern door, the sensation of shame that affected me, occasioned not by reflection on anything evil that had passed in the course of the night's entertainment, but on the resemblance it bore to a debauch. However, a few turns in the Temple, and a breakfast at a neighbouring coffee house, enabled me to overcome it.

In the foregoing pages I have assigned the motives that induced Johnson to the institution of the club, and the writing of the *Rambler*; and here I may add, that his view in both was so far answered, as that the amusements they afforded him contributed, not only to relieve him from the fatigue of his great work the dictionary, but that they served to divert that melancholy, which the public now too well knows was the disease of his mind. For this morbid affection, as he was used to call it, no cause can be assigned; nor will it gratify curiosity to say, it was constitutional, or that it discovered itself in his early youth, and haunted him in his hours of recreation; and it is but a surmise that it might be a latent concomitant of that disease, which, in his infancy, had induced his mother to seek relief from the royal touch. His own conjecture was, that he derived it from his father, of whom he was used to speak as of a man in whose temper and character melancholy was predominant. Under this persuasion, he at the age of about twenty, drew up a state of his case for the opinion of an eminent physician in Staffordshire,[13] and from him received an answer, 'that from the symptoms therein described, he could think nothing better of his disorder, than that it had a tendency to insanity; and without great care might possibly terminate in the deprivation of his rational faculties.' The dread of so great a calamity was one inducement with him to abstain from wine at certain periods of his life, when his fears in this respect were greatest; but it was not without some reluctance that he did it, for he has often been heard to declare, that wine was to him so great a cordial, that it required all his resolution to resist the temptations to ebriety.

It was fortunate for the public, that during a period of two years, the depression of his mind was at no time so great as to incapacitate him for sending forth a number of the *Rambler* on the days on which it became due; nor did any of the essays or discourses therein contained, either in the choice of subjects or the manner of treating them, indicate the least symptom of drooping faculties or lassitude of spirit. Nevertheless, whether the constant meditation on such topics as most frequently occur therein, had not produced in his mind a train of ideas that were now become uneasy to him, or whether, that intenseness of thought which he must have exerted, first, in the conception, and next, in the delivery of such original and noble sentiments as these papers abound with, had not made the relaxation of his mind necessary, he thought proper to discontinue the *Rambler* at a time when its reputation was but in its dawn.

The paper in which this his resolution is announced, is that of March 14, 1752, which concludes the work. As he had given his readers no warning of his intention, they were unprepared for the shock, and had the mortification to receive the tidings and the blow at the same instant, with the aggravation of a sympathetic melancholy, excited by the mournful expressions with which he takes his leave. And though he affects to think the reasons for discontinuing the publication a secret to his readers, it is but too apparent that it was written in the hours of dejection, and that the want of assistance and encouragement was not the weakest of his motives. Of the former of these two he had surely no right to complain, for he was so far from being ever known to wish for assistance, that his most intimate friends seemed to think it would have been presumption to offer it. The want of encouragement indeed might be a justifiable cause of discontent, for I have reason to think that the number of papers taken off hardly amounted to five hundred on any of the days of publication. Nevertheless, the slow circulation of the paper was to be accounted for by other reasons than that the author was never a favourite with the public, a reflection that would have been but excusable, had his imitations of Juvenal become waste paper, or his *Irene*, instead of being suffered to run nine nights, been consigned to oblivion on the first; for it must be considered, that the merits of the *Rambler* were of a kind not likely to recommend it to those who read chiefly for amusement, and of readers, this class will ever be by much the most numerous: the subjects therein discussed are chiefly the weightiest and most important, respecting more our eternal than temporal happiness; and that these were the obstacles to the progress of his paper, himself has unawares confessed in his apology for the conduct of it. 'I have never,' says he, 'complied with temporary curiosity, nor enabled my readers to discuss the topic of the day. I have rarely exemplified my assertions by living characters; in my papers no man could look for censures of his enemies or praises of himself; and they only were expected to peruse them, whose passions left them leisure for abstracted truth, and whom virtue could please by its naked dignity.'

Towards the close of this last paper, he seems to refer to 'the final sentence of mankind,' with a sort of presage, that one more deliberate than that to which he was submitting might be more favourable to his labours. He little thought at this time to what length the justice of mankind would go; that he should be a witness to the publication of the tenth edition of the *Rambler*, or that his heart would ever be dilated, as his friends can testify it was, with the news of its being translated into the Russian language.[14]

Much might be said in commendation of this excellent work; but such suffrages as those here mentioned set it almost above praise. In the author's own opinion it was less estimable than in that of his judges: some merit indeed he claims for having enriched his native language, but in terms so very elegant and modest, that they at once hold forth an exemplar, and convey an apology. 'I have laboured,' says he, 'to refine our language to grammatical purity,[15] and to clear it from colloquial barbarisms, licentious idioms, and irregular combinations. Something perhaps I have added to the elegance of its construction, and something to the harmony of its cadence. When common words were less pleasing to the ear, or less distinct in their signification, I have familiarized the terms of philosophy by applying them to popular ideas, but have rarely admitted any word not authorized by former writers.'—With what success these endeavours of his have been attended is best known to those who have made eloquence their study; and it may go far towards the stamping a lasting character of purity, elegance, and strength on the style of Johnson, to say, that some of the most popular orators of this country now living, have not only proposed it to themselves as a model for speaking, but for the purpose of acquiring the cadence and flow of his periods, have actually gotten whole essays from the *Rambler* by heart.

The concluding paragraph of his farewell paper is so very awful, that I cannot resist the temptation to insert it, and the rather for that it seems to have been written under a persuasion, that Almighty God had been propitious to his labour, and that the solemn address to him which he had composed and offered up, on occasion of his engaging in it, had been heard, and was likely to be accepted.

The essays professedly serious, if I have been able to execute my own intentions, will be found exactly conformable to the precepts of Christianity, without any accommodation to the licentiousness and levity of the present age. I therefore look back on this part of my work with pleasure, which no praise of man shall diminish or augment. I shall never envy the honours which wit and learning obtain in any other cause, if I can be numbered among the writers who have given ardour to virtue, and confidence to truth:

> Celestial pow'rs! that piety regard,
> From you my labours wait their last reward.

The *Rambler*, thus published in numbers, was not suffered to be lost to the world, or to sink into oblivion. As soon as, by the conclusion of it, it became a complete work, it was collected into volumes, and printed in Scotland, and, soon after, also here, and obtained such favour with the public, as was an inducement with Dr. Hawkesworth to an undertaking of the same kind, the publication of a periodical paper called *The Adventurer*. For the carrying on such a work as this, Hawkesworth, though he possessed but a small stock of learning, was more than meanly qualified. He had excellent natural parts, and, by reading the modern English and French authors, had acquired a style, which, by his acquaintance with Johnson, he had improved into a very good one.

He wrote verses, that is to say in English, with ease and fluency, and was better acquainted with the world than most men are who have been bred to no profession.

The subjects of these papers, like those of the *Rambler*, are human life and manners, with a mixture of humour and instructive pleasantry, criticism, and moral and religious exhortation, too various, it must be supposed, for the powers of a single person; they are therefore the produce of different pens, and may owe their merit, in a great measure, to that diversity. The curiosity of the reader is, to a small degree, gratified by the last paper, which assigns to their author, Dr. Joseph Warton, such as have a certain signature, and leaves to Dr. Hawkesworth himself the praise of such as are without any. To the information there given, I add, that the papers marked A. which are said to have come from a source that soon failed, were supplied by Dr. Bathurst, an original associate in the work, and those distinguished by the letter T. by Johnson.[16]

The first number of the *Adventurer* made its appearance on Tuesday, November 7, 1752, and on that weekday, and also on Saturdays, it continued to be published, till the ninth of March, 1754. To point out the many excellent essays contained in it is needless, as they are now collected into volumes, and together with the *Rambler* form a system of moral and economical institution; two of them are to be looked on as curiosities in different ways, Dr. Warton's remarks on *King Lear*, and *The Tempest*, the most learned and judicious critiques in the English language, and the account of a native of Scotland, called Admirable Crichton, dictated from memory by Johnson to Hawkesworth.

As Johnson expected to be believed whenever he either spoke or wrote, he has not vouchsafed to cite any authority for the incredible relation, which the *Adventurer* contains, of the personal and mental endowments of a man who is described as a monster both of erudition and prowess, and in every other view of his character is represented as having passed the limits of humanity. That he had no authority for what he has related of him, would be too much to say, after he has asserted, that he had such as was incontestible, yet having that, he has kept within the bounds of it, and cast a veil over that blaze of glory, which, to gaze on in its naked splendour, would not dazzle but blind the beholder.[17]

That Johnson dictated this number of the *Adventurer*, I have already said: that he did not himself write it, may be thus accounted for; he had doubtless read the history of Crichton in Sir Thomas Urquhart's book, and retained it with that firmness of memory, which held fast almost everything that he met with in books. Supposing him, as we may, too indolent to recur to one that he had formerly read through, and, in the hearing of Hawkesworth, to have related the transactions of so wonderful a man, the latter might catch it as a fit subject for an essay, and give it to the world, as he has done in the *Adventurer*. To which we may add, that Johnson was seldom a narrator of events: his talent was original thinking; in conversation he told stories, and related historical facts with great precision, but rarely sent them abroad in writing.

We are not to suppose, that that soreness of mind, which Johnson seems to have felt at the time of his discontinuing the *Rambler*, was, in the short interval of six months, so completely healed, as to render him a disinterested candidate for praise in this new publication; or that he who had declared, that he could not compose a sermon, gratis, would write an *Adventurer*, without being hired to it: on the contrary, it is certain, that he retained his old maxim, that gain was the only genuine stimulative to literary exertion, and that the assistance he gave to this publication was purchased at two guineas for every number that he furnished; a rate of payment which he had before adjusted in his stipulation for the *Rambler*, and was probably the measure of a reward to his fellow-labourers.

The avowed end of the *Adventurer* being the same with that of the *Rambler*, and the plan and conduct thereof so little different from it, the latter may be considered as a continuation of the former: nevertheless, it may be observed, that in the *Adventurer*, the number of entertaining papers, of portraits, singular characters, and essays of wit, humour, and pleasantry, is greater, in proportion, than in the *Rambler*; and to that diversity it was doubtless owing, that the circulation of it was more diffuse. On the part of the writers it was carried on with great vigour, and, together with the *Rambler*, is likely to remain a lasting evidence of the spirit that dictated, and the public good sense that encouraged, such a series, as they both contain, of religious instruction, economical wisdom, and innocent delight.[18]

Hawkesworth has, almost in terms, declared himself the editor of the *Adventurer*, and that the other contributors thereto were merely auxiliaries; and his zeal for its success may be inferred from the number of papers written by himself, which, upon a comparison, will be found nearly equal to that of all the rest. This zeal was excited by a motive far more strong than any which actuated his co-adjutors, a desire of advantage in his then profession, which ostensibly was that of a governor of a school for the education of young females, by making himself known as a judge of life and manners, and capable of qualifying those of riper years for the important relations of domestic society.

But while he was indulging a well grounded hope to reap this fruit of his studies, a reward of a very different kind courted his acceptance. The Archbishop of Canterbury, Dr. Herring, his diocesan and neighbour, having perused his essays, and informed himself of his general character, made him an offer of a faculty that should raise him above the level of vulgar literati, and, almost without his being conscious of any such exaltation, create him a doctor of both laws, and the honour was accepted.

Among men of real learning, there is but one opinion concerning what are called Lambeth degrees. The right of conferring them is a relic of the power anciently exercised in this country by the legates of the pope, and is, by statute, transferred to the Archbishop of Canterbury. Degrees of this kind are often convenient for clergymen, as they are qualifications for a plurality of livings; but, as they imply nothing more than favour, convey little or no honour.

Hawkesworth was a greater gainer by the *Adventurer* than any of those concerned in it. His success, however, wrought no good effects upon his mind and conduct; it elated him too much, and betrayed him into a forgetfulness of his origin, and a neglect of his early acquaintance; and on this I have heard Johnson remark, in terms that sufficiently expressed a knowledge of his character, and a resentment of his behaviour. It is probable that he might use the same language to Hawkesworth himself, and also reproach him with the acceptance of an academical honour to which he could have no pretensions, and which Johnson, conceiving to be irregular, as many yet do, held in great contempt; thus much is certain, that soon after the attainment of it, the intimacy between them ceased.

The expedients above-mentioned, and the visits of a variety of friends, which his writings had procured him, afforded Johnson great relief, and enabled him to keep at a bay those terrors, which were almost incessantly assailing him, till the beginning of the year 1752, o.s. when it pleased God to try him by a calamity, that was very near realizing all those evils which, for a series of years, he had dreaded; this was the loss of his wife, who, on the 28th day of March, and after seventeen years cohabitation, left him a childless widower, abandoned to sorrow, and incapable of consolation.

Those who were best acquainted with them both, wondered that Johnson could derive no comfort from the usual resources, reflections on the conditions of mortality, the instability of human happiness, resignation to the divine will, and other topics; and the more, when they considered, that their marriage was not one of those which inconsiderate young people call love-matches, and that she was more than old enough to be his mother; that, as their union had not been productive of children, the medium of a new relation between them was wanting; that her inattention to some, at least, of the duties of a wife, was [19] evident in the person of her husband, whose negligence of dress seemed never to have received the least correction from her, and who, in the sordidness of his apparel, and the complexion of his linen, even shamed her. For these reasons I have often been inclined to think, that if this fondness of Johnson for his wife was not dissembled, it was a lesson that he had learned by rote, and that, when he practised it, he knew not where to stop till he became ridiculous. It is true, he has celebrated her person in the word *formosae*, which he caused to be inscribed on her gravestone; but could he, with that imperfection in his sight which made him say, in the words of Milton, he never saw the human face divine,[20] have been a witness of her beauty? which we may suppose had sustained some loss before he married; her daughter by her former husband being but little younger than Johnson himself. As, during her lifetime, he invited but few of his friends to his house, I never saw her, but I have been told by Mr. Garrick, Dr. Hawkesworth, and others, that there was somewhat crazy in the behaviour of them both; profound respect on his part, and the airs of an antiquated beauty on hers. Johnson had not then been used to the company of women, and nothing but his conversation rendered him tolerable among them: it was, therefore, necessary that he should practise his best manners to one, whom, as she was descended from an ancient family, and had brought him a fortune, he thought his superior. This, after all, must be said, that he laboured to raise his opinion of her to the highest, by inserting in many of her books of devotion that I have seen, such endearing memorials as these: 'This was dear Tetty's book'—'This was a prayer which dear Tetty was accustomed to say,' not to mention his frequent recollection of her in his meditations, and the singularity of his prayers respecting her.

To so high a pitch had he worked his remembrance of her, that he requested a divine, of his acquaintance,[21] to preach a sermon at her interment, written by himself, but was dissuaded from so ostentatious a display of the virtues of a woman, who, though she was his wife, was but little known. He intended also to have deposited her remains in the chapel in Tothill Fields, Westminster, but, altering his mind, he committed the disposal of them to his friend Hawkesworth, who buried her in his own parish church of Bromley in Kent, under a black marble stone, on which Johnson himself, a few months before his death, caused the following memorial to be inscribed:

Hic conduntur reliquiae
ELIZABETHAE
Antiqua Jarvisiorum gente,
Peatlingae, apud Leicestrienses, ortae;
Formosae, cultae, ingeniosae, piae;
Uxoris, primis nuptiis, HENRICI PORTER,
Secundis, SAMUELIS JOHNSON;
Qui multum amatam, diuque defletam
Hoc lapide contexit.
Obiit Londini, mense Mart.
A. D. MDCCLIII.

I have been informed, that in his early youth, he entertained a romantic passion, excited possibly by reading the poets, for a young woman of a family and in circumstances far above him; but proofs are wanting that it proceeded to a declaration. In his intercourse with the world, he had become known to many of the female sex, who sought his conversation; [22] but it was never heard that he entertained a passion for anyone, or was in any other sense a lover, than as he was the author of amorous verses. If ever he was in danger of becoming one in reality, it was of a young woman whom he used to call Molly Aston, of whose wit, and of the delight he enjoyed in conversing with her, he would speak with rapture,[23] but this was in the lifetime of Mrs. Johnson, and he was a man too strict in his morals to give any reasonable cause of jealousy to a wife.

The melancholy, which seized Johnson, on the death of his wife, was not, in degree, such as usually follows the deprivation of near relations and friends: it was of the blackest and deepest kind. That affection, which could excite in the mind of Milton the pleasing images described in his sonnet on his deceased wife,

Methought I saw my late espousèd saint,

wrought no such effect on that of Johnson: the apparition of his departed wife was altogether of the terrific kind, and hardly afforded him a hope that she was in a state of happiness.

That these gloomy conceptions were in part owing to the books he had been accustomed to read, I have little doubt. Sundry passages occur in his writings, which induce a suspicion, that his notions of the state of departed spirits were such as are now deemed superstitious; and I will not attempt to vindicate him from the charge of believing some of the many relations extant, that go to prove an intercourse between them and the inhabitants of this earth. These, as they were systematical, and such as he was able to defend by arguments the most specious, I can no better account for, than by a supposition, that in the course of his studies he had been a dabbler in demonology, by which I mean, not the writings of those vulgar authors who relate the intrigues and midnight banquets of witches with infernal spirits, or that teach the difference between black and white witches, and assert the power of them and their agents to harm us, but from those more authentic writers, namely, Mede, and others, whose proofs, that the doctrine of demons made a part of the gentile theology, have induced an opinion, that in these latter times departed spirits have such an existence as the intercourse above-mentioned seems to imply.

Not to dwell longer on so painful a subject, I will dismiss these reflections with an observation, that by the unhappiness of his bodily constitution, and the defect of the organs of sense, he was rendered unsusceptible of almost all those delights which we term pleasures of the imagination, and which help to soothe the mind under affliction; and this melancholy truth I shall attempt to illustrate by the following observations:

With respect to sight, it must be noted, that he was of that class of men, who, from a defect in the visual organs, are termed myops, or nearsighted persons; and farther, that disease had deprived him of the use of one eye, the consequence whereof was, that in lieu of those various delightful prospects which the face of nature affords, the beautiful and the grand, that multiply ideas and administer delight, as well in the reflection as the immediate enjoyment of them, his mind was presented with an universal blank. Nor was his misfortune less, with respect to those objects wherein beauty, symmetry, and harmony of parts and proportions, are resident: to him a statue was an unshapen mass, and a sumptuous edifice a quarry of stone. Of the beauties of painting, notwithstanding the many eulogiums on that art which, after the commencement of his friendship with Sir Joshua Reynolds, he inserted in his writings, he had not the least conception; and this leads me to mention a fact to the purpose, which I well remember. One evening at the club, I came in with a small roll of prints, which, in the afternoon, I had picked up: I think they were landscapes of Perelle, and laying it down with my hat, Johnson's curiosity prompted him to take it up and unroll it; he viewed the prints severally with great attention, and asked me what sort of pleasure such things could afford me; I told him, that as representations of nature, containing an assemblage of such particulars as render rural scenes delightful, they presented to my mind the objects themselves, and that my imagination realized the prospect before me; he said, that was more than his would do, for that in his whole life he was never capable of discerning the least resemblance of any kind between a picture and the subject it was intended to represent.

To the delights of music, he was equally insensible: neither voice nor instrument, nor the harmony of concordant sounds, had power over his affections, or even to engage his attention. Of music in general, he has been heard to say, 'It excites in my mind no ideas, and hinders me from contemplating my own'; and of a fine singer, or instrumental performer, that 'he had the merit of a Canary bird.' [24] Not that his hearing was so defective as to account for this insensibility, but he laboured under the misfortune which he has noted in the life of Barretier, and is common to more persons than in this musical age are willing to confess it, of wanting that additional sense or faculty, which renders music grateful to the human ear.

From this state of his mental and bodily constitution, it must necessarily be inferred, that his comforts were very few, and that his mind had no counterpoise against those evils of sickness, sorrow, and want, which, at different periods of his life he laboured under, and in some of his writings pathetically laments. Of this misfortune himself was sensible, and the frequent reflection thereon wrought in him a persuasion, that the evils of human life preponderated against the enjoyments of it; and this opinion he would frequently enforce by an observation on the general use of narcotics in all parts of the world, as, in the east, and southern countries, opium; in the west, and northern, spirituous liquors and tobacco; [25] and into this principle he resolved most of the temptations to ebriety. To the use of the former of these, himself had a strong propensity, which increased as he advanced in years; his first inducement to it was, relief against watchfulness, but when it became habitual, it was the means of positive pleasure, and as such was resorted to by him whenever any depression of spirits made it necessary. His practice was, to take it in substance, that is to say, half a grain levigated with a spoon against the side of a cup half full of some liquid, which, as a vehicle, carried it down.

With so few resources of delight, it is not to be wondered at, if after the loss of his wife, his melancholy was hardly supportable. Company and conversation were the only reliefs to it, and when these failed him he was miserable. At the club in Ivy Lane, our usual hour of departure was eleven, and when that approached he was frequently tempted to wander the streets, and join in the conversation of those miserable females who were there to be met with. Of these he was very inquisitive as to their course of life, the history of their seduction, and the chances of reclaiming them. The first question he generally asked was, if they could read. Of one who was very handsome, he asked, for what she thought God had given her so much beauty: she answered—'To please gentlemen.' [26]

In the midst of the distresses which, at this period of his life, surrounded him, he found both inclination and the means to be helpful to others. His wife, a short time before her death, had consigned to his care a friend of her own sex, a person of very extraordinary endowments, whom, for a benevolent purpose that will shortly be mentioned, Johnson had invited to a residence in his house: This was Mrs. Anna Williams, whose history is as follows: [27]

Her father, Zachariah Williams, was a surgeon and physician in South Wales, a man of parts and great ingenuity: he had addicted himself to mathematical studies, and having discovered, that the variations of the magnetic needle were equal at equal distances east and west; he entertained a sanguine hope, that he had attained the means of ascertaining the longitude. As London was the place where he thought he should best avail himself of his discovery, he, in the year 1730, left his habitation and business, and, together with his daughter, settled in the metropolis. His first business was, to lay before the commissioners of the longitude the fruits of his studies; but, upon a due examination, they all proved abortive: no proportion whatever of the reward could be assigned him as his due; but, as a kind of recompense for his disappointment, means were found to procure him a maintenance in the Charterhouse, and accordingly he was admitted into that asylum of age and poverty. With all his ingenuity and scientific wisdom, which I have heard his daughter, with an excusable partiality, magnify beyond credibility, he must have been defective in worldly prudence, for, either by the infraction of economical regulations, or some other misconduct, he rendered himself at first obnoxious to censure from the governors, and in the end was obliged to forego all the benefits, to become an outcast, and, at the age of seventy-five, to suffer shipwreck in the wide ocean of the world.

What became of him afterwards I could never learn, save that, in the year 1755, he published in Italian and English a book entitled, *An Account of an Attempt to Ascertain the Longitude at Sea, by an Exact Theory of the Magnetical Needle*, written, as it is supposed, by Johnson, and translated by Mr. Baretti. Of his daughter, I am able to say more, having known her a long time. About ten years after her arrival with her father in London, she was alarmed by the appearance of a cataract on both her eyes, which continued to increase till it totally deprived her of her sight. Before this calamity befell her, she, with the assistance of her father, had acquired a knowledge of the French and Italian languages, and had made great improvements in literature, which, together with the exercise of her needle, at which she was very dexterous, as well after the loss of her sight as before, contributed to support her under her affliction, till a time when it was thought by her friends, that relief might be obtained from the hand of an operating surgeon. At the request of Dr. Johnson, I went with her to a friend of mine, Mr. Samuel Sharp, senior surgeon of Guy's hospital, who before had given me to understand, that he would couch her gratis if the cataract was ripe, but upon making the experiment it was found otherwise, and that the crystalline humour was not sufficiently inspissated for the needle to take effect. She had been almost a constant companion of Mrs. Johnson for some time before her decease, but had never resided in the house: afterwards, for the convenience of performing the intended operation, Johnson took her home, and, upon the failure of that, kept her as the partner of his dwelling till he removed into chambers, first in Gray's Inn, and next in the Temple. Afterward, in 1766, upon his taking a house in Johnson's Court in Fleet Street, he invited her thither, and in that, and his last house in Bolt Court, she successively dwelt for the remainder of her life.

The loss of her sight made but a small abatement of her cheerfulness, and was scarce any interruption of her studies. With the assistance of two female friends, she translated, from the French of Père La Bleterie, the life of the Emperor Julian. In 1755, Mr. Garrick, ever disposed to help the afflicted, indulged her with a benefit play that produced her two hundred pounds; and in 1766, she published by subscription a quarto volume of miscellanies in prose and verse, and thereby increased her little fund to three hundred pounds, which, being prudently invested, yielded an income, that, under such protection as she experienced from Dr. Johnson, was sufficient for her support.

She was a woman of an enlightened understanding; plain, as the women call it, in her person, and easily provoked to anger, but possessing, nevertheless, some excellent moral qualities, among which no one was more conspicuous, than her desire to promote the welfare and happiness of others; and of this she gave a signal proof, by her solicitude in favour of an institution for the maintenance and education of poor deserted females in the parish of St. Sepulchre, London, supported by the voluntary contributions of ladies, and, as the foundation stone of a fund for its future subsistence, she bequeathed to it the whole of that little, which, by the means above-mentioned, she had been able to accumulate. To the endowments and qualities here ascribed to her, may be added a larger share of experimental prudence than is the lot of most of her sex. Johnson, in many exigences, found her an able counsellor, and seldom showed his wisdom more than when he hearkened to her advice. In return, she received from his conversation the advantages of religious and moral improvement, which she cultivated so, as in a great measure to smooth the constitutional asperity of her temper. When these particulars are known, this intimacy, which began with compassion, and terminated in a friendship that subsisted till death dissolved it, will be easily accounted for.

Johnson had but for a short time enjoyed the relief from solitude and melancholy reflection which this friendly attachment afforded him, before he experienced that affliction, which, in the course of nature, is the concomitant of longevity, in the loss of his friend Cave, who finished a useful and well spent life in the month of January, 1754. It might seem that between men so different in their endowments and tempers as Johnson and Cave were, little of true friendship could subsist, but the contrary was the case: Cave, though a man of a saturnine disposition, had a sagacity which had long been exercised in the discrimination of men, in searching into the recesses of their minds, and finding out what they were fit for; and a liberality of sentiment and action, which, under proper restrictions, inclined him not only to encourage genius and merit, but to esteem and even to venerate the possessors of those qualities as often as he met with them: it cannot, therefore, be supposed, but that he entertained a high regard for such a man as Johnson, and, having had a long experience of his abilities and integrity, that he had improved this disposition into friendship. Johnson, on his part, sought for other qualities in those with whom he meant to form connections: had he determined to make only those his friends whose endowments were equal to his own, his life would have been that of a Carthusian; he was therefore more solicitous to contract friendships with men of probity and integrity, and endued with good moral qualities, than with those whose intellectual powers, or literary attainments, were the most conspicuous part of their character; and of the former, Cave had a share, sufficient to justify his choice.

On this mutual regard for each other, as on a solid basis, rested the friendship between Johnson and Cave. It was therefore with a degree of sorrow, proportioned to his feelings towards his friends, which were ever tender, that Johnson reflected on the loss he had to sustain, and became the narrator of the most important incidents of his life. In the account which he has given of his death, it will be readily believed, that what he has related respecting the constancy of his friendship, is true, and that when, as the last act of reason, he fondly pressed the hand that was afterwards employed in recording his memory, his affection was sincere.

By some papers now in my hands it seems that, notwithstanding Johnson was paid for writing the *Rambler*, he had a remaining interest in the copyright of that paper, which about this time he sold. The produce thereof, the pay he was receiving for his papers in the *Adventurer*, and the fruits of his other literary la-

bours, had now exalted him to such a state of comparative affluence, as, in his judgment, made a manservant necessary. Soon
after the decease of Mrs. Johnson, the father of Dr. Bathurst arrived in England from Jamaica, and brought with him a negro
servant, a native of that island, whom he caused to be baptized
and named Francis Barber, and sent for instruction to Barton
upon Tees in Yorkshire: upon the decease of Captain Bathurst,
for so he was called, Francis went to live with his son, who willingly parted with him to Johnson.[28] The uses for which he was
intended to serve this his last master were not very apparent, for
Diogenes himself never wanted a servant less than he seemed to
do: the great bushy wig, which throughout his life he affected
to wear, by that closeness of texture which it had contracted and
been suffered to retain, was ever nearly as impenetrable by a comb
as a quickset hedge; and little of the dust that had once settled
on his outer garments was ever known to have been disturbed by
the brush. In short, his garb and the whole of his external appearance was, not to say negligent, but slovenly, and even squalid;
to all which, and the necessary consequences of it, he appeared
as insensible as if he had been nurtured at the Cape of Good
Hope: he saw that, notwithstanding these offensive peculiarities
in his manners, his conversation had great attractions, and perhaps he might estimate the strength of the one by the degree of
the other, and thence derive that apathy, which, after all, might
have its foundation in pride, and afforded him occasion for triumph over all the solicitudes respecting dress.[29]

Of this negro servant much has been said, by those who knew
little or nothing of him, in justification of that partiality which
Johnson showed for him, and his neglect of his own necessitous
relations. The following particulars are all that are worth relating of him: He stayed with Johnson about five years, that is to
say, till 1758, and then left him, but at the end of two years returned, and was taken again into his service. His first master had,
in great humanity, made him a Christian; and his last, for no
assignable reason, nay, rather in despite of nature, and to unfit
him for being useful according to his capacity, determined to
make him a scholar.

He placed him at a school at Bishop-Stortford, and kept him

there five years; and, as Mrs. Williams was used to say, who would frequently reproach him with his indiscretion in this instance, expended three hundred pounds in an endeavour to have him taught Latin and Greek.[30]

The proposal for the *Dictionary*, and other of his writings, had exhibited Johnson to view in the character of a poet and a philologist: to his moral qualities, and his concern for the interests of religion and virtue, the world were for some time strangers; but no sooner were these manifested by the publication of the *Rambler* and the *Adventurer*, than he was looked up to as a master of human life, a practical Christian and a divine; his acquaintance was sought by persons of the first eminence in literature; and his house, in respect of the conversations there, became an academy. One person, in particular, who seems, for a great part of his life, to have affected the character of a patron of learned and ingenious men, in a letter which I have seen, made him a tender of his friendship in terms to this effect:—'That having perused many of his writings, and thence conceived a high opinion of his learning, his genius, and moral qualities, if Mr. Johnson was inclined to enlarge the circle of his acquaintance, he [the letter writer] should be glad to be admitted into the number of his friends, and to receive a visit from him.'—This person was Mr. Dodington, afterwards Lord Melcombe, the value and honour of whose patronage, to speak the truth, may in some degree be estimated by his diary lately published.* How Johnson received this invitation, I know not: as it was conveyed in very handsome expressions, it required some apology for declining it, and I cannot but think he framed one.[31]

Had Johnson accepted of Mr. Dodington's invitation, it cannot be supposed that he would have been much pleased with the company of * such other persons as it was likely to introduce him to. His declining it seems, therefore, an act of great prudence, and indeed he was exempted from the necessity of seeking connections; for many persons were of Dodington's mind, and were desirous of adding him to the number of their friends. Invitations to dine with such of those as he liked, he so seldom declined, that to a friend of his, he said, 'I never but once, upon a resolution to employ myself in study, balked an invitation out to dinner, and then I stayed at home and did nothing.' Little, however, did that laxity of temper, which this confession seems to imply, retard the progress of the great work in which he was employed; the conclusion, and also the perfection of his *Dictionary*, were objects from which his attention was not to be diverted: the avocations he gave way to were such only as, when complied with, served to invigorate his mind to the performance of his engagements to his employers and the public, and hasten the approach of the day that was to reward his labour with applause.

That day it was his happiness to see; for, by the end of the year 1754, he had completed his copy, not more to his own ease and satisfaction, than to the joy of Millar the bookseller, the principal proprietor of the work, and the guardian or treasurer of the fund out of which the payments were from time to time issued. To say the truth, his joy on the occasion was so great, that he could not refrain from expressing it somewhat intemperately, as appears by the following acknowledgment of the receipt of the last sheet of the manuscript:

Andrew Millar sends his compliments to Mr. Samuel Johnson, with the money for the last sheet of copy of the dictionary, and thanks God he has done with him.

To which Johnson returned this good humoured and brief answer:

Samuel Johnson returns his compliments to Mr. Andrew Millar, and is very glad to find, as he does by his note, that Andrew Millar has the grace to thank God for anything.[32]

The publication of this great work soon followed, as may be imagined, the interchange of these two very laconic epistles; and the month of May, 1755, put the world in possession of a treasure, the value whereof it will require the experience of years to find out. To recommend it to the notice of foreigners, he was desirous it should appear to come from one who had attained academical honours; he therefore applied, by his friend Mr. Thomas Warton, to the university of Oxford for a master's degree, and obtained it by a diploma, dated the tenth day of February, 1755, the tenour whereof is, that the most learned Samuel Johnson, of Pembroke College, having distinguished himself in the literary world by his writings, tending to form the popular manners; and having, for the adorning and settling his native language, compiled, and being about to publish an English dictionary, the chancellor, masters, and scholars of the said university, in solemn convocation assembled, do therefore constitute and appoint the said Samuel Johnson, Master of Arts, and command, that he enjoy and exercise all the rights, privileges, and honours to that degree appertaining.

Upon the receipt of this instrument, Johnson testified his gratitude for the honour done him, in a letter to the vice-chancellor.[33]

So near perfection had the author brought his *Dictionary*, that, upon a review of it previous to his drawing up the preface, he declares, he is unable to detect the casual omission of more than one article, the appellative OCEAN.[34] Nor has he, as I know, been charged with any other defect, or with any misinterpretation of a word, save in an instance or two, where, being moved by party-prejudice, he has imposed significations on a few words that are indefensible. Let these be imputed to a mind agonized, at various periods during the prosecution of this laborious work, with indigence, with sorrow, and pain; and let the piteous description of his circumstances and feelings, which the preface contains, induce us to bury our resentment of a few petulant expressions, in the reflection, that this stupendous compilation was undertaken and completed by the care and industry of a single person.

Upon occasion of publishing the *Dictionary*, Mr. Garrick celebrated the author in the following lines:

Talk of war with a Briton, he'll boldly advance,
That one English soldier will beat ten of France:
Would we alter the boast from the sword to the pen,
Our odds are still greater, still greater our men:
In the deep mines of science though Frenchmen may toil,
Can their strength be compar'd to Locke, Newton, and Boyle?
Let them rally their heroes, send forth all their pow'rs,
Their verse men and prose men; then match them with ours:
First Shakespeare and Milton, like Gods in the fight,

Have put their whole drama and epic to flight;
In satires, epistles, and odes, would they cope.
Their numbers retreat before Dryden and Pope:
And Johnson, well-arm'd like a hero of yore,
Has beat forty French, and will beat forty more.[35]

It has already been mentioned, that Johnson's inducement to this undertaking was the offer of a liberal reward. The term liberal is indefinite, and, after the lapse of twenty years, during which such sums as from three to eight thousand pounds have been paid for copies, would hardly be allowed to fifteen hundred and seventy-five,[36] which was the sum stipulated for the *Dictionary*. Of this, Johnson, who was no very accurate accountant, thought a great part would be coming to him on the conclusion of the work; but upon producing, at a tavern-meeting for the purpose of settling, receipts for sums advanced to him, which were indeed the chief means of his subsistence, it was found, not only that he had eaten his cake, but that the balance of the account was greatly against him. His debtors were now become his creditors: but they, in a perfect consistency with that liberal spirit which, in sundry instances, the great booksellers are known to have exercised towards authors, remitted the difference, and consoled him for his disappointment by making his entertainment at the tavern a treat.

The pointing out the utility of such a work as a vernacular lexicon is needless, and the displaying the merits of that of which I am speaking, is a labour which the suffrage of the public has saved me. The learned world had long wished for its appearance, and the circulation of the book was proportionate to the impatience which the promise of it had excited. Lord Corke, being at Florence at the time when it was published, presented it, in the author's name, to the Academy della Crusca, and that learned body transmitted to him a fine copy of their *Vocabulario*. The French academy also signified their approbation of his labours, by a present of their *Dictionnaire*, of which Mr. Langton was the bearer. To these testimonies of public respect, it is a small but ludicrous addition to say, that Dr. Robertson, the Scots historian, told Johnson, that he had fairly perused his *Dictionary* twice over, and that Johnson was pleased at the hearing it. The *Dictionary* was a library book, and not adapted to common use: the book-sellers knowing this, and being encouraged by its success, easily prevailed on the author to abridge it in two octavo volumes, and made him a liberal recompense.

It was doubtless a great satisfaction to Johnson to have completed this great work; and though we may believe him in the declaration at the end of the preface thereto, that he dismissed it with frigid tranquillity, we cannot but suppose that he was pleased with the reception it met with. One and only one writer, an obscure man named Campbell, a purser of a man of war, who, as well for the malignancy of his heart as his terrific countenance, was called horrible Campbell, attempted to disturb the quiet which possessed him, by animadverting on this and other of his writings: This fellow had abilities for writing, and in a small volume entitled *Lexiphanes*, endeavoured to turn many passages in the *Rambler*, and interpretations in the *Dictionary*, into ridicule: gratifying his spleen also with a number of malevolent censures of Dr. Akenside's *Pleasures of Imagination*. It was the purpose of this libel to provoke both or one of the persons who were the subjects of it, to a controversy, from which, whatever should be the event, he hoped, as it is said Ulysses did in his contest with Ajax, to derive honour.*

> Losing he wins, because his name will be
> Ennobled by defeat, who durst contend with me.
> Dryden.[37]

But in this he was disappointed. Akenside was too proud to dispute with an inferior, and Johnson's silence proceeded not more from his contempt of such an adversary, than from a settled resolution he had formed, of declining all controversy in defence either of himself or his writings. Against personal abuse he was ever armed, by a reflection, that I have heard him utter: 'Alas! reputation would be of little worth, were it in the power of every concealed enemy to deprive us of it';—and he defied all attacks on his writings, by an answer of Dr. Bentley to one who threatened to write him down,—that 'no author was ever written down but by himself.'

His steady perseverance in this resolution afforded him great satisfaction whenever he reflected on it; and he would often felicitate himself, that, throughout his life, he had had firmness enough to treat with contempt the calumny and abuse as well of open as concealed enemies, and the malevolence of those anonymous scribblers, whose trade is slander, and wages infamy.[38]

1756-1760

I F JOHNSON could ever be said to be idle, now was the time. He had, for nine years, been employed in his great work, and had finished it: he had closed the *Rambler*; and the *Adventurer* was closed on him. He had it now in his choice to reassume some one or other of those various literary projects, which he had formed in the early part of his life; * but the powers of his mind, distended by long and severe exercise, became relaxed, and required rest to bring them to their tone, and it was some time before he could resolve on any employment, suited to his abilities, that carried with it any prospect of pleasure, or hope of reward. This remission of his labour, which seemed to be no more than nature herself called for, Johnson, in those severe audits to which it was his practice to summon himself, would frequently condemn, styling it a waste of his time, and a misapplication of the talents with which he was gratefully conscious that God had endowed him. Yet herein was he greatly mistaken; for though Milton says of the servants of God,

> _____thousands at his bidding speed,
> And post o'er land and ocean without rest;

he adds, that

> They also serve who only stand and wait,
>
> Sonnet on his blindness.

Johnson's intellectual faculties could never be unemployed: when he was not writing he was thinking, and his thoughts had ever a tendency to the good of mankind; and that indolence, which, in his hours of contrition, he censured as criminal, needed little expiation.

This recess from literary occupation continued, however, no longer than was absolutely necessary. It has already been shown, that he was not only a friend to such vehicles of literary intelligence as magazines and other epitomes of large works, but that he was a frequent contributor to them. He had occasionally, for Cave's magazine, written the lives of Father Paul Sarpi, Boerhaave, the admirals Drake and Blake, Barretier, and divers other eminent persons; and also, sundry philological essays, particularly a state of the controversy between Crousaz and Warburton respecting the *Essay on Man*, and a vision entitled 'The Apotheosis of Milton.' [1] Cave being now dead, he ceased to furnish articles for that publication, and either voluntarily offered, or suffered himself to be retained as a writer in others of a like kind: accordingly, in 1756, he wrote for *The Universal Visitor, or Monthly Memorialist*, printed for Gardner,[2] two or three letters therein inserted, on the subject of agriculture; and in the same and subsequent year he assumed or submitted to the office of a reviewer, as it is called, for the publisher of a monthly collection, entitled, *The Literary Magazine*, of which one Faden, a printer, was the editor. In this he wrote the address to the public; also, reviews of the following books, viz. Soame Jenyns's *Free Enquiry into the Nature and Origin of Evil*; Dr. Blackwell's *Memoirs of the Court of Augustus*; he wrote also therein, 'Observations on the State of Affairs in 1756,' and the life of the present king of Prussia; and, Hanway's *Journal* coming in his way, which contained in it a severe censure of the practice of tea drinking, he officially, as I may say, and with a degree of alacrity proportioned to his avowed love of that liquor, undertook to criticize the book, and refute the arguments of the author.[3]

Epictetus somewhere advises us to consider the gratification of the calls of hunger and thirst, as acts of necessity; to be performed as it were by the bye, but by no means to be estimated among the enjoyments of life; and by a precept no less than

divine, we are exhorted to take no thought what we shall eat or
what we shall drink. Johnson looked upon the former as a very
serious business, and enjoyed the pleasures of a splendid table
equally with most men. It was, at no time of his life, pleasing to
see him at a meal; the greediness with which he ate, his total
inattention to those among whom he was seated, and his profound silence in the hour of refection, were circumstances that
at the instant degraded him, and showed him to be more a
sensualist than a philosopher. Moreover, he was a lover of tea to
an excess hardly credible; whenever it appeared, he was almost
raving, and by his impatience to be served, his incessant calls for
those ingredients which make that liquor palatable, and the
haste with which he swallowed it down, he seldom failed to make
that a fatigue to everyone else, which was intended as a general
refreshment. Such signs of effeminacy as these, suited but ill with
the appearance of a man, who, for his bodily strength and stature,
has been compared to Polyphemus.

This foible in Johnson's character being known, it will excite
no wonder in the reader to be told, that he readily embraced the
opportunity of defending his own practice, by an examen of
Hanway's book. Accordingly, he began his remarks on it in the
Literary Magazine, Number VII; but receiving from this author
an injunction to forbear proceeding in his censure till a second
edition should appear, he submitted, though it was a prohibition
that could neither be reasonably imposed, nor by any means enforced; yet, such was its effect, that Mr. Hanway's *Journal* was
not remarked on, till he had been allowed every advantage that
could protect it from censure.

Such candour on the part of him, on whose opinion perhaps
many were waiting to form theirs, might have relieved the author
from any dread of unfair treatment; but Johnson, who paid all
proper deference to good intentions, did not think this tacit
indication of the temper in which he sat down to review Mr.
Hanway's *Journal*, sufficient: he, therefore, in resuming the
dispute, promises him, that he shall find no malignity of censure,
and draws a very handsome inference from the contents of his
thirty-two letters, that he is a man whose failings may well be
pardoned for his virtues.

The criticism on this second edition appeared in the *Literary Magazine*, Number XIII, and extends chiefly to Mr. Hanway's arguments against tea and gin: subjects which seem to have inspired him with such enthusiastic eloquence as disdained all the rules of logic, and dictated observations and conclusions, so incoherent and incongruous, as would have stimulated even those, who, in the main, thought with him, to endeavour at correcting his judgment.

But, in Johnson, when writing on the qualities of tea, he met with an opponent on principle; for its antagonist's hatred, however radical or zealous, could not exceed the love its champion bore it; he describes himself as 'a hardened and shameless teadrinker, who has, for many years, diluted his meals with only the infusion of this fascinating plant; whose kettle has scarcely time to cool; who, with tea amuses the evening, with tea solaces the midnights, and with tea welcomes the morning.'

That Mr. Hanway was right in asserting, that the practice of drinking tea is productive of harm among the lower classes of people, must certainly be admitted; and that Johnson was right in denying that it has all the poisonous qualities the *Journal* attributes to it, experience shows. From what has been said on both sides, little can be inferred, but that to some it is noxious, and to others neutral; that those do wrong who persist in the use of it when they find it injurious to their health, and that such as cannot afford the necessaries of life, ought not to indulge in its luxuries.

At Johnson's candid examen, which should not have offended Mr. Hanway, as, by submitting his work to public inspection, he recognized the right of public criticism, the latter was extremely irritated, and very unadvisedly drew his reviewer forth to a second exertion of his argumentative powers, printed in the same magazine, vol. ii., 253, under the title of 'A Reply to a Paper in the *Gazetteer* of May 26, 1757'; in which, with seeming contrition and mock penitence, he requests to know how he has offended, and deprecates the wrath he had excited.—'There are only three subjects,' says he, 'upon which my unlucky pen has happened to venture. Tea, the author of the *Journal*, and the Foundling Hospital.'

Of the author, I unfortunately said, that his injunction was too magisterial. This I said, before I knew he was a governor of the foundlings; but he seems inclined to punish this failure of respect, as the czar of Muscovy made war upon Sweden, because he was not treated with sufficient honours when he passed through the country in disguise. Yet was not this irreverence without extenuation. Something was said of the merit of *meaning well*, and the journalist was declared to be a man *whose failings might well be pardoned for his virtues.* This is the highest praise which human gratitude can confer upon human merit, praise that would have more than satisfied *Titus* or *Augustus,* but which I must own to be inadequate and penurious, when offered to the member of an important corporation.

Unluckily for Mr. Hanway it happened, that while he was labouring for the general good, by reprobating the practice of drinking tea, an institution from which he derived much of his importance, was suffering from want of care. Johnson, in a visit to the Foundling Hospital, observed, that the objects of the charity, however well provided for in other respects, were, in the essential point of religious knowledge, lamentably deficient. To him, who considered wisely that there was no evil from which the governors of the Foundling Hospital could rescue deserted infants, so much to be dreaded as ignorance of this kind, the answers given to his inquiries touching their improvement were very unsatisfactory. Without knowing that Mr. Hanway was concerned in the charge, he, in his former letter, had stated this fact, and followed it by saying, that 'to breed up children in this manner, is to rescue them from an early grave, that they may find employment for the gibbet, from dying in innocence, that they may perish by their crimes.'

The laudable motive which induced Johnson to point out this neglect, and the justice of his remark, did not shield him from unmerited resentment. He was called on to support what he had advanced: his assertion was branded with the epithet of *incredible,* but his observation had produced its effect: he had found means to have it represented to one of the highest names of the society, and a catechist was soon after appointed.

Whoever peruses this controversy, will be forced to confess that, on the part of Johnson, it is conducted, not only with candour, but with great good humour, a circumstance to be remarked in all his polemical writings, and to be wondered at, seeing that in oral disputation his behaviour was so different, as to expose him to the severest censures. His exertions against his adversary were play, not hostility;

> Sporting the lion ramp'd, and in his paw
> Dandled the kid.
> *Paradise Lost*, Book iv., line 343.

About the year 1756, time had produced a change in the situation of many of Johnson's friends, who were used to meet him in Ivy Lane. Death had taken from us M'Ghie; Barker went to settle as a practising physician at Trowbridge; Dyer went abroad; Hawkesworth was busied in forming new connections; and I had lately made one that removed from me all temptations to pass my evenings from home. The consequence was, that our symposium at the King's Head broke up, and he who had first formed us into a society was left with fewer around him than were able to support it.

All this while, the booksellers, who by his own confession were his best friends, had their eyes upon Johnson, and reflected with some concern on what seemed to them a misapplication of his talents. The furnishing magazines, reviews, and even newspapers, with literary intelligence, and the authors of books, who could not write them for themselves, with dedications and prefaces, they looked on as employments beneath him, who had attained to such eminence as a writer; they, therefore, in the year 1756, found out for him such a one as seemed to afford a prospect both of amusement and profit: this was an edition of Shakespeare's dramatic works, which, by a concurrence of circumstances, was now become necessary, to answer the increasing demand of the public for the writings of that author.

Mr. Garrick, who, as everyone knows, was in all that related to Shakespeare an enthusiast, had, by the study of his principal characters, and his own exquisite action, so recommended Shakespeare to the town, that the admiration of him became general even to affectation; many professing to be delighted with the performance and perusal of his plays, who, from their want of literature, and their ignorance of the phraseology of the age in which they were written, could not be supposed capable of construing them. Others there were, in whom a literary curiosity had been excited, by the publication of such editions of this author as tended to settle his text, and by a description of ancient manners and customs of living, to render him intelligible. The first essay of this kind, worth noting, was the edition of Theobald, the defects whereof, in the single opinion of Warburton, were so many and great, as to render that necessary which bears his name.

The two classes of readers, here discriminated, amounted to such a number as encouraged the booksellers to an edition on the plan of the two former, and Johnson was the person, whom, of all others, they thought the fittest to undertake it: the terms settled between them were, that Johnson should receive for his own use the profits arising from a subscription to the first impression, and that the copyright should remain with the then possessors. The first notification of this design was, a proposal drawn up by Johnson, setting forth the incorrectness of the early editions, the original obscurity and subsequent corruptions of the text, the necessity of notes, and the failures of former editors.

A stranger to Johnson's character and temper would have thought, that the study of an author, whose skill in the science of human life was so deep, and whose perfections were so many and various as to be above the reach of all praise, must have been the most pleasing employment that his imagination could suggest, but it was not so: in a visit that he one morning made to me, I congratulated him on his being now engaged in a work that suited his genius, and that, requiring none of that severe application which his *Dictionary* had condemned him to, I doubted not would be executed *con amore.*—His answer was, 'I look upon this as I did upon the *Dictionary*: it is all work, and my inducement to it is not love or desire of fame, but the want of money, which is the only motive to writing that I know of.'—And the event was evidence to me, that in this speech he declared his genuine sentiments; for neither in the first place did he set himself to collect early editions of his author, old plays, translations of histories, and of the classics, and other materials necessary for his purpose, nor could he be prevailed on to enter into that course of reading, without which it seemed impossible to come at the sense of his author. It was provoking to all his friends to see him waste his days, his weeks, and his months so long, that they feared a mental lethargy had seized him, out of which he would never recover. In this, however, they were happily deceived, for, after two years inactivity, they found him roused to action, and engaged—not in the prosecution of the work, for the completion whereof he stood doubly bound, but in a new one, the furnishing a series of periodical essays, entitled, and it may be thought not improperly, *The Idler*, as his motive to the employment was aversion to a labour he had undertaken, though in the execution, it must be owned, it merited a better name.

As Johnson was diverted from his work of Shakespeare, so am I from my purpose of tracing the progress of it, being to relate the occurrences of nine years of his life before I can congratulate the reader on its appearance.

The engagement for the *Idler* was with Newbery the book-seller,[4] a man of a projecting head, a good understanding, and great integrity; and who, by a fortunate connection with Dr. James, the physician, and the honest exertions of his own industry, became the founder of a family. Taking advantage of that rage for intelligence, which the successes of the war had excited, in even the lowest order of the people, he planned a weekly paper, which he called *The Universal Chronicle*, and, as the size of it rendered it susceptible of more matter than the occurrences, during the intervals of its publication, would supply, it was part of his scheme, that it should contain an essay or short discourse on such subjects of morality, or of wit and humour, as, in former instances, had been found to engage the attention of the public. A share in the profits of this paper was Johnson's inducement to the furnishing such a discourse, and, accordingly, it appeared, on Saturday the fifteenth day of April, 1758, and continued to be published on the same day in every week for near two years thence following.

The profits accruing from the sale of this paper, and the subscriptions which, from the year 1756, he was receiving for the edition of Shakespeare by him proposed, were the only known means of his subsistence for a period of near four years, and we may suppose them hardly adequate to his wants, for, upon finding the balance of the account for the *Dictionary* against him, he quitted his house in Gough Square, and took chambers in Gray's Inn; and Mrs. Williams, upon this removal, fixed herself in lodgings at a boarding school in the neighbourhood of their former dwelling.

About this time he had, from a friend who highly esteemed him,[5] the offer of a living, of which he might have rendered himself capable by entering into holy orders: it was a rectory, in a pleasant country, and of such a yearly value as might have tempted one in better circumstances than himself to accept it; but he had scruples about the duties of the ministerial function, that he could not, after deliberation, overcome. 'I have not,' said he, 'the requisites for the office, and I cannot, in my conscience, shear that flock which I am unable to feed.'—Upon conversing with him on that inability which was his reason for declining the offer, it was found to be a suspicion of his patience to undergo the fatigue of catechizing and instructing a great number of poor ignorant persons, who, in religious matters, had, perhaps, everything to learn.

Thus scrupulously did he think of the nature of the ministerial office, and thus did he testify the sincerity of those censures, which he would sometimes pass on the conduct of the generality of the clergy of his time; for though, as a body of men, he held them in great veneration, and was ever ready to defend them against the encroachments of some, and the reproaches of others of the ignorant laity, he exacted from all who had the cure of souls a punctilious discharge of their duty, and held in utter detestation those who, renouncing their garb and clerical character, affected to appear men of the world.

He thought of Dr. Clarke, whose sermons he valued above all other, that he complied too frequently with invitations to dine with persons of high rank, his parishioners, and spent too much of his time in ceremonious visits: differing in this respect from his contemporary Smalridge, the elegant Favonius of the *Tatler*,[6] who, in the height of his reputation as a preacher, was ever ready to visit a sick person in the most obscure alley of Westminster.

In the beginning of the year 1759, and while the *Idler* continued to be published, an event happened, for which it might be imagined he was well prepared, the death of his mother, who had then attained the age of ninety; but he, whose mind had acquired no firmness by the contemplation of mortality, was as little able to sustain the shock as he would have been had this loss befallen him in his nonage. It is conjectured that, for many years before her decease, she derived almost the whole of her support from this her dutiful son, whose filial piety was ever one of the most distinguishable features in his character.[7] Report says, but rather vaguely, that, to supply her necessities in her last illness, he wrote and made money of his *Rasselas*, a tale of his invention, numbered among the best of his writings, and published in the spring of 1759, a crisis that gives credit to such a supposition. No. 41 of the *Idler*, though it pretends to be a letter to the author, was written by Johnson himself, on occasion of his mother's death, and may be supposed to describe, as truly as pathetically, his sentiments on the separation of friends and relations. The fact, respecting the writing and publishing the story of *Rasselas* is, that finding the Eastern tales written by himself in the *Rambler*, and by Hawkesworth in the *Adventurer*, had been well received, he had been for some time meditating a fictitious history, of a greater extent than any that had appeared in either of those papers, which might serve as a vehicle to convey to the world his sentiments of human life and the dispensations of Providence, and having digested his thoughts on the subject, he obeyed the spur of that necessity which now pressed him, and sat down to compose the tale above-mentioned, laying the scene of it in a country that he had before occasion to contemplate, in his translation of Padre Lobo's voyage.

As it was written to raise money, he did not long delay disposing of it; he gave it, as I have been told, to Mr. Baretti, to sell to that bookseller who would give most for it, but the sum he got for it is variously reported.[8] As none of his compositions have been more applauded than this, an examen of it in this place may be not improper, and the following may serve till a better shall appear.[9]

Considered as a specimen of our language, it is scarcely to be paralleled; it is written in a style refined to a degree of immaculate purity, and displays the whole force of turgid eloquence.

But it was composed at a time when no spring like that in the mind of Rasselas urged his narrator; when the heavy hand of affliction almost bore him down, and the dread of future want haunted him. That he should have produced a tale fraught with lively imagery, or that he should have painted human life in gay colours, could not have been expected: he poured out his sorrow in gloomy reflection, and being destitute of comfort himself, described the world as nearly without it.

In a work of such latitude as this, where nothing could be impertinent, he had an opportunity of divulging his opinion on any point that he had thought on: he has therefore formed many conversations on topics that are known to have been subjects of his meditation, and has atoned for the paucity of his incidents by such discussions as are seldom attempted by the fabricators of romantic fiction.

Admitting that Johnson speaks in the person of the victor-disputant, we may, while he is unveiling the hearts of others, gain some knowledge of his own. He has in this Abyssinian tale given us what he calls a dissertation on poetry, and in it that which appears to me a recipe for making a poet, from which may be inferred what he thought the necessary ingredients, and a reference to the passage will tend to corroborate an observation of Mr. Garrick's, that Johnson's poetical faculty was mechanical, and that what he wrote came not from his heart but from his head.

In a following chapter the danger of insanity is the subject of debate; and it cannot but excite the pity of all those who gratefully accept and enjoy Johnson's endeavours to reform and instruct, to reflect that the peril he describes he believed impending over him. That he was conscious of superior talents will surely not be imputed to vanity: how deeply then must he have been depressed by the constant fear that in one moment he might and probably would be, not only deprived of his distinguished endowments, but reduced to a state little preferable, inasmuch as respects this world, to that of brutes! He has traced the misery of insanity from its cause to its effect, and seems to ascribe it to indulgence of imagination: he styles it one of the dangers of solitude; and perhaps to this dread and this opinion was his uncommon love of society to be attributed.

His superstitious ideas of the state of departed souls, and belief in supernatural agency, were produced by a mental disease, as impossible to be shaken off as corporal pain. What it has pleased omnipotence to inflict, we need never seek to excuse; but he has provided against the cavils of those who cannot comprehend how a wise can ever appear a weak man, by remarking, that there is a natural affinity between melancholy and superstition.

In characterizing this performance, it cannot be said, that it vindicates the ways of God to man. It is a general satire, representing mankind as eagerly pursuing what experience should have taught them they can never obtain: it exposes the weaknesses even of their laudable affections and propensities, and it resolves the mightiest as well as the most trivial of their labours into folly.

I wish I were not warranted in saying, that this elegant work is rendered, by its most obvious moral, of little benefit to the reader. We would not, indeed, wish to see the rising generation so unprofitably employed as the prince of Abyssinia; but it is equally impolitic to repress all hope, and he who should quit his father's house in search of a profession, and return unprovided, because he could not find any man pleased with his own, would need a better justification than that Johnson, after speculatively surveying various modes of life, had judged happiness unattainable, and choice useless.

But let those, who, reading *Rasselas* in the spring of life, are captivated by its author's eloquence, and convinced by his perspicacious wisdom that human life and hopes are such as he has depicted them, remember that he saw through the medium of adversity. The concurrent testimony of ages has, it is too true, proved, that there is no such thing as worldly felicity; but it has never been proved, that, therefore we are miserable. Those who look only here for happiness, have ever been and ever will be disappointed: it is not change of place, nor even the unbounded gratification of their wishes, that can relieve them; but if they bend their attention towards the attainment of that felicity we are graciously promised, they will find no such vacuum as distressed Rasselas: the discharge of religious and social duties will afford their faculties the occupation he wanted, and the well-founded expectation of future reward will at once stimulate and support them.

The tale of *Rasselas* was written to answer a pressing necessity, and was so concluded as to admit of a continuation; and, in fact, Johnson had meditated a second part, in which he meant to marry his hero, and place him in a state of permanent felicity: but it fared with this resolution as it did with that of Dr. Young, who, in his estimate of human life, promised, as he had given the dark, so, in a future publication, he would display the bright side of his subject; he never did it, for he had found out that it had no bright side, and Johnson had made much the same discovery, and that in this state of our existence all our enjoyments are fugacious, and permanent felicity unattainable.

Soon after the publication of *Rasselas*, and while he continued to write the *Idler*, Johnson was tempted to engage in a controversy on a subject with which, in the course of his studies, he had acquired but little knowledge, namely, the comparative strength of arches of different forms; the occasion of it was, that after the passing of the act of parliament for building Blackfriars Bridge, a variety of designs for it were tendered to the commissioners, who, after due consideration, reduced them to three. In two of these designs, the construction of the arches was semicircular; in the third, exhibited by Mr. Mylne a Scotsman, it was elliptical.

Whether Johnson thought that the author of this last proposal, as being a native of North Britain, merited to be treated as an intruder, or that he was induced by better motives to oppose his scheme, cannot be determined: this, at least, is certain, that he took up the resolution before he was qualified to debate the question, for I have it from undoubted authority, that, in order thereto, he procured from a person eminently skilled in mathematics and the principles of architecture, answers to a string of questions drawn up by himself, touching the comparative strength of semicircular and elliptical arches. These I myself have seen, and the answers determine in favour of the semicircular.

If the former of the considerations above suggested, was at any time, or in any degree, Johnson's motive for opposing Mr. Mylne, he ought to have reflected, that, at a period when we had no better architects than Vanbrugh, Hawksmoor, James and Kent among us, Campbell and Gibbs, both Scotsmen, had adorned this country with some stately and elegant edifices; and if the latter was his inducement, he should have reflected, that his arguments were not his own, and so far as regards symmetry and correspondence of parts, how little he was qualified to judge of symmetry and the correspondence of parts, whose eye was never capable of comprehending the dome of St. Paul's Cathedral, or the towers of Westminster Abbey. However, armed as he is above said to have been, with reasons against Mr. Mylne's design, he began an attack on it in a letter to the publisher of the *Daily Gazetteer*, inserted in that paper for the first day of December, 1759; and continued it in the succeeding papers of the eighth and fifteenth of the same month. To one or more of these letters, answers were published; in which it was contended, that at Florence there is a bridge that crosses the river Arno, of an elliptical form: but the argument drawn from thence, Johnson had refuted in his first letter, by observing, that the stability thereof is so much doubted, that carts are not permitted to pass over it, and that it has stood two hundred years without imitation. These, and many other arguments, as also the opinion of that excellent mathematician Mr. Thomas Simpson, were not of sufficient weight with the committee for building the bridge to recommend the semicircular arch; Mr. Mylne's design was preferred, and the arches are elliptical.[10]

Neither the writing of his *Rasselas*, nor the event of his mother's death, nor the bridge controversy, stopped the hand of Johnson, nor interrupted the publication of the *Idler*; but the sale of the *Universal Chronicle*, the vehicle that contained it, was in some degree obstructed by the practices of those literary depredators, who subsist by the labours of others, and whose conduct, with respect to the *Idler*, the following paper, evidently drawn up by Johnson, will explain.

London, January 5, 1759. Advertisement. The proprietors of the paper, entitled *The Idler*, having found that those essays are inserted in the newspapers and magazines with so little regard to justice or decency, that the *Universal Chronicle*, in which they first appear, is not always mentioned, think it necessary to declare to the publishers of those collections, that however patiently they have hitherto endured these injuries, made yet more injurious by contempt, they have now determined to endure them no longer. They have already seen essays, for which a very large price is paid, transferred, with the most shameless rapacity, into the weekly or monthly compilations, and their right, at least for the present, alienated from them, before they could themselves be said to enjoy it. But they would not willingly be thought to want tenderness, even for men by whom no tenderness hath been shown. The past is without remedy, and shall be without resentment. But those who have been thus busy with their sickles in the fields of their neighbours, are henceforward to take notice, that the time of impunity is at an end. Whoever shall, without our leave, lay the hand of rapine upon our papers, is to expect that we shall vindicate our due, by the means which justice prescribes, and which are warranted by the immemorial prescriptions of honourable trade. We shall lay hold, in our turn, on their copies, degrade them from the pomp of wide margin and diffuse typography, contract them into a narrow space, and sell them at an humble price; yet not with a view of growing rich by confiscations, for we think not much better of money got by punishment than by crimes; we shall, therefore, when our losses are repaid, give what profit shall remain to the *Magdalens*; for we know not who can be more properly taxed for the support of penitent prostitutes, than prostitutes in whom there yet appears neither penitence nor shame.

He continued this paper to the extent of one hundred and three numbers, and on Saturday the fifth day of April, 1760, closed it with an essay, containing a solemn and very affecting contemplation on the words *this is the last*, in various significations. The concluding paragraph seems to have been written under the pressure of that melancholy, which almost incessantly afflicted him, heightened, perhaps, by the approach of a season of the year, to Christians the most solemn. The reflections, contained in it, are very serious, and so elegantly expressed, that in the hope that the perusal of it will not prove contagious to the reader, I here give it at length.

As the last *Idler* is published in that solemn week which the Christian world has always set apart for the examination of the conscience, the review of life, the extinction of earthly desires, and the renovation of holy purposes; I hope that my readers are already disposed to view every incident with seriousness, and improve it by meditation; and that when they see this series of trifles brought to a conclusion, they will consider that, by outliving the *Idler*, they have passed weeks, months, and years, which are now no longer in their power; that an end must in time be put to everything great as to everything little; that to life must come its last hour, and to this system of being, its last day; the hour at which probation ceases, and repentance will be vain, the day in which every work of the hand, and imagination of the heart, shall be brought to judgment, and an everlasting futurity shall be determined by the past.

The *Idler*, taken as the title of a series of moral and economical essays, is a designation that imports little; or rather, its most obvious meaning is a bad one. Johnson was at a loss for a fitter, but he could hit on no one that had not been pre-occupied. He chose an irony, and meant that his readers should understand by it just the reverse of what it signified; and, in this his intention, he was in little danger of being mistaken, or being charged with idleness by any of those whom he was labouring, by all the powers of reason and eloquence, to make wiser and better.

The plan and conduct of the *Idler* resembles so nearly that of the *Rambler* and the *Adventurer*, that what has been said of each of those publications might serve for a character of this, saving, that, in this latter, admission is given to a greater number of papers, calculated to entertain the mind with pleasing fictions, humorous characters, and varied representations of familiar life, than is to be found in either of the two former, the general effect whereof is, delight, too soon interrupted by their shortness. The second number of the *Idler* contains an invitation to correspondents, and it had the assistance of other hands; but I know but of three papers that can with certainty be said to have been written by any other than Johnson himself; one of the three is No. 67, by Mr. Langton; the other two, No. 76 and 79, are on the subject of painting, and, in an evening hour when his pencil was at rest, were composed by Sir Joshua Reynolds. And here let me take notice, that in the publication of the *Idler*, at least when it was collected into volumes, Johnson and Newbery were joint adventurers, and that they divided equally the profits arising from the sale thereof.

Of these essays, as also the *Rambler*, and those in the *Adventurer* which Johnson wrote, little remains to be remarked, except that, notwithstanding the depth of thinking which they display, and the nervous and elegant style in which they are penned, they were extemporaneous compositions, and hardly ever underwent a revision [11] before they were sent to the press. The original manuscripts of the *Rambler* have passed through my hands, and by the perusal of them I am warranted to say, as was said of Shakespeare by the players of his time, that he never blotted out a line; and I believe without the risk of that retort which Ben Jonson made to them, 'Would he had blotted out a thousand!'

Another circumstance, worthy of notice, is, that in the portraits of singular characters, that occur in the papers written by Johnson, the painting is so strong and lively, that some persons, then living, looking on them as resemblances of themselves, actually charged him with an intention to render them ridiculous, and were hardly appeased by his assurances that he copied no particular subject, but drew from archetypes which his observation had furnished, and his imagination had improved.

Johnson was now become so well known, and had by the *Rambler*, and other of his writings, given such evidences, not only of great abilities, and of his skill in human life and manners, but of a sociable and benevolent disposition, that many became desirous of his acquaintance, and to this they were farther tempted by the character he had acquired of delighting in conversation, and being free and communicative in his discourse. He had removed, about the beginning of the year 1760, to chambers two doors down the Inner Temple lane; and I have been told by his neighbour at the corner, that during the time he dwelt there, more inquiries were made at his shop for Mr. Johnson, than for all the inhabitants put together of both the Inner and Middle Temple. This circumstance in his life leads me to mention, that Richardson possessed, but in a less degree, the like powers of attraction, but they operated chiefly on young females, who, being desirous of instruction in the duties of life, were permitted by their parents and friends to visit and receive from him such lessons of prudence as he was ever ready and well qualified to give them; and it is well known, that many ingenious young women, who resorted to his house as to an academy for tuition, became so improved by his conversation and his extemporary commentaries on his own writings, as afterwards to make a considerable figure in the literary world. And here let me observe, that the benefits of oral instruction, joined with the perusal of such authors as we now put into female hands, may be estimated by the degree of mental improvement at which the sex is at this day arrived, which, as Johnson once remarked to me on receiving a lady's letter, is so great, that in that kind of composition, we who were their teachers, may learn of them.

From this propensity to discursive communication, in which Johnson and Richardson resembled each other, nothing more is to be understood, than that both took pleasure in that interchange of sentiments and opinions, which renders conversation instructive and delightful, for, in other respects, they were men of very different endowments and tempers. Richardson being bred to a mechanic occupation, had no learning, nor more reading than was sufficient to enable him to form a style easy and intelligible, and a little raised above that of vulgar narrative. His sentiments were his own, and of this he was so sensible, and also of the originality and importance of many of them, that he would ever be talking of his writings, and the words *sentiment* and *sentimentality* became, not only a part of the cant of his school, but were adopted by succeeding writers, and have been used to recommend to some readers sentimental journeys, sentimental letters, sentimental sermons, and a world of trash, which, but for this silly epithet, would never have attracted notice.

Richardson's conversation was of the preceptive kind, but it wanted the diversity of Johnson's, and had no intermixture of wit and humour. Richardson could never relate a pleasant story, and hardly relish one told by another: he was ever thinking of his own writings, and listening to the praises which, with an emulous profusion, his friends were incessantly bestowing on them, he would scarce enter into free conversation with anyone that he thought had not read *Clarissa*, or *Sir Charles Grandison*, and at best, he could not be said to be a companionable man.

Those who were unacquainted with Richardson, and had read his books, were led to believe, that they exhibited a picture of his own mind, and that his temper and domestic behaviour could not but correspond with that refined morality which they inculcate; but in this they were deceived. He was austere in the government of his family, and issued his orders to some of his servants in writing only. His nearest female relations, in the presence of strangers, were mutes, and seemed to me, in a visit I once made him, to have been disciplined in the school of Ben Jonson's Morose, whose injunction to his servant was, 'Answer me not but with your leg.' [12] In short, they appeared to have been taught to converse with him by signs; and it was too plain to me, that on his part, the most frequent of them were frowns and gesticulations, importing that they should leave his presence. I have heard it said, that he was what is called a nervous man; and how far nervosity, with so good an understanding as he is allowed to have possessed, will excuse a conduct so opposite to that philanthropy which he laboured to inculcate, I cannot say: his benevolence might perhaps have taken another direction, and in other instances be very strong; for I was once a witness to his putting into the hand of Mr. Whiston the bookseller, ten guineas for the relief of one whom a sudden accident had made a widow.

Johnson's mind was never occupied on trifles; his speculations were grand and noble, his reading various and extensive, and, on some subjects, profound. As he professed always to speak in the best and most correct phrase, rejecting all such common and vulgar combinations of speech as are in use only till others equally affected and insignificant are invented, his conversation style bore a great resemblance to that of his writings, so that, in his common discourse, he might seem to incur the censure which Bishop Burnet casts on the Lord Chancellor Nottingham, of being too eloquent; but so far were his hearers from thinking so, that many wished for the power of retaining as well the colloquial form as the substance of his conversations; and some there were, who to that end,* made commonplaces of his sayings, his precepts, and his apophthegms; but the want of judgment in the selection of them, has rendered most of the collections of this kind, that I have ever seen, of little worth.

Gesticular mimicry and buffoonery he hated, and would often huff Garrick for exercising it in his presence; but of the talent of humour he had an almost enviable portion. To describe the nature of this faculty, as he was wont to display it in his hours of mirth and relaxation, I must say, that it was ever of that arch and dry kind, which lies concealed under the appearance of gravity, and which acquiesces in an error for the purpose of refuting it. Thus, in the *Rambler*, No. 1, he tells his readers, very gravely, that it is one among many reasons for which he purposes to entertain his countrymen, that he hopes not much to tire those whom he shall not happen to please, and if he is not commended for the beauty of his works, to be at least pardoned for their brevity.[13]

A friend of his used often to visit him, who, though a man of learning and great good sense, had a style of conversing so peculiarly eloquent and verbose, as to be sometimes unintelligible: Johnson had a mind one day to give me a specimen of it, and assuming his manner, he, in a connected speech on a familiar subject, uttered a succession of sentences, in language resembling the style of metaphysics, but, though fluent, so obscured by parentheses and other involutions, that I was unable to collect from it a single idea. After he had for five minutes continued this gibberish, he said, 'This is the manner in which **** entertains me whenever he comes here.'[14]

In the same vein of humour he once ridiculed Hervey's meditations on a flower garden and other subjects,[15] in the following extemporaneous reflections on a pudding:

Let us seriously reflect on what a pudding is composed of. It is composed of flour that once waved in the golden grain, and drank the dews of the morning—of milk pressed from the swelling udder by the gentle hand of the beauteous milkmaid, whose beauty and innocence might have recommended a worse draught; who, whilst she stroked the udder, indulged no ambitious thoughts of dwelling in palaces, and formed no schemes for the destruction of her fellow-creatures—milk which is drawn from the cow, that useful animal, that eats the grass of the field, and supplies us with that which made the greatest part of the food of that age, which the poets have agreed to call golden.

It is made with an egg, that miracle of nature, which the theoretical Burnet has compared to creation—an egg that contains water within its beautiful smooth surface, and an unformed mass which, by the incubation of the parent, becomes a regular animal, furnished with bones and sinews, and covered with feathers.

Let us consider—can there be anything wanting to complete this meditation on a pudding—if more is wanting, more may be found. It contains salt, which preserves the sea from putrefaction; salt, which is made the image of intellectual excellence, contributes to the formation of a pudding.

He excelled also in the talent of burlesque versification, and upon occasion of a discourse at Sir Joshua Reynolds's on Dr. Percy's *Reliques of Ancient English Poetry*, in which the beautiful simplicity of many of the ballads therein contained was remarked with some exaggeration, Johnson contended, that what was called simplicity was, in truth, inanity; and, to illustrate his argument, and ridicule that kind of poetry, uttered the following impromptu:

> As with my hat upon my head,
> I walk'd along the Strand,
> I there did meet another man,
> With his hat in his hand.

And it being at a tea conversation, he, addressing himself to Miss Reynolds, went on rhyming thus;

> I pray thee, gentle Renny dear,
> That thou wilt give to me,
> With cream and sugar temper'd well,
> Another dish of tea.
>
> Nor fear that I, my gentle maid,
> Shall long detain the cup,
> When once unto the bottom I
> Have drank the liquor up.
>
> Yet hear, at last, this mournful truth,
> Nor hear it with a frown,
> Thou canst not make the tea so fast,
> As I can gulp it down.

With these powers of instructing and delighting those with whom he conversed, it is no wonder that the acquaintance of Johnson was sought by many; and I will not say, either that he set so great a value on his time, as not to be accessible to all who wished for the pleasure of it, or that his vanity was not gratified by the visits of bishops, of courtiers, senators, scholars, travellers, and women.

In his conversation with the last in this enumeration, he had such a felicity as would put vulgar gallantry out of countenance. Of the female mind, he conceived a higher opinion than many men, and though he was never suspected of a blameable intimacy with any individual of them, had a great esteem for the sex. The defect in his powers of sight rendered him totally insensible to the charms of beauty; but he knew that beauty was the attribute of the sex, and treated all women with such an equable complacency, as flattered every one into a belief, that she had her share of that or some more valuable endowment. In his discourses with them, his compliments had ever a neat and elegant turn; they were never direct, but always implied the merit they were intended to attest.

In this enjoyment of himself and his friends, his engagements to the public were forgotten: his critical talents lay dormant, and not any, nor all of those who wished to see his Shakespeare, could rouse his attention to the prosecution of that work; yet was he ready, at the call of almost anyone, to assist, either by correction, or by a preface, or dedication, in the publication of works not his own. Dr. Madden, so well known by his premiums for the encouragement of Protestant working schools in Ireland, and other instances of beneficence in favour of that country, in the year 1745 published a panegyrical poem on Archbishop Boulter; some years after, being minded to re-publish it, he submitted it to Johnson's correction, and I found among his books a copy of the poem, with a note, in a spare leaf thereof, purporting, that the author had made him a visit, and, for a very few remarks and alterations of it, had presented him with ten guineas. Such casual emoluments as these Johnson frequently derived from his profession of an author. For the dedication to his present Majesty, of Adams's book on the use of the globes,[16] he was, as himself informed me, gratified with a present of a very curious meteorological instrument, of a new and ingenious construction.

About this time, as it is supposed, he, for sundry beneficed clergymen that requested him, composed pulpit discourses, and for these, he made no scruple of confessing, he was paid: his price, I am informed, was a moderate one, two guineas; and such was his notion of justice, that having been paid, he considered them so absolutely the property of the purchaser, as to renounce all claim to them. He reckoned that he had written about forty sermons; but, except as to some, knew not in what hands they were —'I have,' said he, 'been paid for them, and have no right to inquire about them.' [17]

1760-1764

I HAVE NOW brought him to the year 1760, the fifty-first of his age. He had nothing to depend on for subsistence but the labour of his brain; and that apprehension, touching the duration of his rational powers, which throughout his life haunted him, increased the terrors of approaching age. The accession of our present gracious sovereign to the throne, and the bounty exercised by him towards Johnson, dispelled this gloomy prospect, and placed him in such a state of affluence as his utmost industry would hardly ever have enabled him to arrive at. Lord Bute was the minister at the time; and the person employed to notify to Johnson his Majesty's intention to reward him for his literary labours with a pension of 300£. a year, was his friend Mr. Murphy. Upon receiving the news, Johnson was in doubt what answer to return, being, perhaps, disturbed with the reflection, that whatever he might deserve from the public, he had very little claim to the favour of any of the descendants of the House of Hanover; and desired that Mr. Murphy would give him till next day to deliberate upon a message so unexpected. At the end thereof he signified his willingness to accept it.[1]

It was, by Johnson and his friends, thought fit, that he should return thanks for this distinguishing mark of the royal favour, and that Lord Bute, who may be supposed to have been instrumental in procuring it, was the proper person to convey them. Accordingly, he waited on his lordship for the purpose, and, being admitted to him, testified his sense of the obligation; but having done this, he thought he had done enough, and never after could be prevailed on to knock at his door.

He had now suffered himself to be enrolled in the list of pensioners, and was become obnoxious to the censures of those, who, looking upon a perpetual enmity to government and its ministers as a proof of public virtue, endeavoured to have it believed, that all favours dispensed by the crown, even when meant as the rewards of merit, or the encouragement of learning, of ingenuity, or industry, were but the wages of iniquity. Johnson, it is true, had laid himself open to reproach, by his interpretation of the word *pension* in his *Dictionary*,[2] written, it is evident, at a time when his political prejudices were strongest, and he found himself in a predicament similar to that of Dr. Sherlock, who, at the Revolution, was a non-juror to King William, but, after deliberating on his refusal as a case of conscience, took the side that made for his interest, but against his reputation. But who, except the Great Searcher of Hearts, can know, that in the case of Sherlock or Johnson, either made a sacrifice of his conscience? Or, seeing that the grant of Johnson's pension was confessedly unconditional, and bound him neither to the renunciation of any of his political principles, nor the exercise of his pen in the defence of any set of men or series of measures, who will have the face to say, that his acceptance of it was criminal; or that it was in the power of anyone to pervert the integrity of a man, who, in the time of his necessity, had, from scruples of his own raising, declined the offer of a valuable ecclesiastical preferment, and thereby renounced an independent provision for the whole of his life?

It is yet difficult, if not impossible, to justify Johnson, both in the interpretation given by him of the word *pension*, and in his becoming a pensioner: in one instance or the other he was wrong, and either his discretion or integrity must be given up: in the former, he seems, in some of his actions, to have been wanting, in the latter never: not only charity, but reason, therefore, directs us in the opinion we are to form of an act which has drawn censure on his conduct, and proves nothing more than that he was not equally wise at all times.[3]

The addition of three hundred pounds a year, to what Johnson was able to earn by the ordinary exercise of his talents, raised him to a state of comparative affluence, and afforded him the means of assisting many whose real or pretended wants had formerly excited his compassion. He now practised a rule which he often recommended to his friends, always to go abroad with a quantity of loose money to give to beggars, imitating therein, though I am confident without intending it, that good but weak man, old Mr. Whiston, whom I have seen distributing, in the streets of London, money to beggars on each hand of him, till his pocket was nearly exhausted.

He had, early in his life, been a dabbler in physic, and laboured under some secret bodily infirmities that gave him occasion once to say to me, that he knew not what it was to be totally free from pain. He now drew into a closer intimacy with him a man, with whom he had been acquainted from the year 1746, one of the lowest practitioners in the art of healing that ever sought a livelihood by it: him he consulted in all that related to his health, and made so necessary to him as hardly to be able to live without him.

The name of this person was Robert Levett. An account of him is given in the *Gentleman's Magazine* for February, 1785: [4] an earlier than that, I have now lying before me, in a letter from a person in the country to Johnson, written in answer to one in which he had desired to be informed of some particulars respecting his friend Levett, then lately deceased. The substance of this information is as follows:

He was born at Kirk Ella, a parish about five miles distant from Hull, and lived with his parents till about twenty years of age. He had acquired some knowledge of the Latin language, and had a propensity to learning, which his parents not being able to gratify, he went to live as a shopman with a woollen draper at Hull: with him he stayed two years, during which time he learned from a neighbour of his master somewhat of the practice of physic: at the end thereof he came to London, with a view possibly to improve himself in that profession; but by some strange accident was led to pursue another course, and became steward, or some other upper servant, to the then Lord Cardigan [or Cadogan]; and having saved some money, he took a resolution to

travel, and visited France and Italy for the purpose, as his letters
mention, of gaining experience in physic, and, returning to London with a valuable library which he had collected abroad, placed
one of his brothers apprentice to a mathematical-instrument
maker, and provided for the education of another. After this he
went to Paris, and, for improvement, attended the hospitals in
that city. At the end of five years he returned to England, and
taking lodgings in the house of an attorney in Northumberland
Court, near Charing Cross, he became a practicer of physic. The
letter adds, that he was about seventy-eight at the time of his
death.

I here add a dictum of Johnson respecting Levitt, viz. that his
external appearance and behaviour were such, that he disgusted
the rich, and terrified the poor.

But notwithstanding these offensive particulars, Johnson, whose
credulity in some instances was as great as his incredulity in
others, conceived of him as of a skillful medical professor, and
thought himself happy in having so near his person one who was
to him, not solely a physician, a surgeon, or an apothecary, but
all. In extraordinary cases he, however, availed himself of the assistance of his valued friend Dr. Lawrence, a man of whom, in
respect of his piety, learning, and skill in his profession, it may
almost be said, the world was not worthy, inasmuch as it suffered
his talents, for the whole of his life, to remain, in a great measure,
unemployed, and himself to end his days in sorrow and obscurity.[5]

The sincere and lasting friendship that subsisted between
Johnson and Levett, may serve to show, that although a similarity
of dispositions and qualities has a tendency to beget affection, or
something very nearly resembling it, it may be contracted and
subsist where this inducement is wanting; for hardly were ever
two men less like each other, in this respect, than were they.
Levett had not an understanding capable of comprehending the
talents of Johnson: the mind of Johnson was therefore, as to him,
a blank; and Johnson, had the eye of his mind been more penetrating than it was, could not discern, what did not exist, any
particulars in Levett's character that at all resembled his own.
He had no learning, and consequently was an unfit companion
for a learned man; and though it may be said, that having lived

some years abroad, he must have seen and remarked many things that would have afforded entertainment in the relation, this advantage was counterbalanced by an utter inability for continued conversation, taciturnity being one of the most obvious features in his character: the consideration of all which particulars almost impels me to say, that Levett admired Johnson because others admired him, and that Johnson in pity loved Levett, because few others could find anything in him to love.

And here I cannot forbear remarking, that, almost throughout his life, poverty and distressed circumstances seemed to be the strongest of all recommendations to his favour. When asked by one of his most intimate friends, how he could bear to be surrounded by such necessitous and undeserving people as he had about him, his answer was, 'If I did not assist them no one else would, and they must be lost for want.' Among many others whom he thus patronized, was a worthless fellow, a dancing master by profession, and an assistant in teaching to the famous Noverre, the favourite of Garrick. This man, notwithstanding the nature of his employment, which was a genteel one, and led to no such connections, delighted in the company and conversation of marshal's-court attorneys, and of bailiffs and their followers, and others of a lower class, sharpers and swindlers, who, when they had made him drunk, would get him to sign notes and engagements of various kinds, which, he not being able to discharge, they had him arrested upon, and this was so frequently the case, that much of his time was passed in confinement. His wife, through Mrs. Williams, got at Johnson, and told him her tale, which was, that her husband was, at that instant, detained for a small debt in a sponging house, and he conceiving it to be a piteous one, and an additional proof that in human life the evil accidents outnumber the good, sent her to me for advice. I heard her story, and learned from it, that all the merit of the fellow lay in his heels, that he had neither principle nor discretion, and, in short, was a cully, the dupe of everyone that would make him drunk. I therefore dismissed her with a message to Johnson to this effect: that her husband made it impossible for his friends to help him, and must submit to his destiny. When I next saw Johnson, I told him that there seemed to be as exact a fitness between the character of this man and his associates, as is between the web of a spider and the wings of a fly, and I could not but think he was born to be cheated. Johnson seemed to acquiesce in my opinion; but I believe, before that, had set him at liberty by paying the debt.

Another of Johnson's distressed friends was Mr. Edmund Southwell, a younger brother of Thomas Lord Southwell, of the kingdom of Ireland. This gentleman, having no patrimony, was, in his younger days, a cornet of horse; but having in a duel, into which he was forced, slain his antagonist, he quitted the service, and trusted to Providence for a support. He was a man of wonderful parts, of lively and entertaining conversation, and well acquainted with the world; he was also a brother in affliction with Johnson, that is to say, he laboured under a depression of mind, occasioned by the misadventure above-mentioned, that often approached to insanity. Being without employment, his practice was to wander about the streets of London, and call in at such coffee houses, for instance, the Smyrna and Cocoa Tree in Pall Mall, and Child's and Batson's in the city, as were frequented by men of intelligence, or where anything like conversation was going forward: in these he found means to make friends, from whom he derived a precarious support. In the city he was so well known, and so much beloved and pitied, that many, by private donations, relieved his wants.* A gentleman of great worth in the city, who knew and pitied his distresses, procured, unknown to him, from a lady famous for her beneficence, a pension of a hundred pounds a year, which he lived but a few years to receive.

Johnson was a great lover of penitents, and of all such men as, in their conversation, made professions of piety; of this man he would say, that he was one of the most pious of all his acquaintance, but in this, as he frequently was in the judgment he formed of others, he was mistaken. It is possible that Southwell might, in his conversation, express such sentiments of religion and moral obligation, as served to show that he was not an infidel, but he seldom went sober to bed, and as seldom rose from it before noon.

He was also an admirer of such as he thought well bred men. What was his notion of good breeding I could never learn. If it was not courtesy and affability, it could to him be nothing; for he was an incompetent judge of graceful attitudes and motions, and of the ritual of behaviour. Of Lord Southwell, the brother of the above person, and of Tom Hervey, a profligate, worthless man,* who had nothing in his external appearance that could in the least recommend him, he was used to say, they were each of them a model for the first man of quality in the kingdom.⁶ In this method of estimating behaviour, he seemed to think that good breeding is a faculty, which, like fencing, dancing, and other bodily exercises, must be learned before they can be practised; whereas, it is obvious, that this quality is nothing more than artificial benevolence, and that politeness, which it is the employment of the instructors of youth to teach, is but a substitute for those dispositions of mind, which, whoever possesses, and takes care to cultivate, will have very little need of foreign assistance in the forming of his manners.

He once mentioned to me a saying of Dr. Nicholls, and highly commended it, viz. that it was a point of wisdom to form intimacies, and to choose for our friends only persons of known worth and integrity; and that to do so had been the rule of his life. It is, therefore, difficult to account for the conduct of Johnson in the choice of many of his associates, and particularly of those who, when his circumstances became easy, he suffered to intrude on him. Of these he had some at bed and board, who had elbowed through the world, and subsisted by lying, begging, and shifting; all which he knew, but seemed to think never the worse of them. In his endeavours to promote the interests of people of this class, he, in some instances, went such lengths as were hardly consistent with that integrity, which he manifested on all other occasions; for he would frequently, by letters, recommend those to credit, who could obtain it by no other means, and thereby enabled them to contract debts which he had good reason to suspect, if they ever could, they never would pay.

These connections exposed him to trouble and incessant solicitation, which he bore well enough; but his inmates were enemies to his peace, and occasioned him great disquiet: the jealousy that subsisted among them rendered his dwelling irksome to him, and he seldom approached it, after an evening's conversation

abroad, but with the dread of finding it a scene of discord, and of
having his ears filled with the complaints of Mrs. Williams of
Frank's neglect of his duty and inattention to the interests of
his master, and of Frank against Mrs. Williams, for the authority
she assumed over him, and exercised with an unwarrantable severity. Even those intruders who had taken shelter under his roof,
and who, in his absence from home, brought thither their children,
found cause to murmur; their provision of food was scanty, or
their dinners ill dressed; all which he chose to endure rather than
put an end to their clamours, by ridding his house of such thank-
less and troublesome guests. Nay, so insensible was he of the
ingratitude of those whom he suffered thus to hang on him, and
among whom he may be said to have divided an income which
was little more than sufficient for his own support, that he would
submit to reproach and personal affront from some of them;
even Levett would sometimes insult him, and Mrs. Williams,
in her paroxysms of rage, has been known to drive him from her
presence.

Who, that reflects on Johnson's pusillanimity in these instances,
can reconcile it to that spirit which prompted him, or with those
endowments which enabled him to maintain a superiority over
all with whom he conversed? or to that seeming ferocity of temper
that gave occasion to some to consider him as an animal not to
be approached without terror? or account for the inconsistency
above noted, otherwise than by resolving it into those principles
that dictated patience, under all the provocations of a female
tongue, to Socrates? In truth, there was more asperity in his manner of expression than in his natural disposition; for I have heard
that, in many instances, and in some with tears in his eyes, he
has apologized to those whom he had offended by contradiction
or roughness of behaviour.

To this inconsistency of character it must be imputed, that he
failed to attract reverence and respect from those who lived in
greatest intimacy with him. There was wanting in his conduct
and behaviour that dignity which results from a regular and orderly course of action, and by an irresistible power commands esteem. He could not be said to be a staid man, nor so to have adjusted in his mind the balance of reason and passion, as to give

occasion to say, what may be observed of some men, that all they do is just, fit, and right; and although he was strict, and even punctilious, in the practice of the great duties of morality, he trusted but little to his domestic conduct, to his method of employing his time, and governing his family, for the good opinion he wished the world to entertain of him, but, in these particulars, gave way to the love of ease, and to self-indulgence, little regarding, in his own practice, those counsels of prudence, those economical maxims, and those reflections on the shortness of human life, with which his writings abound. To a lady, who signified a great desire to increase her acquaintance with authors, conceiving that more might be learned from their conversation and manner of living, than from their works—'Madam,' said he, 'the best part of an author will always be found in his writings.'—And to a person, who once said he paid little regard to those writers on religion or morality, whose practice corresponded not with their precepts, he imputed a want of knowledge of mankind, saying, it was gross ignorance in him not to know, that good principles and an irregular life were consistent with each other.

This was a secret which, without much mischief, might have been revealed in conversation, but Johnson has thought fit to send it abroad in the fourteenth number of the *Rambler*, with this apology:

We are not to wonder that most fail, amidst tumult, and snares, and dangers, in the observance of those precepts which they lay down in solitude, safety, and tranquillity, with a mind unbiased, and with liberty unobstructed. It is the condition of our present state to see more than we can attain; the exactest vigilance and caution can never maintain a single day of innocence, much less can the utmost efforts of incorporated mind reach the summits of speculative virtue.

He farther says,

it is recorded of Sir Matthew Hale, that he, for a long time, concealed the consecration of himself to the stricter duties of religion, lest, by some flagitious and shameful action, he should bring piety into disgrace;

and upon this his conduct he suggests, that 'it may be prudent for a writer, who apprehends that he shall not enforce his own maxims by his domestic character, to conceal his name that he may not injure them.'

In this passage, Johnson seems to prepare his readers for that contrariety which is often observed between the lives of authors and their writings, or, which is much the same, between preceptive and practical wisdom and virtue, as if they were scarcely consistent with each other; whereas, had his acquaintance lain, at this time, as in the latter part of his life it did, with persons of rank and condition, he might have formed different notions on the subject, and been convinced, that all ages, and even the present, have afforded examples of men, in whom learning and parts, and even wit, were but auxiliaries to qualities more estimable.

The above facts and observations are meant to show some of the most conspicuous features and foibles in Johnson's character, and go to prove, not only that his ferocity was not so terrific, as that anyone endued with temper, and disposed to moderation and forbearance, might not only withstand, but overcome it, but that he had a natural imbecility [7] about him, arising from humanity and pity to the sufferings of his fellow creatures, that was prejudicial to his interests; and also, that he neither sought nor expected praise for those acts of beneficence which he was daily performing, nor looked for any retribution from those who were nourished by his bounty. Indeed, they were such creatures as were incapable of being awed by a sense of his worth, or of discerning the motives that actuated him; they were people of the lowest and vulgarest minds, whom idleness had made poor, and liberality impudent, and what is to be expected from such, is known to all that are, in the slightest degree, acquainted with the world.

This history of learning furnishes us with many examples of men who have deviated from the study of polite literature to that of the hermetic science, or, in plainer English, to that sublimer chemistry which leads to the transmutation of metals; and those who may have heard that Johnson exercised himself in chemical processes, may perhaps think, that his view therein was suddenly to become the possessor of immense riches; but I am able to obviate this suspicion, and assure them, that his motive thereto was only curiosity, and his end mere amusement. At the time he frequented the club in Ivy Lane, Dyer was going through a course of chemistry under Dr. Pemberton, of Gresham College, and would sometimes give us such descriptions of processes as were very entertaining, particularly to Johnson, who would listen to them attentively. We may suppose, that, in the course of his reading, he had acquired some knowledge of the theory of the art, and that he wished for an opportunity of reducing that knowledge into practice; he thought that time now come, and though he had no fitter an apartment for a laboratory than the garret over his chambers in the Inner Temple, he furnished that with an alembic, with retorts, receivers, and other vessels adapted to the cheapest and least operose processes. What his aims were, at first, I know not, having forgotten the account he once gave me of the earliest of his chemical operations; but I have since learned, that they dwindled down to mere distillation, and that from substances of the simplest and coarsest sort, namely, peppermint, and the dregs of strong beer, from the latter whereof he was able to extract a strong but very nauseous spirit, which all might smell, but few chose to taste.

Johnson had now considerably extended the circle of his acquaintance, and added to the number of his friends sundry persons of distinguished eminence: among them were, Sir Joshua Reynolds, Mr. Edmund Burke, Mr. Beauclerk, and Mr. Langton. With these he passed much of his time, and was desirous of being still closer connected. How much he delighted in convivial meetings, how he loved conversation, and how sensibly he felt the attractions of a tavern, has already been mentioned; and it was but a natural consequence of these dispositions, that he should wish for frequent opportunities of indulging them in a way that would free him from domestic restraints, from the observance of hours, and a conformity to the regimen of families. A tavern was the place for these enjoyments, and a weekly club was instituted for his gratification and the mutual entertainment and delight of its several members. The first movers in this association were Johnson and Sir Joshua Reynolds: the number of persons included in it was nine: the place of meeting was the Turk's Head in Gerard Street: the day Monday in every week, and the hour of assembling seven in the evening. To this association I had the honour of being invited. The members were,

Johnson,
Sir Joshua Reynolds,
Mr. Edmund Burke,
Christ. Nugent, M.D.,
Oliver Goldsmith, M.B.

Mr. Topham Beauclerk,
Mr. Bennet Langton,
Mr. Anthony Chamier, and
Myself.

As some of the persons above-mentioned are happily yet living, and are too eminently known to receive honour from anything I am able to say of them, I shall content myself with giving the characters of such of them as are now no more.

Dr. Nugent was a physician, of the Romish communion, and rising into practice with persons of that persuasion. He was an ingenious, sensible, and learned man, of easy conversation, and elegant manners. Johnson had a high opinion of him, and always spoke of him in terms of great respect.

Goldsmith is well known by his writings to have been a man of genius and of very fine parts; but of his character and general deportment, it is the hardest task anyone can undertake to give a description. I will, however, attempt it, trusting to be excused if, in the spirit of a faithful historian, I record as well his singularities as his merits.[8]

There are certain memoirs of him extant, from which we learn, that his inclination, co-operating with his fortunes, which were but scanty, led him into a course of life little differing from vagrancy, that deprived him of the benefits of regular study: it however gratified his humour, stored his mind with ideas and some knowledge, which, when he became settled, he improved by various reading; yet, to all the graces of urbanity he was a stranger. With the greatest pretensions to polished manners he was rude, and, when he most meant the contrary, absurd. He affected Johnson's style and manner of conversation, and, when he had uttered, as he often would, a laboured sentence, so tumid as to be scarce intelligible, would ask, if that was not truly Johnsonian; yet he loved not Johnson, but rather envied him for his parts; and once entreated a friend to desist from praising him, 'for in doing so,' said he, 'you harrow up my very soul.'

He had some wit, but no humour, and never told a story but he spoiled it. The following anecdotes will convey some idea of the style and manner of his conversation:

He was used to say he could play on the German flute as well as most men;—at other times, as well as any man living. But, in truth, he understood not the character in which music is written, and played on that instrument, as many of the vulgar do, merely by ear. Roubiliac the sculptor, a merry fellow, once heard him play, and minding to put a trick on him, pretended to be charmed with his performance, as also, that himself was skilled in the art, and entreated him to repeat the air, that he might write it down. Goldsmith readily consenting, Roubiliac called for paper, and scored thereon a few five-lined staves, which having done, Goldsmith proceeded to play, and Roubiliac to write; but his writing was only such random notes on the lines and spaces as anyone might set down who had ever inspected a page of music. When they had both done, Roubiliac showed the paper to Goldsmith, who looking it over with seeming great attention, said, it was very correct, and that if he had not seen him do it, he never could have believed his friend capable of writing music after him.

He would frequently preface a story thus:—'I'll now tell you a story of myself, which some people laugh at, and some do not.'—[9]

At the breaking up of an evening at a tavern, he entreated the company to sit down, and told them if they would call for another bottle they should hear one of his *bons mots*:—they agreed, and he began thus:—'I was once told that Sheridan the player, in order to improve himself in stage gestures, had looking glasses, to the number of ten, hung about his room, and that he practised before them; upon which I said, then there were ten ugly fellows together.'—The company were all silent: he asked why they did not laugh, which they not doing, he, without tasting the wine, left the room in anger.

In a large company he once said, 'Yesterday I heard an excellent story, and I would relate it now if I thought any of you able to understand it.' The company laughed, and one of them said, 'Doctor, you are very rude'; but he made no apology.

He once complained to a friend in these words:—'Mr. Martinelli is a rude man: I said in his hearing, that there were no good writers among the Italians, and he said to one that sat near him, that I was very ignorant.'

'People,' said he, 'are greatly mistaken in me: a notion goes about, that when I am silent I mean to be impudent; but I assure you, gentlemen, my silence arises from bashfulness.'

Having one day a call to wait on the late Duke, then Earl of Northumberland, I found Goldsmith waiting for an audience in an outer room; I asked him what had brought him there: he told me an invitation from his lordship. I made my business as short as I could, and, as a reason, mentioned, that Dr. Goldsmith was waiting without. The earl asked me if I was acquainted with him: I told him I was, adding what I thought likely to recommend him. I retired, and stayed in the outer room to take him home. Upon his coming out, I asked him the result of his conversation:—'His lordship,' says he, 'told me he had read my poem,' meaning *The Traveller*, 'and was much delighted with it; that he was going Lord Lieutenant of Ireland, and that, hearing that I was a native of that country, he should be glad to do me any kindness.'—And what did you answer, asked I, to this gracious offer? 'Why,' said he, 'I could say nothing but that I had a brother there, a clergyman, that stood in need of help: as for myself, I have no dependence on the promises of great men: I look to the booksellers for support; they are my best friends, and I am not inclined to forsake them for others.'

Thus did this idiot in the affairs of the world, trifle with his fortunes, and put back the hand that was held out to assist him! Other offers of a like kind he either rejected or failed to improve, contenting himself with the patronage of one nobleman, whose mansion afforded him the delights of a splendid table, and a retreat for a few days from the metropolis.

While I was writing the *History of Music*, he, at the club, communicated to me some curious matter: I desired he would reduce it to writing; he promised me he would, and desired to see me at his chambers: I called on him there; he stepped into a closet, and tore out of a printed book six leaves that contained what he had mentioned to me.

As he wrote for the booksellers, we, at the club, looked on him as a mere literary drudge, equal to the task of compiling and translating, but little capable of original, and still less of poetical composition: he had, nevertheless, unknown to us, written and addressed to the Countess, afterwards Duchess, of Northumberland, one of the finest poems of the lyric kind that our language has to boast of, the ballad 'Turn Gentle Hermit of the Dale'; and surprised us with *The Traveller*, a poem that contains some particulars of his own history. Johnson was supposed to have assisted him in it; but he contributed to the perfection of it only four lines: his opinion of it was, that it was the best written poem since the time of Pope.

Of the booksellers whom he styled his friends, Mr. Newbery was one. This person had apartments in Canonbury House, where Goldsmith often lay concealed from his creditors. Under a pressing necessity he there wrote his *Vicar of Wakefield*, and for it received of Newbery forty pounds.[10]

Of a man named Griffin, a bookseller in Catherine Street in the Strand, he had borrowed by two and three guineas at a time, money to the amount of two hundred pounds; to discharge this debt, he wrote the *Deserted Village*, but was two years about it. Soon after its publication, Griffin declared, that it had discharged the whole of his debt.

His poems are replete with fine moral sentiments, and bespeak a great dignity of mind; yet he had no sense of the shame, nor dread of the evils, of poverty. In the latter he was at one time so involved, that for the clamours of a woman, to whom he was indebted for lodging, and for bailiffs that waited to arrest him, he was equally unable, till he had made himself drunk, to stay within doors, or go abroad to hawk among the booksellers a piece of his writing, the title whereof my author does not remember.[11] In this distress he sent for Johnson, who immediately went to one of them, and brought back money for his relief.

In his dealings with the booksellers, he is said to have acted very dishonestly, never fulfilling his engagements. In one year he got of them, and by his plays, the sum of 1800£. which he dissipated by gaming and extravagance, and died poor in 1774.

He that can account for the inconsistencies of character above-noted, otherwise than by showing, that wit and wisdom are seldom found to meet in the same mind, will do more than any of Gold-smith's friends were ever able to do. He was buried in the Temple Church yard. A monument was erected for him in the poets' corner in Westminster Abbey, by a subscription of his friends, and is placed over the entrance into St. Blase's Chapel. The inscription thereon was written by Johnson. This I am able to say with certainty, for he showed it to me in manuscript.

The members of our club that remain to be spoken of, were persons of less celebrity than him above-mentioned, but were better acquainted with the world, and qualified for social intercourse. Mr. Beauclerk, was the son of Lord Sidney Beauclerk of the St. Alban's family, and took his Christian name from Mr. Topham of Windsor, the famous collector of pictures and drawings. To the character of a scholar, and a man of fine parts, he added that of a man of fashion, of which his dress and equipage showed him to be emulous. In the early period of his life he was the exemplar of all who wished, without incurring the censure of foppery, to become conspicuous in the gay world. Travel, and a long residence at Rome, and at Venice, had given the last polish to his manners, and stored his mind with entertaining information. In painting and sculpture his taste and judgment were accurate; in classic literature, exquisite; and in the knowledge of history, and the study of antiquities, he had few equals. His conversation was of the most excellent kind; learned, witty, polite, and, where the subject required it, serious; and over all his behaviour there beamed such a sunshine of cheerfulness and good humour, as communicated itself to all around him. He was a great collector of books, and left at his death a library, which, at a sale by auction, yielded upwards of five thousand pounds.

Mr. Anthony Chamier was descended from a French Protestant family, that has produced one or more very eminent divines, and were refugees in this country at the end of the last century. He was bred to the profession of a stockbroker; but, having had a liberal education, his deportment and manner of transacting business distinguished him greatly from most others of that calling. He had acquired a knowledge of the modern languages, particularly of the Spanish, in the study whereof he took great delight. His connections, at his setting out in the world, were of the best kind, for very early in his life, he was employed by those liberal-minded brothers the Van Necks, whose riches, and general munificence, have ranked them in the same class of wealthy men with the Fuggers of Augsburg, a company of money dealers, who, in their time, held the balance of the Antwerp exchange, and by their transactions at that mart, influenced the politics of all the courts of Europe. By his dealings in the funds, and, it was supposed, with the advantage of intelligence which, previous to the conclusion of the peace before the last, he had obtained, he acquired such a fortune as enabled him, though young, to quit business, and become, what indeed he seemed by nature intended for, a gentleman. At the beginning of his present majesty's reign, he had a prospect of going secretary to an embassy to Spain, and was preparing for it, by the improvement of himself in the language of that country; but a change in the appointment of an ambassador kept him at home, and gave him opportunity of becoming acquainted with Lord Weymouth, who, upon his being made secretary of state, took him for one of his undersecretaries. In this station he was continued by his successor Lord Hilsborough, and remained till the time of his death.

It was Johnson's original intention, that the number of this our club should not exceed nine; but Mr. Dyer, a member of that in Ivy Lane, before spoken of, and who for some years had been abroad, made his appearance among us, and was cordially received. By the recommendation of Mr. Belchier the banker, and member for Southwark, he had obtained an appointment to be one of the commissaries in our army in Germany; but, on the conclusion of the peace, he returned to England, very little the better for an employment which few have been known to quit without having made a fortune.

The hours which Johnson spent in this society seemed to be the happiest of his life: he would often applaud his own sagacity in the selection of it, and was so constant at our meetings as never to absent himself.[12] It is true, he came late, but then he stayed late, for, as has been already said of him, he little regarded hours. Our evening toast was the motto of Padre Paolo, 'Esto perpetua.' A lady, distinguished by her beauty, and taste for literature,[13] invited us two successive years to a dinner at her house. Curiosity was her motive, and possibly a desire of intermingling with our conversation the charms of her own. She affected to consider us as a set of literary men, and perhaps gave the first occasion for distinguishing the society by the name of the Literary Club, an appellation which it never assumed to itself.

At these our meetings, Johnson, as indeed he did everywhere, led the conversation, yet was he far from arrogating to himself that superiority, which, some years before, he was disposed to contend for. He had seen enough of the world to know, that respect was not to be extorted, and began now to be satisfied with that degree of eminence to which his writings had exalted him. This change in his behaviour was remarked by those who were best acquainted with his character, and it rendered him an easy and delightful companion. Our discourse was miscellaneous, but chiefly literary. Politics, the most vulgar of all topics, were alone excluded. On that subject most of us were of the same opinion. The British lion was then licking his wounds, and we drank to the peace of Old England.[14]

The institution of this society was in the winter of 1763,[15] at which time Mr. Garrick was abroad with his wife, who, for the recovery of her health, was sent to the baths at Padua. Upon his return, he was informed of our association, and trusted, that the least intimation of a desire to come among us, would procure him a ready admission, but in this he was mistaken. Johnson consulted me upon it, and when I could find no objection to receiving him, exclaimed:—'He will disturb us by his buffoonery';— and afterwards so managed matters, that he was never formally proposed, nor, by consequence, ever admitted.[16]

This conduct of Johnson gave me, for the first time, to understand, that the friendship between him and Garrick was not so strong as it might be supposed to be: it was not like that of David and Jonathan; it passed not the love of women, and hardly exceeded the strength of an adventitious intimacy: Garrick had a profound veneration for the learning and talents of Johnson, but was used to complain to me, that he was capricious in his friendship, and, as he termed it, coquettish in his display of it. Johnson, on his part, hated the profession of a player, and perhaps might contemplate with indignation, that disposition of the public, which assigns to those who minister to their pleasures, greater rewards than to those whose employment it is to supply their most essential wants. He might possibly reflect that, in his outset in life as an instructor of youth, his hopes were bounded by the prospect of five hundred pounds a year, and that the mimetic powers of Garrick, for under that denomination he ranked all his excellencies, produced to the possessor of them an income of four thousand.

These are such excuses for Johnson's coolness towards an old friend as charity might suggest; but, alas! it had a deeper root, and it is to be feared that it sprung from envy, a passion, which he sometimes was candid enough to confess he was subject to, and laboured through his life to eradicate. His behaviour to Garrick was ever austere, like that of a schoolmaster to one of his scholars,[17] and he flattered himself, that in all he said and did, he stood in awe of his frown.—'I was,' said Johnson, once to a friend, 'last night, behind the scenes at Drury Lane, and met Davy dressed for his part. I was glad to see him; but I believe he was ashamed to see me.'—A supposition hardly to be admitted, even if he had been dressed in the rags of Drugger.[18]

Garrick took his rejection very patiently, and showed his resentment of it no otherwise, than by inquiring of me, from time to time, how we went on at the club. He would often stop at my gate, in his way to and from Hampton, with messages from Johnson relating to his Shakespeare, then in the press, and ask such questions as these:—'Were you at the club on Monday night?'—'What did you talk of?'—'Was Johnson there?'—'I suppose he said something of Davy—that Davy was a clever fellow in his way, full of convivial pleasantry; but no poet, no writer, ha?'—I was vexed at these inquiries, and told him, that this perpetual solicitude about what was said of him, was unnecessary, and could only tend to disturb him; that he might well be content with that share of the public favour which he enjoyed, that he had nothing to do but to possess it in quietness, and that too

great an anxiety to obtain applause would provoke envy, and tend
to intercept, if not totally deprive him of it.

The greatest of Mr. Garrick's foibles was, a notion of the importance of his profession: he thought that Shakespeare and himself were, or ought to be, the objects of all men's attention. When
the King of Denmark was in England, he received an order from
the Lord Chamberlain to entertain that monarch with an exhibition of himself in six of his principal characters. In his way to
London, to receive his instructions, he called on me, and told
me this as news. I could plainly discern in his looks the joy that
transported him; but he affected to be vexed at the shortness of
the notice, and seemed to arraign the wisdom of our councils,
by exclaiming—'You see what heads they have!'

Johnson's objection to the admission of Garrick may seem to
be cynical, and to have arisen from jealousy or resentment, but it
admits of palliation: the truth is, that Garrick was no disquisitor;
his reading had been confined, and he could contribute but little
to the pleasures of sober and instructive conversation. Even his
knowledge of the world was derived through the medium of the
dramatic writers, who, all men know, are not guides to be trusted;
and, in his intercourse with mankind, and manner of conducting
business, he frequently betrayed such ignorance and inattention,
as the following instance will illustrate.[19]

There stood near the dwelling of Mr. Garrick at Hampton, and
adjoining to his garden next the river, a small house, the owner
and occupier whereof was Mr. Peele a bookseller, who had retired from business. Mr. Peele had often said, that as he knew
it would be an accommodation to Mr. Garrick, he had given directions, that at his decease he should have the refusal of it. A
man in the neighborhood had set his eye upon it, and formed
a scheme to make it his own. He had got intelligence that there
was a relation or friend of Mr. Peele's living in the country, and
immediately on Mr. Peele's death applied to his executors, pretending that he had a commission from him to purchase the house
at any price; and, upon this suggestion, procured a conveyance
of it to a person nominated by him, but under a secret trust for
himself. Mr. Garrick, seeing himself thus balked of his hopes, and
in danger of being troubled with an ill neighbour, thought he

had nothing to do but to complain. He told his sad story to me, and in a lucky hour; for, just before his entering my house, I had been reading the life of the Lord Keeper Guildford, and therein a case of a similar fraud, against which his lordship decreed. Upon hearing Mr. Garrick's story, I searched farther, and found the case in law language in Vernon's *Chancery Reports,* and giving him a note of it, told him he might file a bill in chancery, and, on the authority of that determination, hope for relief. About six months after, I being in town, a message came to me in the evening from Mr. Garrick, signifying, that his cause was to come on the next morning, and requesting me to furnish him with a note of a case that I had formerly mentioned to him as resembling his own. Astonished at his remissness, and knowing that no time was to be lost, I immediately borrowed the book I had referred him to, and giving it my servant, went with it to Drury Lane Theatre, where, upon inquiry, I was informed, that he was busily employed in exhibiting an imitation of a spectacle then recent, the procession of the coronation of his present majesty, in an afterpiece to the play for that night. I waited in an outer room till all was over, when in entered Mr. and Mrs. Garrick, and, after giving him time to recover from his fatigue, I told him what I had been doing to help him in his distress, and produced the book; but his thoughts were so wholly taken up by the pageant he was come from, which seemed still to be passing before his eyes, that he could scarcely attend to me, but asked Mrs. Garrick twenty questions about it, how it went off, and whether she did not think the applause of the audience great. He then turned to me, took from me the book, and said he should lay it before his counsel. The book was returned in a few days, but I heard nothing of the decree of the court till some months after, when meeting with his brother George, in the court of requests, I asked him how the cause had gone—'Oh,' said he, 'with us:—the first purchase is decreed fraudulent, and the defendant is condemned in costs.'

Mr. Garrick's forgetfulness and inattention, in a concern that gave him some uneasiness, is not to be accounted for by those who believe, contrary to the fact, that he was ever sufficiently awake to his own interest, nor, indeed, by any who were not well acquainted with his character. In all that related to the theatre he was very acute; but in business of other kinds, a novice. His profession was of such a nature, as left him no intervals of thought or cool deliberation: his mind was either elevated to the highest pitch of intension, or let down to the lowest degree of remission. In the former state, it was inflated by the ideas with which the course of his reading had stored his memory; in the latter, it sunk into an indolent levity, which indulged in jokes, in mimicry, and witticisms.

In the first of these situations, I have described him by the relation of his conduct in a lawsuit: in a season of vacuity, he was another man, easy and cheerful, and disposed, out of everything he saw or heard, to extract mirth. The following story I give as an instance of his pleasantry, at times when the business of the theatre did not occupy his thoughts.

Living at Twickenham, at about two miles distance from his house at Hampton, I made him, as I frequently did when in the country, an afternoon visit. It was in the month of August, and I found him and Mrs. Garrick in the garden, eating figs. He complained that the wasps, which that year were very numerous, had left him very few; and, talking farther about those noxious insects, told me he had heard, that a person near Uxbridge, having swallowed one of them in a draught of liquor, had died of the sting. I told him it was true; for that at a turnpike meeting at Uxbridge I had dined with the apothecary that had attended him, and he had assured me of the fact.—'I believe it,' said Mr. Garrick, 'and have been persuading this lady,' pointing to Mrs. Garrick, 'to do so; but I cannot convince her, and yet, she can believe the story of St. Ursula and the eleven thousand virgins!'— Mrs. Garrick, it is no secret, is of the Romish persuasion.

Davies, in his life of Garrick,[20] has mentioned a variety of particulars that do honour to his memory. Among others, he gives several instances of liberality to his friends. Johnson would frequently say, that he gave away more money than any man of his income in England: and his readiness to give the profits of a night to public charities, and to families and individuals in distress, will long be remembered. He was the first that attempted to reform the stage, by banishing from it all profaneness and immorality, and by expunging from the plays acted at his theatre, every expression capable of any other than a good meaning. And whereas it had for many years been the custom, at one or more of the theatres, to indulge the mob, in the evening of the Lord Mayor's day, with the representation of *The London Cuckolds*, a comedy written by Ravenscroft in times of great licentiousness, and abounding in scenes of vulgar humour, he paid a handsome compliment to the citizens, and showed his regard for the welfare of youth, by discontinuing the practice, and substituting in its place the affecting tragedy of *George Barnwell*,[21] a play adapted to the situation and circumstances of city apprentices, and affording an instructive lesson of discretion and morality.

Notwithstanding the perpetual competition between him and Rich, for the favour of the town, they lived together upon the most friendly terms. Rich, who was never celebrated either for his wit or his understanding, once made him a very elegant compliment: the occasion was this: Rich had improved his house at Covent Garden, by altering the disposition of the seats, so as to accommodate a greater number of spectators than formerly it would, and Mr. Garrick wishing to see these improvements, Mr. Rich invited him to his house, and went with him all over it. In the course of their survey, Mr. Garrick asked, in the language of the theatre, what sum of money the house would hold.—'Sir,' said Mr. Rich, 'that question I am at present unable to answer; but were Mr. Garrick to appear but one night on my stage, I should be able to tell to the utmost shilling.' After all that has been said of Mr. Garrick, envy must allow, that he owed his celebrity to his merit; and yet, of that himself seemed so diffident, that he practised sundry little, but innocent arts, to insure the favour of the public.

Besides Mr. Garrick, there were others that were desirous of becoming members of this our club, the fame whereof had spread abroad, and induced many, who hoped to acquire a reputation for literature, to wish for an admission among us. That unfortunate divine, as he was called, Dr. William Dodd, was one of the number, and made a secret effort for this purpose. This person, at that time, dwelt with his wife in an obscure corner of Hounslow Heath, near a village called Worton; but kept, in a back lane near him, a girl who went by the name of Kennedy. His pretensions to learning, and especially to classical erudition, were very great; and he had in his house a few young gentlemen, who, at very expensive rates, were committed to his care, as to an academy, for instruction. A brother of his wife's rented some land of me, and of him I learned from time to time many particulars respecting his character and manner of living, which latter, as he represented it, was ever such as his visible income would no way account for. He said that he was the most importunate suitor for preferment ever known; and that himself had been the bearer of letters and messages to great men, soliciting promotion to vacant livings, and had hardly escaped kicking downstairs. Dodd's wish to be received into our society was conveyed to us only by a whisper, and that being the case, all opposition to his admission, became unnecessary.

 OHNSON WAS now at ease in his circumstances: he wanted his usual motive to impel him to the exertion of his talents, necessity, and he sunk into indolence. Whoever called in on him at about midway, found him and Levett at breakfast, Johnson in dishabille, as just risen from bed, and Levett filling out tea for himself and his patron alternately, no conversation passing between them. All that visited him at these hours were welcome. A night's rest, and breakfast, seldom failed to refresh and fit him for discourse, and whoever withdrew went too soon. His invitations to dinners abroad were numerous, and he seldom balked them. At evening parties, where were no cards, he very often made one; and from these, when once engaged, most unwillingly retired.

In the relaxation of mind, which almost anyone might have foreseen would follow the grant of his pension, he made little account of that lapse of time, on which, in many of his papers, he so severely moralizes. And, though he was so exact an observer of the passing minutes, as frequently, after his coming from church, to note in his diary how many the service took up in reading, and the sermon in preaching; he seemed to forget how many years had passed since he had begun to take in subscriptions for his edition of Shakespeare. Such a torpor had seized his faculties, as not all the remonstrances of his friends were able to cure: applied to some minds, they would have burned like caustics, but Johnson felt them not: to other objects he was sufficiently attentive, as I shall presently show.

In the performance of the engagement I am under, I find myself compelled to make public, as well those particulars of Johnson that may be thought to abase as those that exalt his character. Among the former, may be reckoned the credit he for some time gave to the idle story of the Cock Lane ghost, concerning which the following facts are the least unworthy of being noted. In the month of January, 1762, it was reported, that at a house in Cock Lane near West Smithfield, there were heard certain noises, accompanied with extraordinary circumstances, tending to the discovery of the death of a young woman who was said to have been destroyed by poison. The agent in this business was a girl, who pretended that the spirit of the deceased appeared to her, and terrified her with the noises above-mentioned. This report drew many persons to the house, who, being thus assembled, put several questions to the girl, and received answers, as from the ghost, describing the circumstances of the poisoning, and a promise, by an affirmative signal, that it would attend one of the querists into the vault under the Church of St. John, Clerkenwell, where the body was deposited, and give a token of its presence by a knock upon the coffin: it was therefore determined to make trial of the existence or veracity of the supposed spirit; and it was then advertised, that the person, to whom the promise was made, was about to visit the vault; and accordingly the whole company present adjourned to the church. He who had a claim to the performance of the promise, and most of the company, went into the vault, and solemnly required the signal; but nothing more ensued. The person accused of the poisoning, with several others, then descended the vault, but no effect was perceived. It was, therefore, the opinion of the whole assembly, that the girl had some art of making or counterfeiting particular noises, and that there was no agency of any higher cause.

Johnson, whose sentiments with respect to supernatural interpositions are discoverable in many parts of his writings, was prompted by curiosity to visit this place, and wait for the appearance of the ghost. Mr. Saunders Welch, his intimate friend, would have dissuaded him from his purpose, urging, that it would expose him to ridicule; but all his arguments had no effect; he went to the house, and, as it is supposed, into the church, and gave countenance to the vulgar expectation, that the ghost would appear; but at length, being convinced that the whole transaction was an imposture, he drew up, as may be inferred from the style and advertisement at the end of the paper, an account of the detection thereof, published in the *Gentleman's Magazine* for February, 1762.

Soon after this, the imposture being more clearly and even to demonstration detected, the persons concerned in it were prosecuted, and underwent a punishment suited to their offence.

What Mr. Welch foretold, in his advice to Johnson, touching this imposture, was now verified: he was censured for his credulity; his wisdom was arraigned, and his religious opinions resolved into superstition. A reverend divine of the time, who had taken effectual care by his conduct to avoid the like imputations, but was enough distinguished by a greater folly, political enthusiasm, exhibited him to ridicule in a satirical poem, and revived the remembrance of that engagement to the public, which, by this, and other instances of the laxity of his mind, he seemed not much inclined to fulfill.[1]

Nor was this all: that facetious gentleman Mr. Foote, who, upon the strength and success of his satirical vein in comedy, had assumed the name of the modern Aristophanes, and at his theatre had long entertained the town with caricatures of living persons, with all their singularities and weaknesses, thought that Johnson at this time was become a fit subject for ridicule, and that an exhibition of him in a drama, written for the purpose, in which himself should represent Johnson, and in his mien, his garb, and his speech, should display all his comic powers, would yield him a golden harvest. Johnson was apprised of his intention; and gave Mr. Foote to understand, that the licence, under which he was permitted to entertain the town, would not justify the liberties he was accustomed to take with private characters, and that, if he persisted in his design, himself would be a spectator of his disgrace, and would, by a severe chastisement of his representative on the stage, and in the face of the whole audience, convince the world, that, whatever were his infirmities, or even his foibles, they should not be made the sport of the public, or the means of gain to anyone of his profession.[2] Foote, upon this intimation, had discretion enough to desist from his purpose. Johnson entertained no resentment against him, and they were ever after friends.

Johnson was insensible to the effects of this abuse; but the poem above-mentioned had brought to remembrance, that his edition of Shakespeare had long been due. His friends took the alarm, and, by all the arts of reasoning and persuasion, laboured to convince him, that, having taken subscriptions for a work in which he had made no progress, his credit was at stake. He confessed he was culpable, and promised from time to time to begin a course of such reading as was necessary to qualify him for the work: this was no more than he had formerly done in an engagement with Coxeter, to whom he had bound himself to write the life of Shakespeare; but he never could be prevailed on to begin it, so that, even now, it was questioned whether his promises were to be relied on. For this reason, Sir Joshua Reynolds, and some other of his friends, who were more concerned for his reputation than himself seemed to be, contrived to entangle him by a wager, or some other pecuniary engagement, to perform his task by a certain time, and this, together possibly with some distrust of the continuance of his mental powers, set him to work; but, as he had been remiss in making collections for the purpose, he found it an irksome task. Theobald declares, that to settle the text of his author, and to elucidate obscure passages in him, he had found it necessary to peruse a great number of plays and other publications, to the very titles of most whereof it is certain Johnson was a stranger. He, it is true, had read as many old English books as came in his way, but he had never sought after any such; he was no collector, and in fact was destitute of materials for his work. All therefore that he did, or could do, after the waste of so much time, was, to read over his author in the former editions, and solicit help from his friends; who, if he is not mistaken in his assertion, were but slack in offering him assistance. To me, among others, he did the honour of sending for such notes as he thought I might have made in the course of my reading. Mr. Garrick was his messenger, as he frequently passed by my gate in the country;

and, though I was at that time deeply engaged in the *History of Music*, I furnished him with a few remarks, which, unimportant as they are, he thought fit to insert. Others, more valuable, he got from such of his friends as were at leisure to assist him.

The year 1765 gave to the world an edition of Shakespeare's dramatic works by Samuel Johnson, the greatest proficient in vernacular erudition, and one of the ablest critics of his time. Much had been expected from it, and little now appeared to have been performed; a few conjectural emendations of the text, and some scattered remarks on particular passages, were all that was presented to our view that had any pretence to novelty, except some general observations, which serve to illustrate the beauties, and mark the defects, of the several plays, and are inserted at the end of each.

For the apparent meagreness of the work, the paucity of the notes, and other evidences of the editor's want of industry, and, indeed, unfitness for the office of a scholiast, so far as it regards the illustration of the text, some atonement, it must be confessed, is made by the preface, wherein, as if the author had reserved himself for one great effort of his genius, all the powers of eloquence and critical erudition are displayed. In truth, it is an essay on dramatic poesy in general, in which, with a degree of perspicacity that had never before been exercised on the subject, he has exhibited the perfections of his author in a blaze of splendour that distracts us with its radiance. To attemper our admiration, he has, however, thought fit to note the slumbers of even this great genius, his violations of historical truth, his deviations from dramatic regularity, his low conceits, and the frequent recurrence of scenes that suspend actions of importance, and, wherever interposed, are excrescences; and this not in a style of perfunctory disquisition, but with such a degree of asperity as critics discover when they are criticizing the works of a rival.

For thus detracting from the merit of his favourite, Mr. Garrick was to the highest degree exasperated with Johnson: he reproached him, though not to his face, with want of feeling and the knowledge of human nature, of which, he said, he understood nothing, but what he had learned from books:—'All that he writes,' added he, 'comes from his head: Shakespeare, when he sat down to write, dipped his pen into his own heart.'

Johnson seemed to be conscious that this work would fall short of the expectations it had raised, and endeavoured to ward off the censure of the public by an insinuation in the preface, that his friends had been backward in furnishing him with assistance. The passage is pretty strongly pointed, and is here given in his own words.

Having classed the observations of others, I was at last to try what I could substitute for their mistakes, and how I could supply their omissions. I collated such copies as I could procure, and wished for more, but have not found the collectors of these rarities very communicative. Of the editions which chance or kindness put into my hands, I have given an enumeration, that I may not be blamed for neglecting what I had not the power to do.

Few there were who saw this passage, and knew that Mr. Garrick had the earliest editions of all Shakespeare's plays, but construed this into a reproach on him; in that sense he understood it, and it gave him great offence. To clear himself of the imputation of a conduct so unfriendly, he protested to me, that his collection had ever been accessible to Johnson, and that himself had signified, that any or all the books in it were at his service; and, farther to convince me, he, at the next visit I made him, called in his man Charles, and bade him relate to me his instructions respecting the use of his library, or the loan of books to Johnson.— 'Sir,' said the man, 'I was told to let Mr. Johnson have whatever books he wanted; but he never applied for any.' [3]

To say the truth, Mr. Garrick was rather forward in offering the use of his library to the writers of the time: he did it to Mr. Whalley, when editing the works of Ben Jonson; and to Dr. Percy, the collector and publisher of the *Reliques of Ancient English Poetry*. His view, as I conjecture, was, to receive, in return for his kindness, thanks, with perhaps some additional compliment; and in these two instances he was gratified with both. I imagine that Johnson was unwilling to buy the favour intended him at that price, and that therefore he declined it.

We are not to suppose that the publication of Shakespeare, a work undertaken without any impulse, and executed with reluctance, would greatly add to the literary reputation of Johnson; yet such was the character he had acquired by his *Dictionary*, and other of his writings, that the heads of the university of Dublin were moved to testify their sense of his merits; and accordingly, on the twenty-third day of July, 1765, he was, by them, presented with a diploma, creating him doctor in both laws; a distinction the more to be valued, as it was unsolicited, and a voluntary testimony of the esteem in which he was held by that learned body. The causes assigned for bestowing it are contained in the following words, part of the instrument, 'ob egregiam scriptorum elegantiam et utilitatem.' [4]

His great affection for our own universities, and particularly his attachment to Oxford, prevented Johnson from receiving this honour as it was intended, and he never assumed the title which it conferred. He was as little pleased to be called Doctor in consequence of it, as he was with the title of Domine, which a friend of his once incautiously addressed him by. He thought it alluded to his having been a schoolmaster; and, though he has ably vindicated Milton from the reproach that Salmasius meant to fix on him, by saying that he was of that profession,[5] he wished to have it forgot, that himself had ever been driven to it as the means of subsistence, and had failed in the attempt.

Johnson was now arrived at the fifty-sixth year of his age, and had actually attained to that state of independence, which before he could only affect. He was now in possession of an income that freed him from the apprehensions of want, and exempted him from the necessity of mental labour. He had discharged his obligations to the public, and, with no encumbrance of a family, or anything to control his wishes or desires, he had his mode of living to choose. Blest with what was to him a competence, he had it now in his power to study, to meditate, and to put in practice a variety of good resolutions, which, almost from his first entrance into life, he had been making. Some specimens of these have been given in a collection of prayers and devotional exercises lately published by his direction,[6] to which I could add a great number. They are the effusions of a fervent piety, and the result of most severe examinations of himself in his hours of retirement; and have for their objects, early rising, a good use of time, abstinence, the study of the Scriptures, and a constant attendance on divine worship; in the performance of all which duties he seems to construe his frequent interruptions into criminal remissness. One extract from his diary I however here insert, for the purpose of showing the state of his mind at about the beginning of the year 1766.

Since the last reception of the Sacrament, I hope I have no otherwise grown worse, than as continuance in sin makes the sinner's condition more dangerous. Since last New Year's Day, I have risen every morning by eight, at least, not after nine: which is more superiority over my habits than I have ever before been able to obtain. Scruples still distress me. My resolution, with the blessing of God, is, to contend with them, and, if I can, to conquer them.

My resolutions are,

To conquer scruples.
To read the Bible this year.
To try to rise more early.
To study divinity.
To live methodically.
To oppose idleness.
To frequent divine worship.

It was a frequent practice with him, in his addresses to the divine Majesty, to commemorate and recommend to mercy his wife and departed friends; and the knowledge thereof has induced a suspicion, that he adopted the Romish tenet of Purgatory. To clear his memory from this imputation, I am necessitated to mention a few particulars which I learned from him in conversation, that may serve to show, that no such conclusion is to be drawn from his practice in this respect; for that his acquiescence therein arose from a controversy, which, about the year 1715, was agitated between certain divines of a Protestant communion, that professed to deny, not less than they did the doctrine of transubstantiation, that of purgatory.[7]

These were, the non-juring clergy of the time; of whom, and also of their writings, Johnson was ever used to speak with great respect. One of them, Dr. Thomas Brett, was a man profoundly skilled in ritual literature, as appears by a dissertation of his, printed, together with a collection of ancient liturgies, in 1720; [8] and he, as I infer from the style of the book and the method of reasoning therein, wrote a tract entitled, *Reasons for Restoring Some Prayers and Directions, as They Stand in the Communion-service of the First English Reformed Liturgy, Compiled by the Bishops in the Second and Third Years of King Edward VI.*[9]

He first shows, that the recommending the dead to the mercy of God is nothing of the remains of popery, but a constant usage of the primitive church; and for this assertion, he produces the authority of Tertullian, who flourished within an hundred years after the death of the apostle St. John, and also, the authority of St. Cyprian, St. Cyril, St. Ambrose, St. Epiphanius, St. Chrysostom, and St. Augustine, by citations from the several writings of those fathers.

He then argues, that this custom neither supposes the modern purgatory, nor gives encouragement to libertinism and vice; that the ancient church believed the recommending the dead a serviceable office; that the custom seems to have gone upon this principle, that supreme happiness is not to be expected till the resurrection, and that the interval between death and the end of the world is a state of imperfect bliss; the church, therefore, concludes he, might believe her prayers for good people would improve their condition, and raise the satisfactions of this period.

This tract was, with great acuteness, and no less learning, answered by another non-juring divine, in one entitled *No Sufficient Reasons for Restoring Some Prayers and Directions of King Edward the Sixth's Liturgy.* A reply was given to it, and the controversy was carried on to a great length; the result of it was, a schism among the non-jurors; those, for restoring the prayers, compiled a new communion-office; others, who were against widening the breach with the national church, chose to abide by the present form; and this diversity of sentiments and practice was, as Johnson once told me, the ruin of the non-juring cause.

In the study of this controversy, which I have reason to think interested Johnson very deeply, he seems to have taken part with Dr. Brett and the separatists his followers, whose conduct is accounted for and vindicated, in the dissertation on liturgies abovementioned.

Such as are disposed to charge Johnson with weakness and superstition, and are so weak as to insinuate that, because he recommended his deceased wife and friends to the divine mercy, (though with the qualifying words, 'so far as it may be lawful') he must have been popishly affected, or a believer in the doctrine of purgatory, may hence learn to be less severe in their censures, and lament their ignorance of ecclesiastical history, which would have taught them, that the practice prevailed long before popery was established, or purgatory thought of; and that, though it may not upon the whole be defensible, there is more to be said for it, than many of the enemies to his memory are able to answer.[10]

And to those of his friends, who think that, for the sake of his reputation, the prayers and meditations, in which these sentiments have appeared, should have been suppressed, it ought surely to be an answer, that they were put into the hands of the reverend divine, who, to my knowledge, attended him with great affection and assiduity through his last illness, with an express charge to commit them to the press, and who, if he had forborne this friendly office, had deprived a charitable and laudable institution of a benefit, which the performance of it was intended to confer.[11]

With a view to improve the leisure he now enjoyed, and seemingly determined to reform those habits of indolence, which, in the former part of his life, he had contracted, he removed from the Temple into a house in Johnson's Court, Fleet Street, and invited thither his friend Mrs. Williams. An upper room, which had the advantages of a good light and free air, he fitted up for a study, and furnished with books, chosen with so little regard to editions or their external appearance, as showed they were intended for use, and that he disdained the ostentation of learning. Here he was in a situation and circumstances that enabled him to enjoy the visits of his friends, and to receive them in a manner suitable to the rank and condition of many of them. A silver standish, and some useful plate, which he had been prevailed on to accept as pledges of kindness from some who most esteemed him, together with furniture that would not have disgraced a better dwelling, banished those appearances of squalid indigence, which, in his less happy days, disgusted those who came to see him.

In one of his diaries he noted down a resolution to take a seat in the church; this he might possibly do about the time of this his removal. The church he frequented was that of St. Clement Danes, which, though not his parish church, he preferred to that of the Temple, which I recommended to him, as being free from noise, and, in other respects, more commodious. His only reason was, that in the former he was best known. He was not constant in his attendance on divine worship; but, from an opinion peculiar to himself, and which he once intimated to me, seemed to wait for some secret impulse as a motive to it.

I could never collect from his discourse, that he was drawn to public worship by the charms of pulpit eloquence, or any affection for popular preachers, who, in general, are the worst; nor can I form any judgment of the value he set on it, having never been present with him at church but once, and that at a time, when, in compliment to him, as it may be supposed, the preacher gave us a sermon, that read like a Saturday's *Rambler*,[12] and was, by many, soon discovered to have been cast in the same mold, or, in other words, of Johnson's composing; but he seemed to think it a duty to accept in good part the endeavours of all public instructors, however meanly qualified for the office, and ever to forbear exercising his critical talents on the effusions of men inferior in learning and abilities to himself.*

The Sundays which he passed at home were, nevertheless, spent in private exercises of devotion,[13] and sanctified by acts of charity of a singular kind: on that day he accepted of no invitation abroad, but gave a dinner to such of his poor friends as might else have gone without one.

He had little now to conflict with but what he called his morbid melancholy, which, though oppressive, had its intermissions, and left him the free exercise of all his faculties, and the power of enjoying the conversation of his numerous friends and visitants. These reliefs he owed in a great measure to the use of opium, which, as I have elsewhere mentioned, he was accustomed to take in large quantities, the effect whereof was generally such an exhilaration of his spirits as he sometimes suspected for intoxication.

I am now about to mention a remarkable era of his life, distinguished by a connection that, for many years, was a source of great satisfaction and comfort to him. It was a friendship, contracted, as his diary imports, in 1765, with Mr. Thrale, a brewer, in Southwark, who, though a follower of a trade, which in other countries is lightly thought of, yet as in this it implies great opulence, and the power of conducing in various ways to the interests of the community, ranked as a gentleman. He had received the benefit of an university education, and was a representative in parliament, as his father had been, for the above-mentioned borough; and in every view of his character, could not but be deemed a valuable addition to the number of Johnson's friends. To his villa at Streatham, in Surrey, Johnson was invited, not as a guest, but as a resiant, whenever he was disposed to change the town for the country air: for his accommodation, an apartment was allotted; for his entertainment, a library was furnished with such books as himself chose, and little was wanting to persuade him, that, when at Streatham, he was at home. He soon experienced the salutary effects of his new abode, and there is little doubt that to it he was indebted for some years of his life.

It might have been expected that Johnson, in the easy circumstances in which he had for some time felt himself, and with such a love of independence as he affected, would have declined obligations that he was unable to repay, at least in kind; but he knew that friendship weighs not in a balance the favours it confers. Mr. Thrale's tenders carried in them all the evidences of sincerity, and he had the example of men, equally wise with himself, to justify his acceptance of such invitations as were now made him. The only obligation they subjected him to was, that of supporting his character, and, in a family where there were many visitants, furnishing such conversation as was to be expected from a man who had distinguished himself by his learning, his wit, and his eloquence. This, it must be confessed, was a burdensome task to one who, like others, must be supposed to have had his sombrous intervals, and, in the hour of repletion, to wish for the indulgence of being silent, or, at least, of talking like other men. To be continually uttering apophthegms, or speeches worthy of remembrance, was more than could have been expected of Socrates.

Besides the conveniences for study, with which he was furnished at Streatham, he had opportunities of exercise, and the pleasure of airings and excursions. He was once prevailed on by Mr. Thrale to join in the pleasures of the chase, in which he showed himself a bold rider, for he either leaped, or broke through, many of the hedges that obstructed him. This he did, not because he was eager in the pursuit, but, as he said, to save the trouble of alighting and remounting. He did not derive the pleasure or benefit from riding that many do: it had no tendency to raise his spirits; and he once told me that, in a journey on horseback, he fell asleep. In the exercise of a coach he had great delight; it afforded him the indulgence of indolent postures, and, as I discovered when I have had him in my own, the noise of it assisted his hearing.

It cannot be supposed but that these indulgences were a great relief to Johnson in his declining years; they, nevertheless, indisposed him for meditation and reflection; and, as he has noted in his diary, assigning for the reason the irregularity of the family, it broke his habit of early rising, which he had persisted in from New Year's Day, 1765, to about the midsummer following.[14] It is possible that the family, had they been disposed to it, might with equal truth have complained, that he was little less irregular, and that, if they obliged him to break his resolution of early rising, he often prevented their retiring to rest, at a seasonable hour, that he might not want the gratification of tea.

About this time, Johnson had the honour of a conversation with his majesty, in the library, at the queen's house.[15] Whether the occasion of it was accidental, or otherwise, I have never been informed; but from this account of it, given by him, it afforded him great satisfaction. He spoke to me of the king's behaviour in terms of the highest gratitude and approbation, and described it as equalling in grace and condescension what might have been expected from Lewis the fourteenth, when the manners of the

French court were in the highest state of cultivation. The public are already in possession of the handsome compliment which his majesty made him; I will, nevertheless, give it here a place: he asked Johnson if he intended to give the world any more of his compositions; Johnson answered, he believed he should not, for that he thought he had written enough; 'I should have thought so too,' replied his majesty, 'if you had not written so well.'

1768-1775

OHNSON WAS now approaching towards sixty. He was an exact computer of time, and, as his essays abundantly show, regretted deeply the lapse of those minutes that could not be recalled, and though, in his own judgment of himself, he had been criminal in the waste of it, he was ever resolving to subtract from his sleep those hours which are fittest for study and meditation. Numberless are the resolutions that I meet with in his diaries, for a series of years back, to rise at eight; but he was unable, for any long continuance, to perform them, a weakness, less inexcusable than he thought it, for he was ever a bad sleeper, and was sufficiently sensible of his infirmity, in that respect, to have allayed his scrupulosity, had he not been a most rigorous judge of his actions. To impress the more strongly on his mind the value of time, and the use it behoved every wise man to make of it, he indulged himself in an article of luxury, which, as far as my observation and remembrance will serve me, he never enjoyed till this late period of his life: it was a watch, which he caused to be made for him, in the year 1768, by those eminent artists Mudge and Dutton: it was of metal, and the outer case covered with tortoise shell; he paid for it seventeen guineas. On the dial plate thereof, which was of enamel, he caused to be inscribed, in the original Greek, these words of our blessed Saviour, Νυξ γαρ ερχεται,[1] but with the mistake of a letter μ for ν: the meaning of them is, 'For the night cometh.' This, though a memento of great im-

portance, he, about three years after, thought pedantic; he, therefore, exchanged the dial plate for one in which the inscription
was omitted.

In the same year, 1768, upon the establishment of the royal
academy of painting, sculpture, &c. Johnson was nominated professor of ancient literature, an office merely honorary, and conferred on him, as it is supposed, upon the recommendation of
the president, Sir Joshua Reynolds.

In the variety of subjects on which he had exercised his pen,
Johnson had hitherto forborne to meddle with the disputes of
contending factions, which is all, that, at this day, is to be understood by the word *politics*. He was ever a friend to government,
in a general sense of the term, as knowing what benefits society
derives from it; and was never tempted to write on the side of
what is called opposition, but at a period of his life, when experience had not enabled him to judge of the motives which induce
men to assume the characters of patriots. In the year 1769, he
saw with indignation the methods which, in the business of
Wilkes,[2] were taken to work upon the populace, and, in 1770,
published a pamphlet, entitled *The False Alarm*, wherein he
asserts, and labours to show, by a variety of arguments founded
on precedents, that the expulsion of a member of the House of
Commons, for such offences as he had been convicted of, was
both just and seasonable, and that no such calamity as the subversion of the constitution, was to be feared from an act, that
had usage, which is the law of parliament, to warrant it. The non-
acquiescence of the people interested in the question, is therefore branded by him with folly and madness, in the following
animated expressions:—

Every artifice of sedition has been since practised to awaken discontent, and inflame indignation. The papers of every day have been
filled with the exhortations and menaces of faction. The madness
has spread through all ranks and both sexes; women and children
have clamoured for Mr. Wilkes; honest simplicity has been cheated
into fury, and only the wise have escaped the infection.

To ridicule the conduct of opposition, he adopts a term, invented by the leaders thereof, and calls the conjuncture of events,

at the time of which he is speaking, an *alarming crisis*, but endeavours to abate the fears of its termination, by alluding to parliamentary decisions apparently partial, and sometimes oppressive; and showing that the vexation excited by injustice, suffered, or supposed to be suffered, by any private man or single community, was local and temporary. This position he illustrates by the following observation:

We have found by experience, that though a squire has given ale and venison in vain, and a borough has been compelled to see its dearest interests in the hands of him whom it did not trust, yet the general state of the nation has continued the same. The sun has risen, and the corn has grown, and whatever talk has been of the danger of property, yet he that ploughed the field commonly reaped it, and he that built the house was master of the door.

In a tone more grave, he addresses such as are capable of conviction, and tells them—that

they have as much happiness as the condition of life will easily receive; and that a government, of which an erroneous, or unjust, representation of one county only, is the greatest crime that interest can discover, or malice can upbraid, is a government approaching nearer to perfection than any that experience has shown, or history related.

The pamphlet concludes with some shrewd remarks on the support given to faction by the sectaries, and that frigid neutrality of the Tories in this business, which he censures in these words: 'They do not yet consider that they have at last a king, who knows not the name of a party, and who wishes to be the common father of his people.'

It was not to be imagined, that a publication, so unpopular as this, would long remain unanswered. Of many answers to it, one alone seemed to Johnson worthy of a reply; [3] but, in a consultation with his friends, he was advised to forbear. Had he engaged in a vindication of *The False Alarm*, the world might possibly have been entertained with a specimen of his abilities in controversial writing, in which there is little doubt that he would have displayed the temper and perspicuity of Hooker, the strength of Chillingworth, and the dexterity of Hoadly, though, in truth, he was no friend to controversy; his opinion on that subject being, that it seldom produced conviction, that an impotent argument against a book was best refuted by silence, and that it is want of policy to give immortality to that which must of itself expire.

In the next succeeding year, a subject of more general importance to the interests of this country engaged his attention: it was a question between us and the court of Spain, touching the prediscovery, and, consequently, the right of dominion over certain islands in the South Seas, known to us by the name of Pepys's or Falkland's Islands, and to the Spaniards by that of the Malouines, spots of earth so inconsiderable, as Johnson asserts, that in the desert of the ocean they had almost escaped human notice; and which, if they had not happened to make a seamark, had perhaps never had a name. Lord Anson, in his voyage, had noticed these islands, and the relator thereof [4] had recommended them as necessary to the success of any future expedition against the coast of Chile, and, of such importance, that the possession of them would produce many advantages in peace; and in war would make us masters of the South Sea. In 1748, our ministry sent out a few sloops, for a fuller knowledge of Pepys's and Falkland's Islands, and for further discoveries in the South Sea; but, upon a remonstrance of Wall, the Spanish ambassador here, maintaining the right of his master to the exclusive dominion of the South Sea, they relinquished part of their original design, and our purpose of settling there was disowned. Thus the matter rested, till Lord Egmont was appointed to the direction of our naval operations, who, in the year 1765, sent out an expedition, the commander whereof took possession of Falkland's Island in the name of his Britannic majesty, and placed a garrison in a place of defence, to which he gave the appellation of Port Egmont. In this settlement, we were soon after disturbed; for Madariaga, a Spanish commodore, with five frigates and a train of artillery, appearing before the island, obliged our people to capitulate, and obtained possession. This event was no sooner known at our court, than hostilities against Spain were resolved on, and a powerful fleet was assembled: these preparations brought on a conference between Prince Masserano, the Spanish ambassador here, and our minister, and a subsequent negotiation at Madrid, between Mr. Harris our minister there, and the Marquis Grimaldi: the result was, a disavowal on the part of Spain of the violent enterprise of Buccarelli, the governor of Buenos Ayres, who had sent the force that dispossessed the English, and a promise to restore the port and fort called Egmont, with all the artillery and stores therein, but with a declaration, that this engagement should not affect the question of the prior right of sovereignty of the Malouines, otherwise called Falkland's Islands.

The acquiescence of our court in these concessions of that of Madrid, and the reference of a disputable question to the Greek calends, furnished the leaders of faction with a new topic for clamour, and war became the cry. The heavy burthen of debt, incurred by the last, was no reason against a new one, and millions were to be expended, and thousands murdered, for the titular sovereignty of an island, which Johnson thus strongly and even poetically characterizes:—

A bleak and gloomy solitude, an island thrown aside from human use, stormy in winter, and barren in summer: an island which not the southern savages have dignified with habitation; where a garrison must be kept in a state that contemplates with envy the exiles of Siberia; of which the expense will be perpetual, and the use only occasional, and which, if fortune smile upon our labours, may become a nest of smugglers in peace, and in war the future refuge of buccaneers.

These are his sentiments respecting the incommodities of this contested settlement: against the advantages suggested by the relator of Anson's expedition, whom he represents as having written under the influence of a heated imagination, he opposes the following arguments, founded in true policy and sound morality:

That such a settlement may be of use in war, no man that considers its situation will deny. But war is not the whole business of life; it happens but seldom, and every man, either good or wise, wishes that its frequency were still less. That conduct which betrays designs of future hostility, if it does not excite violence, will always generate malignity; it must forever exclude confidence and friendship, and continue a cold and sluggish rivalry, by a sly reciprocation of indirect injuries, without the bravery of war, or the security of peace.

The advantage of such a settlement in time of peace is, I think, not easily to be proved. For, what use can it have but of a station for contraband traders, a nursery of fraud, and a receptacle of theft? . . .

Government will not, perhaps, soon arrive at such purity and excellence, but that some connivance at least will be indulged to the triumphant robber and successful cheat. He that brings wealth home, is seldom interrogated by what means it was obtained. This, however, is one of those modes of corruption with which mankind ought always to struggle, and which they may, in time, hope to overcome. There is reason to expect, that as the world is more enlightened, policy and morality will at last be reconciled, and that nations will learn not to do what they would not suffer.[5]

To silence this clamour, to defeat the purposes of a wicked and malevolent faction, to allay the thirst for human blood, and to bring the deluded people to a sense of their true interest, was the aim of Johnson in writing this most judicious pamphlet: he succeeded in his endeavour, the miseries of war were averted, the contractors disappointed, and a few months restored the populace to the use of their understandings.

In a review of the several particulars herein before related, it will appear, that Johnson's course of life was very uniform. London was a place of residence which he preferred to all others, as affording more intelligence, and better opportunities of conversation than were elsewhere to be found, and he was but little delighted either with rural scenes or manners. Novelty, and variety of occupations, it is true, were objects that engaged his attention, and from these he never failed to extract information. Though born and bred in a city, he well understood both the theory and practice of agriculture, and even the management of a farm: he could describe, with great accuracy, the process of malting; and, had necessity driven him to it, could have thatched a dwelling. Of field recreations, such as hunting, setting, and shooting, he would discourse like a sportsman, though his personal defects rendered him, in a great measure, incapable of deriving pleasure from any such exercises.

But he had taken a very comprehensive view of human life and manners, and, that he was well acquainted with the views and pursuits of all classes and characters of men, his writings abundantly show. This kind of knowledge he was ever desirous of increasing, even as he advanced in years: to gratify it, he was accessible to all comers, and yielded to the invitations of such of his friends as had residences in the country, to vary his course of living, and pass the pleasanter months of the year in the shades of obscurity.

In these visits, where there were children in the family, he took great delight in examining them as to their progress in learning, or, to make use of a term almost obsolete, of apposing them. To this purpose, I once heard him say, that in a visit to Mrs. Percy, who had the care of one of the young princes, at the queen's house, the Prince of Wales, being then a child,[6] came into the room, and began to play about; when Johnson, with his usual curiosity, took an opportunity of asking him what books he was reading, and, in particular, inquired as to his knowledge of the scriptures: the prince, in his answers, gave him great satisfaction; and, as to the last, said, that part of his daily exercises was to read Ostervald. In many families into which he went, the fathers were often desirous of producing their sons to him for his opinion of their parts, and of the proficiency they had made at school, which, in frequent instances, came out to be but small. He once told me, that being at the house of a friend, whose son on his school vacation was come home, the father spoke of this child as a lad of pregnant parts, and said, that he was well versed in the classics, and acquainted with history, in the study whereof he took great delight. Having this information, Johnson, as a test of the young scholar's attainments, put this question to him: —'At what time did the heathen oracles cease?'—The boy, not in the least daunted, answered:—'At the dissolution of religious houses.'

By the exercise of such offices as these; by his disposition to encourage children in their learning, and joining admonition to instruction, to exhort them to obedience to their parents and teachers, Johnson rendered himself a welcome guest in all the families into which he was admitted, and, in various ways, did he employ his talents in the gratification of his friends. A gentleman, with whom he had maintained a long and strict friendship, had the misfortune to lose his wife, and wished Johnson, from the outlines of her character, which he should give him, and his own knowledge of her worth, to compose a monumental inscription for her: he returned the husband thanks for the confidence he placed in him, and acquitted himself of the task in the * fine eulogium, now to be seen in the parish church of Watford in Hertfordshire.[7]

He had long been solicited by Mr. James Boswell, a native of Scotland,[8] and one that highly valued him, to accompany him in a journey to the Hebrides, or Western islands of that kingdom, as to a part of the world in which nature was to be viewed in her rudest and most terrific form; and where, whatever was wanting to delight the eye, or soothe the imagination, was made up by objects that could not fail to expand it, and turn delight into astonishment; and being now, in the year 1773, his own master, having no literary engagement to fulfill, he accepted the invitation. He began the tour proposed, in the autumn of the year above-mentioned, and, computing from the eighteenth day of August, when he left Edinburgh, to the ninth of November, when he returned thither, completed it in eleven [9] weeks and six days; and, at his return to England, drew up and published an account of it.[10]

The islands which Johnson and his friend saw, though few in comparison with the whole number, were some of the most considerable of the Hebrides; and his manner of describing them and the inhabitants, as also, his reception, is entertaining; but it is not enough particular to render it intelligible to a stranger. In the relation of historical facts, and local circumstances, Johnson delighted not: whatever intelligence came in his way, furnished him with matter for reflection, and his book is rather a disquisition on Hebridian manners, than such a description of the islands and the people as it was in his power to give.

I have some reason to think that, in writing the account of his journey to the Western islands, Johnson had in his eye one of the most delightful books of the like kind in our language, Maund-rell's *Journey from Aleppo to Jerusalem.* The motives that induced him to undertake a labour so formidable to a man of his age, as his tour must be thought, I will not inquire into: doubtless, curiosity was one of them; but, it was curiosity directed to no peculiar object. He was neither an antiquary nor a naturalist; he had little acquaintance with the treasures which lie below the surface of the earth; and for the study of botany he never dis-covered the least relish. If any particular subject may be said to have engaged his attention, it must have been the manners of a people of whom he knew little but by report, the knowledge whereof might furnish him with new topics for reflection and disquisition, an exercise of his mental powers which, of all others, he most delighted in. That in this employment he has conducted himself with that impartiality which becomes a lover of truth, the natives of the kingdom he visited deny; and, that he carried out of this country the temper of a man who hoped for an hospitable reception among strangers, few are so hardy as to assert. Accord-ingly, we find in his narrative an intermixture, not only of praise and blame, but of gratitude and invective.

The volume which this tour gave birth to may properly be called a dissertation, for it has scarcely any facts, and consists chiefly in propositions which he hunts down, and enlivens with amusing disquisition. As he says himself, on another occasion, the nega-tive catalogue of particulars is very copious: what he did not see, what he could not learn, what he would not believe, what he did not inquire about, and what he is not sure of, altogether form a considerable enumeration. Yet the merit of this tract is great; for, though I will admit that no one going his route could derive from him direction or intelligence; though no remembrance could be refreshed, nor remarks corroborated; because his web was spun, not from objects that presented themselves to his view, but from his own pre-existent ideas; I am convinced, that everybody must have regretted the omission, had he, for any reason, withheld so entertaining a series of reflections.

From a tour to which he had no stronger an incentive, from which he was so little able to extract pleasure, and which had oc-casioned a suspension of the enjoyments he found in a metropolis,

it seems at first wonderful, that he should have returned satisfied: that he did so is certain; and it must be attributed to the
gratification he felt in the respect that had been paid to him, in
seeing the celebrity he had acquired, and in increasing the stock
of his ideas.

Had Johnson been more explicit in his acknowledgments of the
hospitable and courteous treatment he experienced from a people,
who had reason to look on him rather as a spy than a traveller,
and might have said to him—'To discover the nakedness of the
land are ye come,'—he would have given a proof, that he had, in
some degree, overcome his prejudices against them and their country; but they seemed to be unconquerable.

Johnson's prejudices were too strong to permit him to extend
his philanthropy much beyond the limits of his native country,
and the pale of his own church; and, that he was unable to conquer his habits of thinking and judging, is the only apology that
can be offered for his asperity towards the people whose country
and manners he has taken upon him to describe; or that he has
forborne to display any such generous sentiments respecting the
inhabitants of Scotland as others have done who have visited that
country.

I must here observe, as it was a circumstance that gave him
some trouble after his return to England, that during his stay
in the Hebrides, Johnson was very industrious in his inquiries
touching the Earse language, with a view to ascertain the degree
of credit due to certain poems then lately published and ascribed to Ossian, an ancient bard, who, till then, had scarce been
heard of. His opinion, upon the question of their genuineness, is
pretty decisive, and will appear best in his own words.

I suppose my opinion of the poems of Ossian is already discovered.
I believe they never existed in any other form than that which we
have seen. The editor, or author, never could show the original; [11] nor
can it be shown by any other. To revenge reasonable incredulity by refusing evidence, is a degree of insolence with which the world is
not yet acquainted; and stubborn audacity is the last refuge of guilt.
It would be easy to show it, if he had it; but whence could it be
had? It is too long to be remembered, and the language formerly had
nothing written. He has doubtless inserted names that circulate in

popular stories, and may have translated some wandering ballads, if any can be found; and the names, and some of the images, being recollected, make an inaccurate auditor imagine, by the help of Caledonian bigotry, that he has formerly heard the whole. . . .

I have yet supposed no imposture, but in the publisher; yet, I am far from certainty, that some translations have not been lately made, that may now be obtruded as parts of the original work. Credulity on one part is a strong temptation to deceit on the other, especially to deceit of which no personal injury is the consequence, and which flatters the author with his own ingenuity. The Scots have something to plead for their easy reception of an improbable fiction: they are seduced by their fondness for their supposed ancestors. A Scotchman must be a very sturdy moralist, who does not love Scotland better than truth; he will always love it better than inquiry: and, if falsehood flatters his vanity, will not be very diligent to detect it. Neither ought the English to be much influenced by Scotch authority; for of the past and present state of the whole Earse nation, the Lowlanders are, at least, as ignorant as ourselves. To be ignorant is painful; but it is dangerous to quiet our uneasiness by the delusive opiate of hasty persuasion.

But this is the age in which those who could not read, have been supposed to write; in which the giants of antiquated romance have been exhibited as realities. If we know little of the ancient Highlanders, let us not fill the vacuity with Ossian. If we have not searched the Magellanick regions, let us, however, forbear to people them with Patagons.

No sooner did this strong and unequivocal declaration of Johnson's opinion of the poems of Ossian appear, than Mr. James Macpherson, the publisher of them, not only repelled the charge of forgery therein contained, but, in a letter to the author of it, threatened him with corporal chastisement. If Mr. Macpherson had known his man, he would probably have forborne the thought of such a revenge. To show his contempt of him and all that he was able to do that could hurt him, Johnson returned the following brief but spirited answer:

No date.[12]

Mr. James Macpherson,

I received your foolish and impudent letter.—Any violence that shall be attempted upon me, I will do my best to repel; and what I cannot do for myself, the law shall do for me; for I will not be hindered from exposing what I think a cheat, by the menaces of a ruffian. What would you have me retract? I thought your work an imposture; [13] I think so still; and, for my opinion, I have given reasons which I here dare you to refute.—Your abilities, since your Homer, are not so formidable; and, what I hear of your morality, inclines me to credit rather what you shall prove, than what you shall say.

Whether Johnson was apprehensive that his adversary would put his threat in execution, or that he meant to show all who came to see him, that he stood upon his guard, he provided himself with a weapon, both of the defensive and offensive kind. It was an oak plant of a tremendous size; a plant, I say, and not a shoot or branch, for it had had a root, which being trimmed to the size of a large orange, became the head of it. Its height was upwards of six feet, and from about an inch in diameter at the lower end, increased to near three: this he kept in his bedchamber, so near the chair in which he constantly sat, as to be within reach.

But this precaution for his defence turned out to be unnecessary. Johnson's letter, above inserted, put an end to the dispute between him and Macpherson; but, by other persons, it was continued with a degree of asperity equal to that which was shown in the controversy concerning the genuineness of Phalaris's epistles, and with as much acuteness as that which tended to ascertain the question, whether the poems lately ascribed to Rowley are not forgeries.[14] Moderators have also interposed, as there did in the dispute about the authenticity of the Sybilline oracles, and with as little success: the world remains, and is likely ever to remain, without satisfaction in respect of either the one or the other.[15]

Before this time, Johnson had undertaken to revise the former edition of his Shakespeare, and extend his plan, by admitting the corrections and illustrations of various other commentators. He therefore, in conjunction with Mr. George Steevens, published in 1773, a new edition of that author, in ten octavo volumes, which was republished with additions in 1778.

In 1774, the parliament having been dissolved, and Mr. Wilkes persisting in his endeavours to become a representative in that which was about to be chosen, Johnson addressed to the electors of Great Britain a pamphlet, entitled *The Patriot*; [16] the design whereof is to guard them from imposition, and teach them to distinguish that which of itself seems sufficiently obvious, the difference between true and false patriotism; but the madness of the people was then at its height, and they needed to be told how often in their lucid intervals they had lamented the deceits practised on them by artful and designing men. With this view, he describes a patriot, as one whose public conduct is regulated by one single motive, the love of his country; who, as an agent in parliament, has, for himself, neither hope nor fear, neither kindness nor resentment, but refers everything to the common interest. These, and other marks of patriotism by him pointed out, he allows to be such as artifice may counterfeit, or folly misapply; but he enumerates several characteristical modes of speaking and acting, which may prove a man not to be a patriot; which discrimination he illustrates in sundry instances, by pointed references to the conduct of many of those men who were courting the favour of the people.

Johnson published also in 1775, a pamphlet entitled, *Taxation No Tyranny*, an answer to the resolutions and address of the American Congress; in which, as the ground of his argument, he assumes as self-evident, the following proposition:

In all the parts of human knowledge, whether terminating in science merely speculative, or operating upon life private or civil, are admitted some fundamental principles, or common axioms, which, being generally received, are little doubted, and being little doubted, have been rarely proved.

Of these gratuitous and acknowledged truths, it is often the fate to become less evident by endeavours to explain them, however necessary such endeavours may be made by the misapprehensions of absurdity, or the sophistries of interest. It is difficult to prove the principles of science, because notions cannot always be found more intelligible than those which are questioned. It is difficult to prove the principles of practice, because they have, for the most part, not been discovered by investigation, but obtruded by experience; and the demonstrator will find, after an operose deduction, that he has been trying to make that seen, which can only be felt.

Of this kind is the position that *the supreme power of every community has the right of requiring from all its subjects such contri-*

butions as are necesssary to the public safety or public prosperity, which was considered by all mankind as comprising the primary and essential condition of all political society, till it became disputed by those zealots of anarchy, who have denied to the parliament of Britain the right of taxing the American colonies.

With much wit does he ridicule, and with force of reasoning refute, the arguments founded on the inability of the Americans to bear taxation, their powers of resistance, the stubbornness of their tempers, and the profits accruing to this country by its commerce with them: these, he tells us, are used only as auxiliaries to that other, which, as he briefly states it, is—'that to tax the colonies is usurpation and oppression, an invasion of natural and legal rights, and a violation of those principles which support the constitution of the English government.'

He next considers the legal consequences of migration from a mother country, and afterwards proceeds to an examination of that fallacious position, that from an Englishman nothing can be taken but by his own consent, and of the argument grounded thereon, that the Americans, being unrepresented in parliament, cannot be said to have consented in their corporate capacity, and that, refusing their consent as individuals, they cannot legally be taxed.

Of this he says, that

it is a position of a mighty sound, but that every man that utters it, with whatever confidence, and every man that hears it, with whatever acquiescence, if consent be supposed to imply the power of refusal, feels to be false, for that, in wide extended dominions, the business of the public must be done by delegation, and the choice of delegates is by a select number of electors, who are often far from unanimity in their choice; and where the numbers approach to equality, almost half must be governed, not only without, but against their choice.

Of those, who are not electors, he says:—'they stand idle and helpless spectators of the commonweal, wholly unconcerned in the government of themselves.' The resolution of the Congress, that their ancestors, who first settled the colonies, were, at the time of their emigration from the mother country, entitled to all the rights, liberties, and immunities of free and natural born subjects within the realm of England, he admits; but granting it, he contends, that their boast of original rights is at an end, and that, by their emigration, they sunk down into colonists, governed by a charter; and that though, by such emigration, they had not forfeited, surrendered, or lost, any of those rights, they had lost them by natural effects, that is to say, had abandoned them.— 'A man,' says he,

can be but in one place at once; he cannot have the advantages of multiplied residence. He that will enjoy the brightness of sunshine, must quit the coolness of the shade. And though an emigrant, having a right to vote for a knight or burgess, by crossing the Atlantic does not nullify that right, he renders the exertion of it no longer possible.

'But the privileges of an American,' adds he, 'scorn the limits of place; they are part of himself, and cannot be lost by departure from his country; they float in the air, or glide under the ocean.'

The above citations are evidences of Johnson's skill in political controversy, and are but slight specimens of that species of oratory which delights the ear, and convinces the understanding. With respect to logical precision, and strength of argument, the tracts, from whence they are severally taken, defy all comparison; and, as they abound in wit, and discover nothing of that acrimony which disgraces former controversies, the Disciplinarian and Bangorian not excepted,[17] may be considered as standing exemplars of polemical eloquence, and political ratiocination.

The friends of sedition and rebellion were highly exasperated against Johnson for his interfering, by these publications, in the debate of political questions: they were provoked to see such talents as his employed in exposing the malignity of faction, and detecting the artifices of those, who, by specious oratory and false reasoning, were courting popularity, and deluding the inhabitants of this country into a resignation of their rights. It was not, said they, for a man of his abstracted genius, a philosopher, a moralist, and a poet, to concern himself in the contentions between a

parent-state and its offspring. The muses, gentle creatures! are of
no party: they

─────────────────────── in a ring
Ay round about Jove's altar sing.

Il Penseroso

And, in conformity to this character, it behoved him to be a
silent spectator of all that was passing, and leave the agitation of
political questions to men, whose malevolence comprehended in
it all the qualifications necessary in the course of such a warfare.

But Johnson was of another mind: he was conscious of his own
abilities, and felt within himself such powers of reasoning, such
a knowledge of the principles of civil policy, as qualified him for
a contest, not with American planters, or colony agents, but with
tumid orators, factious lawyers, and interested selfish merchants.
And, in this exercise of his pen, he was not less sincere than formidable. Admitting him to be a Tory, he was a friend to both
the ecclesiastical and civil establishment of his country; and he
thought it his duty, as a good subject, when the legislative authority was denied, to refute the arguments of such as resisted
it.

It has been insinuated, that in his vindication of the measures
of government, as contained in the several pamphlets before cited,
Johnson had an eye rather to the obligation which his pension
implied, than to the questions in debate. This, if it could be
proved, might be an objection to his integrity, but sets him but
on a level with his opponents, whose apparent and known motive
to opposition and clamour was the desire of popularity, as a means,
whereby the ambitious among them hoped to attain power, and
the indigent to acquire places or emoluments; and who will say,
that an itch for vulgar applause is not as corrupt a motive to an
action as any that can be imputed to one in Johnson's situation?
But with matters of opinion, motives have nothing to do: arguments alone are the weapons of controversy. With respect to
the first pamphlet, *The False Alarm*, the question there agitated
was, whether the expulsion of a member of one of the houses of
parliament, by a majority of votes, imported a design on the liber-

ties of the people; and impartial posterity, which must decide upon it, will look no farther than to the reasoning of each party.

Of those who endeavour at this time to excite suspicions of this nature, it may be truly said, that they understand neither the constitution, nor the politics of this country; nor do they know, that the former is now so amended by the concessions which, since the Restoration, have been made by the crown to the people, that less is to be feared from princes, or their ministers, who are ever responsible for their conduct, than from artful and designing men, stimulated by ambition, or provoked by disappointment, and furnished with the fascinating powers of popular eloquence.

I forbear to animadvert on the two next succeeding pamphlets, *Falkland's Islands*, and *The Patriot*; but shall observe, that the last of the four, *Taxation No Tyranny*, has not only never received an answer, but the converse of the proposition has never yet been so proved, by arguments founded on legal principles, as to make a vindication of Johnson's reasoning necessary, for any other purpose, than that of preventing the ignorant from being misled. The principle assumed by Johnson, that 'the supreme power of every community has the right of requiring from all its subjects such contributions as are necessary to the public safety, or public prosperity,' is as self-evident, as that obedience is due from children to parents, and is not refuted by the assertion, that the consent of those who are required thus to contribute, is necessary, for, were it so, what becomes of the right? Neither is the position, that taxation and representation are correlative, to be admitted as a principle of the English constitution, seeing it does not, nor ever did, exist as a part of it; and that the far greater number of the subjects of England, men who are not freeholders to a certain amount, copyholders, who are a third of the landholders in this kingdom, and all women, are unrepresented in parliament, and bound by laws enacted by the representatives of others, but in no sense of themselves. In cities, and boroughs, the representation is often of the meanest of the people; in London, for instance, where a mechanic, if he be a liveryman, has a vote, and a freeholder, wanting that qualification, though assessed ever so high to the land tax, has none.

This assertion might possibly have place in a state about to

be founded, as none ever was or is likely to be, on solemn agreement, or that political fiction called an original contract; but, the
constitution of a state already formed, is to be taken as we find
it. Nor has any one of those who deny the right of a mother country to tax its colonies, attempted to prove an exemption, by any
other arguments than are to be found in Mr. Locke's *Essay on
Government*, a discourse of general import, and which applies
to no existing constitution on earth.

The above tracts, as they contain no evidence of a personal attachment of the author to those who, at the respective times of
their appearance, had the direction of the public councils, are
a refutation of all those slanders which they drew on him; and,
as the subjects of them, severally, are questions of the greatest
national importance, sufficiently distinguish him from those hireling scribblers, who, in the contests of factions, are retained on the
side of either party, and whom the vulgar style political writers.
In like manner did Addison and Hoadly employ their talents:
they were both friends of government, and wrote in defence of
the public measures, and not only escaped obloquy, but were
and still are celebrated as lovers of their country.

I have hitherto forborne to speak, otherwise than in general
terms, of Johnson's political principles; but, the task of reviewing the tracts above cited, has revived in my memory many of
his sentiments, which, at different times, he communicated to
me, on the subjects of government, the English constitution, and
the motives to party opposition. That he was a Tory, he not only
never hesitated to confess, but, by his frequent invectives against
the Whigs, was forward to proclaim: yet, was he not so besotted
in his notions, as to abet what is called the patriarchal scheme,
as delineated by Sir Robert Filmer and other writers on government; nor, with others of a more sober cast, to acquiesce in the
opinion that, because submission to governors is, in general terms,
inculcated in the Holy Scriptures, the resistance of tyranny and
oppression is, in all cases, unlawful: he seemed rather to adopt
the sentiments of Hooker on the subject, as explained by Hoadly,
and by consequence, to look on submission to lawful authority
as a moral obligation: he, therefore, condemned the conduct of
James the second during his short reign; and, had he been a sub-

ject of that weak and infatuated monarch, would, I am persuaded, have resisted any invasion of his right or unwarrantable exertion of power, with the same spirit, as did the president and fellows of Magdalen College, or those conscientious divines the seven bishops.[18] This disposition, as it leads to Whiggism, one would have thought, might have reconciled him to the memory of his successor, whose exercise of the regal authority among us merited better returns than were made him; but, it had no such effect: he never spoke of King William but in terms of reproach, and, in his opinion of him, seemed to adopt all the prejudices of Jacobite bigotry and rancour.

For the English constitution, as originally framed,[19] he ever expressed a profound reverence. He understood it well, and had noted in his mind the changes it had at various periods undergone, that is to say, first, in the reign of Hen. VII. when the yeomanry were put into a state of competition with the nobility; afterwards, when by the abolition of tenures, and the putting down the court of wards and liveries, occasion was given to Sir Harbottle Grimston to say that, in that transaction, neither did the crown know what it lost, nor the people what they had gained; and lastly, by the erecting a moneyed, in opposition to the landed, interest, and the introduction of the science and practice of funding.

He, therefore, looked not on Magna Charta as the palladium of our liberties, (knowing full well, that * very little of the whole statute will apply to the constitution in its now improved state;) but to the subsequent concessions of the crown in favour of the people, such as are the petition of right, the habeas corpus act, the bill of rights, and numerous other statutes of a like beneficial tendency.

To party opposition he ever expressed great aversion; and, of the pretences of patriots, always spoke with indignation and contempt. He partook of the short-lived joy that infatuated the public, when Sir Robert Walpole ceased to have the direction of the national councils, and trusted to the professions of Mr. Pulteney and his adherents, who called themselves the country party, that all elections should thenceforward be free and uninfluenced, and that bribery and corruption, which were never practised but by courtiers and their agents, should be no more. A few weeks, nay, a few days, convinced Johnson, and indeed all England, that what had assumed the appearance of patriotism, was personal hatred and inveterate malice in some, and in others, an ambition for that power, which, when they had got it, they knew not how to exercise. A change of men, and in some respect, of measures, took place: Mr. Pulteney's ambition was gratified by a peerage; [20] the wants of his associates were relieved by places, and seats at the public boards; and, in a short time, the stream of government resumed its former channel, and ran with a current as even as it had ever done.

Upon this development of the motives, the views, and the consistency of the above-mentioned band of patriots, Johnson once remarked to me, that it had given more strength to government than all that had been written in its defence, meaning thereby, that it had destroyed all confidence in men of that character. Little did he then think, that the people of this country would again be deluded, by fallacious reasoning and specious eloquence, into a fruitless expenditure of more than one hundred millions, or that statues would ever be erected to eternize the memory of a minister, of whom, in 1771, he said it would be happy if the nation should dismiss him to nameless obscurity; [21] and of whom an able and experienced statesman once said, it would have been good for this country if he had never been born.

History has been said to be philosophy teaching by example, and well would it be for mankind, if they would convert events into precepts, and not postpone their care to prevent evils, till their own experience shall have brought them home to themselves. New generations of men arise in succession, who, in the nonage of their faculties, are credulous, weak, and open to deceit: these, unhackneyed in the ways of the world, trust to the professions of all who pretend a friendship for them; and, when they are told they are ill governed, are as ready, as were the Israelites of old, to murmur against their rulers. And let all be said that can of a principle in men invested with power, to abuse it and become tyrants, the history of the world will inform us, that there is also a disease, which the Scriptures emphatically term, the madness of the people, from which evils greater than from despotism are

to be feared, and that government, even where it is best administered, subsists more by force than by the consent of those who
derive benefit from it. What an advantage, then, does this disposition in a people give to ambitious men, endowed with that
kind of eloquence, which fascinates without conviction, and, while
it delights, stupefies!

His frequent reflections on the politics of this country, and the
willingness of the people to be deceived, had begot in Johnson
such an apathy, as rendered him deaf to the calls of those who
were watching over our dearest rights. When the cry was loudest
against general warrants, he took not the alarm; and, when they
were declared illegal, he protested to me, that he would, at no
time of his life, have given half a crown to be forever indemnified
against their operation. The question of the legality of that kind
of process is now at an end, and I will not arraign the decision
that condemned it; but it will ever remain a question, whether
we have not lost more by it than we have gained.[22]

The publication of Johnson's political tracts, exhibited him to
the world in a new character: he ceased now to be considered as
one who, having been occupied in literary studies, and more conversant with books than with men, knew little of active life, the
views of parties, or the artifices of designing men: on the contrary,
they discovered that he had, by the force of his own genius, and
the observations he had made on the history of our own and other
countries, attained to such skill in the grand leading principles
of political science, as are seldom acquired by those in the most
active and important stations, even after long experience; and
that, whatever opinions he might have formed on this subject,
he had ability by strong reasoning to defend, and by a manly
and convincing eloquence to enforce.

Mr. Thrale, a man of slow conceptions, but of a sound judgment, was not one of the last that discerned in his friend this
talent, and believing, that the exercise of it might redound to the
benefit of the public, entertained a design of bringing Johnson
into parliament. We must suppose that he had previously determined to furnish him with a legal qualification, and Johnson,
it is certain, was willing to accept the trust. Mr. Thrale had two
meetings with the minister, who, at first, seemed inclined to find

him a seat; but, whether upon conversation he doubted his fitness for his purpose, or that he thought himself in no need of his assistance, the project failed.

Had it succeeded, and Johnson become a member of the House of Commons, as he was one of the most correct speakers ever known,[23] he would undoubtedly have exhibited to that assembly a perfect model of senatorial eloquence; and might probably have prevented the introduction therein of a great number of words, phrases, and forms of speech, to which neither dictionaries, nor the example of any English writer of authority, have given a sanction.

Johnson was a little soured at this disappointment: he spoke of Lord North in terms of asperity, as indeed he did of all those ministers whose councils indicated a want of spirit to carry into action the measures which were resolved on as expedient: in which particular, the above minister must surely be exculpated, whose designs, it is too well known, were blasted by those to whom the execution of them was committed. Of the abilities of Mr. Grenville, he also entertained but a mean opinion, for his giving up the Manila ransom.[24]—'Grenville,' he would say, 'if he could have got the Manila ransom, was able to have counted the money, but he knew not how to enforce the payment of it.' Of Sir Robert Walpole, notwithstanding that he had written against him in the early part of his life, he had a high opinion: he said of him, that he was a fine fellow, and that his very enemies deemed him so before his death: he honoured his memory for having kept this country in peace many years, as also for the goodness and placability of his temper; of which Pulteney, Earl of Bath, thought so highly, that, in a conversation with Johnson, he said, that Sir Robert was of a temper so calm and equal, and so hard to be provoked, that he was very sure he never felt the bitterest invectives against him for half an hour. To the same purpose, Johnson related the following anecdote, which he said he had from Lord North: Sir Robert having got into his hands some treasonable letters of his inveterate enemy, Will. Shippen, one of the heads of the Jacobite faction, he sent for him, and burned them before his face. Some time afterwards, Shippen had occasion to take the oaths to the government in the House of Commons, which, while he was doing, Sir Robert, who stood next him, and knew his principles to be the same as ever, smiled:—'Egad Robin,' said Shippen, who had observed him, 'that's hardly fair.'

It is not a little wonderful, that Sir Robert Walpole could preserve such an equanimity under the greatest provocations, as he is known to have done, or that he could entertain a kindness for anyone, seeing he is known to have asserted, that every man has his price; to which I will add, from unquestionable authority, that some time before his death, he uttered this sentiment— 'that so great is the depravity of the human heart, that ministers, who only could know it, were, in charity to mankind, bound to keep it a secret.'—Agreeable to this of Dr. Young,

> Heav'n's Sovereign saves all Beings but himself,
> That hideous sight, a naked human heart.
> *Night Thoughts*, 'Narcissa.'

1775-1780

I N THE year 1775, Johnson received from the university of Oxford the highest testimony of esteem, which that learned body could confer, in a diploma creating him a doctor in the faculty of law. The instrument bears date the thirtieth day of March, in the above year.[1]

In the summer of the same year, Johnson accepted of an invitation from his friend Mr. Thrale, to make one of a party with him and his wife, in a tour to Paris. No memoirs of this journey, in his own handwriting, are extant;[2] nor is the want thereof to be regretted, unless it were certain, that he was enough master of the French language to be able to converse in it,[3] and that he had noted down the reflections he may be supposed to have made in a visit to a strange country, and a residence among a people whose national character differs from our own. His garb and mode of dressing, if it could be called dressing, had long been so inflexibly determined, as to resist all the innovations of fashion. His friends had therefore great difficulty in persuading him to such a compliance in this respect, as might serve to keep them in countenance, and secure him from the danger of ridicule: he yielded to their remonstrances so far as to dress in a suit of black and a Bourgeois wig, but resisted their importunity to wear ruffles.[4]

In the course of this narrative it has been shown, that although, and that by his own declarations, the literary faculties of Johnson were, at most times, inert, and that he could seldom be stimulated to the exercise of his pen, but by the immediate prospect of gain; yet, he was ever ready to assist the publication of any work that had either novelty or any intrinsic worth, with a life of the author, a dedication, preface, or an introduction tending to recommend it, as in the case of Ascham's pieces, the last edition of Sir Thomas Browne's *Christian Morals*, and Kennedy's *Scripture Chronology*, and many more, all of which he ushered into the world, and, for aught that appears, without any recompense. With a like benevolent disposition, he was ready to assist with a prologue, or an epilogue, the representation of a play written by a friend; or with an occasional address of the same kind, under circumstances that put it in his power to promote the interests of the family of a deceased author: accordingly, he wrote, for his friend Goldsmith, a prologue to a comedy written by him, called *The Good-natured Man*, and acted in 1768; and, for the granddaughter of Milton, a prologue to *Comus*, exhibited on the fifth day of April, 1750.

The same good office he performed for the wife and children of Mr. Hugh Kelly, the author of a comedy called, *A Word to the Wise*, which, in the year 1770, was brought on the stage, but, by the malice of a party, was obstructed in the representation, and consigned to oblivion. This person, it is said, was originally a staymaker, but being a man of wit and parts, he quitted that unmanly occupation, and having, as we must suppose, some slender means to enable him thereto, he betook himself to reading and study, and, at a time when the discipline of the inns of court was scandalously lax, got himself called to the bar, and practised at the quarter-sessions under me, but with little success. In aid of this profession, he became the conductor of a paper called *The Public Ledger*, and took up that precarious one of a writer for the stage, in which he met with some encouragement, till it was insinuated, that he was a pensioner of the minister, and, therefore, a fit object of patriotic vengeance. He died in the year 1769, and leaving a wife and five children unprovided for, the proprietors of Covent Garden Theatre, in 1777, with their usual generosity, permitted to be acted at their house, for the benefit of his family, the comedy above-mentioned; and, to soften the

hearts of the audience, Johnson was easily prevailed on to write
upon the occasion the following very fine lines:

> This night presents a play, which public rage,
> Or right or wrong, once hooted from the stage:
> From zeal, or malice, now no more we dread,
> For English vengeance *wars not with the dead*.
> A generous foe regards with pitying eye
> The man whom fate has laid where all must lie.
> To wit, reviving from its author's dust,
> Be kind, ye judges, or at least be just:
> Let no renew'd hostilities invade,
> Th' oblivious grave's inviolable shade.
> Let one great payment every claim appease,
> And him who cannot hurt, allow to please;
> To please by scenes, unconscious of offence,
> By harmless merriment, or useful sense.
> Where aught of bright or fair the piece displays,
> Approve it only—'tis too late to praise.
> If want of skill or want of care appear,
> Forbear to hiss—the poet cannot hear.
> By all, like him, must praise and blame be found,
> At last, a fleeting gleam, or empty sound.
> Yet then shall calm reflection bless the night,
> When liberal pity dignified delight;
> When pleasure fired her torch at virtue's flame,
> And mirth was bounty with an humbler name.

In the year 1777, he was induced, by a case of a very extraordinary nature, to the exercise of that indiscriminate humanity,
which, in him, was obedient to every call.[5] A divine of the Church
of England, Dr. William Dodd, already mentioned in the course
of this account, and who had assisted in the education of the
present Earl of Chesterfield, having, by his extravagance, involved himself in difficulties, had recourse to the following, among
many other expedients, to raise money. As a pretended agent for
this nobleman, and in consideration of the sum of 600£. he
forged the hand of the earl to the grant of an annuity, chargeable on his estate, which forgery being detected, Dodd was con-

victed of felony, and sentenced to the usual punishment for such offences. The public were, at first, very little interested in the fate of a man, who, besides the arts he had practised to make himself conspicuous as a man of letters, had rendered himself scandalous, by an offer, to the first law officer in the kingdom, of a large sum of money, for a presentation to a valuable rectory; but, by various artifices, and particularly, the insertion of his name in the public papers, with such palliatives as he and his friends could invent, never without the epithet of *unfortunate*, they were betrayed into such an enthusiastic commiseration of his case, as would have led a stranger to believe, that himself had been no accessary to his distresses, but that they were the inflictions of Providence.

Great endeavours were used with the earl, to prevail on him to desist from a prosecution, but without effect. His lordship preferred a bill of indictment for felony, and the same being found before me at Hicks's Hall, upon the evidence of himself, and other witnesses, Dodd was, at the Old Bailey, arraigned thereon, and convicted.

The speech he made to the court and jury, while at the bar, was penned by Johnson; but the evidence on the trial, was so very full and clear, that the jury hesitated not in the least to pronounce him guilty of the indictment; and, no circumstances of alleviation appearing, they did not, as juries seldom fail to do where that is the case, recommend him as an object of that clemency, which his majesty is ever ready to exert, in favour of those who have the least claim to it.

A petition to the throne for a pardon, was an expedient that naturally suggested itself, but, as it required the utmost powers of eloquence to palliate his offence, he found means to interest Dr. Johnson in his behalf, and easily procured from him two of the most energetic compositions of the kind ever seen, the one a petition from himself to the king, the other, a like address from his wife to the queen, severally conceived in the terms following:

To the King's most excellent Majesty.

Sir,
It is most humbly represented to your majesty by William Dodd, the unhappy convict now lying under sentence of death:

That William Dodd, acknowledging the justice of the sentence denounced against him, has no hope or refuge but in your majesty's clemency.

That though to recollect or mention the usefulness of his life, or the efficacy of his ministry, must overwhelm him, in his present condition, with shame and sorrow; he yet humbly hopes, that his past labours will not wholly be forgotten; and that the zeal with which he has exhorted others to a good life, though it does not extenuate his crime, may mitigate his punishment.

That debased as he is by ignominy, and distressed as he is by poverty, scorned by the world, and detested by himself, deprived of all external comforts, and afflicted by consciousness of guilt, he can derive no hopes of longer life, but that of repairing the injury he has done to mankind, by exhibiting an example of shame and submission, and of expiating his sins by prayer and penitence.

That for this end, he humbly implores from the clemency of your majesty, the continuance of a life legally forfeited; and of the days which, by your gracious compassion, he may yet live, no one shall pass without a prayer, that your majesty, after a long life of happiness and honour, may stand, at the day of final judgment, among the merciful that obtain mercy.

So fervently prays the most distressed and wretched of your majesty's subjects,

William Dodd.

To the Queen's most excellent Majesty.

Madam,

It is most humbly represented by Mary Dodd, wife of Dr. William Dodd, now lying in prison under sentence of death:

That she has been the wife of this unhappy man more than twenty-seven years, and has lived with him in the greatest happiness of conjugal union, and the highest state of conjugal confidence.

That she has been a constant witness of his unwearied endeavours for public good, and his laborious attendance on charitable institutions. Many are the families whom his care has delivered from want; many are the hearts which he has freed from pain, and the faces which he has cleared from sorrow.

That, therefore, she most humbly throws herself at the feet of the queen, earnestly entreating, that the petition of a distressed wife asking mercy for a husband, may be considered as naturally soliciting the compassion of her majesty; and that, when her wisdom has com-

pared the offender's good actions with his crime, she will be pleased
to represent his case to our most gracious sovereign, in such terms as
may dispose him to mitigate the rigour of the law.

So prays your majesty's most dutiful subject and supplicant,

Mary Dodd.

To the first of these petitions, but not without difficulty, Mrs.
Dodd first got the hands of the jury that found the bill against
her husband, and after that, as it is supposed, of the jury that
tried him. It was then circulated about, and all the while the cry
for mercy was kept up in the newspapers, and the merits and sufferings of the unfortunate divine were so artfully represented by
paragraphs therein inserted, that, in a short space of time, no
fewer than twenty-three thousand names were subscribed thereto.
Moreover, letters and addresses, written also by Johnson, implor-
ing their interposition, were sent to the minister and other great
persons.

While Dodd was waiting the event of the petitions, his wife
and friends were not idle. Dr. Johnson told me, that they had
offered Akerman, the keeper of Newgate, a thousand pounds to
let him escape; and that failing, that a number of them, with
banknotes in their pockets, to the amount of five hundred pounds,
had watched for a whole evening, about the door of the prison,
for an opportunity of corrupting the turnkey, but could not succeed in the attempt.

When all hopes of a favourable answer to either of the petitions
were at an end, Johnson drew up for publication a small collection of what are called *Occasional Papers by the Late William
Dodd, LL.D.* and five hundred copies thereof were printed for
the benefit of his wife; but she, conscious that they were not of
her husband's writing, would not consent to their being published;
and the whole number, except two or three copies, was suppressed.
The last office he performed for this wretched man, was the composing a sermon, which he delivered in the chapel of Newgate,
on Friday, 6th June, 1777, and which was soon after published
with the title of *The Convict's Address*.

Johnson had never seen the face of Dodd in his life.[6] His wife
had found her way to him during his confinement, and had interested him so strongly in his behalf, that he lamented his fate,

as he would have done that of an intimate friend under the like circumstances. He was deeply concerned at the failure of the petitions; and asked me at the time, if the request contained in them was not such an one as ought to have been granted to the prayer of twenty-three thousand subjects? to which I answered, that the subscription of popular petitions was a thing of course, and that, therefore, the difference between twenty and twenty thousand names was inconsiderable. He further censured the clergy very severely, for not interposing in his behalf, and said, that their inactivity arose from a paltry fear of being reproached with partiality towards one of their own order.

Here I cannot forbear remarking, an inconsistency in the opinion of Johnson respecting the case of Dodd. He assisted in the solicitations for his pardon, yet, in his private judgment, he thought him unworthy of it, having been known to say, that had he been the adviser of the king, he should have told him that, in pardoning Dodd, his justice, in remitting the Perreaus to their sentence, would have been called in question.

Of his great humanity the above instances might serve as proofs: here follows another, which has lately come to my knowledge.

While he was at Paris, in a visit to a convent in that city, he met with an Englishman, the librarian thereof, an ecclesiastic of the Romish communion, named Compton, who, with the accustomed civility shown to strangers by persons in his station, produced to him the books of greatest rarity in his custody, and in many other ways gratified his curiosity, and assisted him in his researches. This person, a short time after, came to England, and renounced the errors of popery; but finding no friends, and being in great distress, communicated his wants to the superior of the monks in London, who for some time supplied them; till, having received instructions from France no longer to patronize an apostate, he was obliged to leave him to his fortunes. In this extremity, Mr. Compton recollected his casual acquaintance at Paris with Johnson, and conceiving a hope of assistance from him, found him out and made him a visit. Johnson, at the first interview, heard his story, and, with the warmest expressions of tenderness and esteem, put into his hand a guinea, assuring him, that he might expect support from him till a provision for him could be found, and which he would make it his business to seek. In pursuance of this promise, Johnson furnished him with decent apparel, and afterwards applied to the present Bishop of London, who recognized him as a presbyter of the Church of England,[7] and licensed him to preach throughout his diocese. Moreover, he allowed money for his support, till about the beginning of last year, when he got to be morning preacher in the Church of Allhallows on the Wall, London, and soon after, upon an attestation to his character for three years back, by two clergymen of reputation, he was chosen lecturer of the united parishes of St. Alban's Wood Street, and St. Olave Silver Street, London.

About this time, Dr. Johnson changed his dwelling in Johnson's Court, for a somewhat larger in Bolt Court, Fleet Street, where he commenced an intimacy with the landlord of it, a very worthy and sensible man, some time since deceased, Mr. Edmund Allen the printer. Behind it was a garden, which he took delight in watering; a room on the ground floor was assigned to Mrs. Williams, and the whole of the two pair of stairs floor was made a repository for his books; one of the rooms thereon being his study. Here, in the intervals of his residence at Streatham, he received the visits of his friends, and, to the most intimate of them, sometimes gave, not inelegant dinners.

Being at ease in his circumstances, and free from that solicitude which had embittered the former part of his life, he sunk into indolence, till his faculties seemed to be impaired: deafness grew upon him; long intervals of mental absence interrupted his conversation, and it was difficult to engage his attention to any subject. His friends, from these symptoms, concluded, that his lamp was emitting its last rays, but the lapse of a short period gave them ample proofs to the contrary.

In the year 1774, the long-agitated question of literary property received a final decision, on an appeal to the supreme judicature of this kingdom, whereby it was, in effect, declared, that such property was merely ideal, and existed only in imagination. The immediate consequence of this determination was, a scramble of the lowest and least principled of the booksellers, for the jewel thus cast among them. Regardless of that obvious rule of natural justice, which gives the possessor a right to what he has purchased, they printed books, for the copyright whereof very large sums had been paid by booksellers, who, for their liberality to authors, and the encouragement by them given to voluminous works, had been looked on and acknowledged as the patrons of literature. Among these numerous depredators was one, who projected an edition of the English poets, which, by advertisements conceived in the most hyperbolical terms, and calculated to impose upon the credulity of the ignorant, was obtruded on the public.[8]

The booksellers, against whose interest this intended publication was likely to operate, derived their right to the works of many of the poets, included in the above design, by mesne assignments, from those ever respectable men the Tonsons, who had purchased them of their authors. To check this attempt therefore, they determined themselves to publish an edition of the poets, and, in order to obtain for it a preference, engaged Johnson to write the lives of all, or the chief of them; and he undertook and executed the task with great alacrity, and in a manner that argued not the least decline of his faculties.

When Johnson had determined on this work, he was to seek for the best mode of executing it. On a hint from a literary lady of his acquaintance and mine, [9] he adopted, for his outline, that form in which the Countess D'Aunois has drawn up the memoirs of the French poets, in her *Recueils des Plus Belles Pièces des Poëtes François*; and the foundation of his work was, the lives of the dramatic poets by Langbaine, and the lives of the poets at large by Winstanley, and that more modern one than either, their lives by Giles Jacob, whose information, in many instances, was communicated by the persons themselves. Nevertheless, the materials which Johnson had to work on were very scanty. He was never a sedulous inquirer after facts or anecdotes, nor very accurate in fixing dates: Oldys was the man of all others the best qualified for such an employment; Johnson's talent was disquisition; a genius like his, disdained so servile a labour. Whenever, therefore, he found himself at a loss for such intelligence as his work required, he availed himself of the industry of a friend or two, who took pleasure in furnishing him with such particulars as are to be found in the lives of Addison, Prior, Pope, Swift, Gay, and a few others, whose persons, habits, and characters, some yet, or very lately living, were able, either from their own knowledge, or authenticated tradition, to describe.

The book came abroad in the year 1778, in ten small volumes, and no work of Johnson has been more celebrated.[10] It has been said to contain the soundest principles of criticism, and the most judicious examen of the effusions of poetic genius, that any country, not excepting France, has to show; and so much of this is true, that, in our perusal of it, we find our curiosity, as to facts and circumstances, absorbed in the contemplation of those penetrating reflections and nice discriminations, which are far the greater part of it.

It is, nevertheless, to be questioned, whether Johnson possessed all the qualities of a critic, one of which seems to be a truly poetic faculty. This may seem a strange doubt, of one who has transfused the spirit of one of Mr. Pope's finest poems into one written by himself in a dead language, and, in two instances, nearly equalled the greatest of the Roman satirists. By the poetic faculty, I mean that power which is the result of a mind stored with beautiful images, and which exerts itself in creation and description: of this Johnson was totally devoid. His organs, imperfect as they were, could convey to his imagination but little of that intelligence which forms the poetic character, and produces that enthusiasm which distinguishes it. If we try his ability by Shakespeare's famous description;

> The poet's eye, in a fine frenzy rolling,
> Doth glance from Heaven to earth, from earth to Heaven;
> And, as imagination bodies forth
> The forms of things unknown, the poet's pen
> Turns them to shapes, and gives to airy nothing
> A local habitation, and a name.[11]

he will appear deficient. We know that he wanted this power; that he had no eye that could be said to roll or glance, and, therefore, that all his conceptions of the grandeur and magnificence of external objects, of beautiful scenes, and extensive prospects, were derived from the reports of others, and consequently were but the feeble impressions of their archetypes; so that it may be questioned whether, either waking or sleeping,

Such sights as youthful poets dream,[12]

were ever presented to his view.

This defect in his imaginative faculty, may well account for the frigid commendation which Johnson bestows on Thomson, and other of the descriptive poets, on many fine passages in Dryden, and on the 'Henry and Emma' of Prior. Moral sentiments, and versification, seem chiefly to have engaged his attention, and on these his criticisms are accurate, but severe, and not always impartial. His avowed fondness for rhyme is one of the blemishes in his judgment: he entertained it in opposition to Milton, and cherished it through the whole of his life; and it led him into many errors. Dryden had his doubts about the preference of rhyme to blank verse; and I have heard Johnson accuse him for want of principle in this respect, and of veering about in his opinion on the subject. No such imputation could fasten on himself.

That Johnson had no sense of the harmony of musical sounds, himself would frequently confess, but this defect left him not without the power of deriving pleasure from metrical harmony, from that commixture of long and short quantities, which the laws of prosody have reduced to rule, and from whence arises a delight in those whose ear is unaffected by consonance. The strokes on the pulsatile instruments, the drum for instance, though they produce monotonous sounds, have, if made by rule, mathematical ratios of duple and triple, with numberless fractions, and admit of an infinite variety of combinations, which give pleasure to the auditory faculty; but of this Johnson seems also to have been insensible. That his own numbers are so harmonious as, in general, we find them, must have been the effect of his sedulous attention to the writings of Dryden and Pope, and the discovery of some secret in their versification, of which he was able to avail himself.

If Johnson be to be numbered among those poets in whom the powers of understanding, more than those of the imagination, are seen to exist, we have a reason for that coldness and insensibility which he so often discovers in the course of this work; and, when we recollect that he professed himself to be a fastidious critic, we are not to wonder, that he is sometimes backward in bestowing applause on passages that seem to merit it. In short, he was a scrupulous estimator of beauties and blemishes, and possessed a spirit of criticism, which, by long exercise, may be said to have become mechanical. So nicely has he balanced the one against the other, that, in some instances, he has made neither scale preponderate, and, in others, by considering the failings of his authors as positive demerit, he has left some celebrated names in a state of reputation below mediocrity. A spirit like this, had before actuated him in his preface to Shakespeare, in which, by a kind of arithmetical process, subtracting from his excellencies his failings, he has endeavoured to sink him in the opinion of his numerous admirers, and to persuade us, against reason and our own feelings, that the former are annihilated by the latter.

His censures of the writings of Lord Lyttelton, and of Gray, gave great offence to the friends of each: the first cost him the friendship of a lady, whose remarks on the genius of Shakespeare have raised her to a degree of eminence among the female writers of this time; [13] and the supposed injury done by him to the memory of Gray, is resented by the whole university of Cambridge. The character of Swift he has stigmatized with the brand of pride and selfishness, so deeply impressed, that the marks thereof seem indelible. In the praises of his wit, he does him no more than justice; of his moral qualities, he has made the most; and of his learning, of which Swift possessed but a very small portion, he has said nothing. Few can be offended at Johnson's account of this man, whose arrogance and malevolence were a reproach to human nature; and in whose voluminous writings little is to be found, that can conduce to the improvement or benefit of mankind, or, indeed, that it beseemed a clergyman to publish.

In his own judgment of the lives of the poets, Johnson gave the preference to that of Cowley, as containing a nicer investigation and discrimination of the characteristics of wit, than is elsewhere to be found. Others have assigned to Dryden's life the preeminence. Upon the whole, it is a finely written, and an entertaining book, and is likely to be coeval with the memory of the best of the writers whom it celebrates.

To the life of Pope, he thought proper to adjoin a criticism on the epitaphs of that poet, written some years before, and inserted in a monthly pamphlet, entitled *The Visitor*, in which he detects a great number of faulty passages, and puerile sentiments.[14]

All that is necessary to remark on his examen of Pope's epitaphs is, that, in one instance, it was productive of a singular event, the total erasure of that epitaph on Sir Godfrey Kneller's monument in Westminster Abbey, which had long been objected to, as being a very indifferent imitation of Cardinal Bembo's famous distich on Raphael; and it seems that the author thought so, for, in the later editions of his works, he has omitted it.

After he had finished the lives of the poets, Johnson, contemplating the strength of his mental powers, was so little sensible of any decay in them, that he entertained a design of giving to the world a translation of that voluminous work of Thuanus, the history of his own times, an undertaking surely too laborious for one who had nearly completed the age of man, and whose mind was generally occupied by subjects of greater importance than any that relate to this world. But, in this estimate of his abilities, he soon found himself deceived. Sleepless nights, and the use of opium, which he took in large quantities, alternately depressed and raised his spirits, and rendered him an incompetent judge of his own powers, so that, had he pursued his resolution, he would, doubtless, have sunk under the burden of so great a labour.

It may farther be questioned whether, upon trial, he would not have found himself unequal to the task of transfusing into an English version the spirit of his author. Johnson's talent was original thinking, and though he was ever able to express his own sentiments in nervous language, he did not always succeed in his attempts to familiarize the sense of others: his translation of Père Lobo's voyage has little to recommend it but the subject matter. Among his papers was found, a translation from Sallust of the *Bellum Catilinarium*, so flatly and insipidly rendered, that the suffering it to appear would have been an indelible disgrace to his memory.[15]

1781-1784

WE MUST now take our leave of Johnson as an author, and view him as a man worn out with literary labour and disease, contemplating his dissolution, and exerting all his powers to resist that constitutional malady which now, more than ever, oppressed him. To divert himself from a train of thinking which often involved him in a labyrinth of doubts and difficulties touching a future state of existence, he solicited the frequent visits of his friends and acquaintance, the most discerning of whom could not but see, that the fabric of his mind was tottering; and, to allay those scruples and terrors which haunted him in his vacant hours, he betook himself to the reading of books of practical divinity, and, among the rest, the writings of Baxter, and others of the old Puritan and non-conforming divines. Of Baxter, he entertained a very high opinion, and often spoke of him to me as a man of great parts, profound learning, and exemplary piety: he said, of the office for the communion drawn up by him and produced at the Savoy Conference, that it was one of the finest compositions of the ritual kind he had ever seen.[1] It was a circumstance to be wondered at, that a high-churchman, as Johnson ever professed himself to be, should be driven to seek for spiritual comfort in the writings of sectaries; men whom he affected, as well to condemn for their ignorance, as to hate for their principles; but, as his acquaintance with the world, and with the writings of such men as Watts, Foster, Lardner, and Lowman, increased, these prejudices were greatly softened. Of the early Puritans, he thought their want of general learning was atoned for by their skill in the Scriptures, and the holiness of their lives; and, to justify his opinion of them, and their writings, he once cited to me a saying of Howell in one of his letters, that to make a man a complete Christian, he must have the works of a Papist, the words of a Puritan, and the faith of a Protestant.² At times when he was most distressed, I recommended to him the perusal of Bishop Taylor's *Rules and Exercises of Holy Living and Dying*, and also, his *Ductor Dubitantium*, a book abounding in erudition, and most aptly suiting his circumstances. Of the former, though he placed the author at the head of all the divines that have succeeded the fathers, he said, that in the reading thereof, he had found little more than he brought himself; and, at the mention of the latter, he seemed to shrink. His Greek testament was generally within his reach, and he read much in it. He was completely skilled in the writings of the fathers, yet was he more conversant with those of the great English churchmen, namely, Hooker, Usher, Mede, Hammond, Sanderson, Hall, and others of that class. Dr. Henry More, of Cambridge, he did not much affect: he was a Platonist, and, in Johnson's opinion, a visionary. He would frequently cite from him, and laugh at, a passage to this effect:—'At the consummation of all things, it shall come to pass, that eternity shall shake hands with opacity.' He had never, till I mentioned him, heard of Dr. Thomas Jackson, of Corpus Christi College, Oxon. Upon my recommendation of his works, in three folio volumes, he made me a promise to buy and study them, which he lived not to perform. He was, for some time, pleased with Kempis's tract *De Imitatione Christi*, but at length laid it aside, saying, that the main design of it was to promote monastic piety, and inculcate ecclesiastical obedience. One sentiment therein, he, however, greatly applauded, and I find it adopted by Bishop Taylor, who gives it in the following words:—

It is no great matter to live lovingly with good-natured, with humble and meek persons; but he that can do so with the froward, with the willful, and the ignorant, with the peevish and perverse, he only hath true charity. Always remembering, that our true solid peace, the peace of God, consists, rather in compliance with others, than in being complied with; in suffering and forbearing, rather than in contention and victory.[3]

In the course of these studies, he exercised his powers of eloquence, in the composition of forms of devotion, adapted to his circumstances and the state of his mind at different times. Of these, a specimen has lately been given to the public. He also translated into Latin many of the collects in our liturgy. This was a practice which he took up in his early years, and continued through his life, as he did also the noting down the particular occurrences of each day thereof, but in a loose and desultory way, in books of various forms, and in no regular or continued succession.

He seemed to acquiesce in that famous saying of John Valdesso, which induced the Emperor Charles the fifth to resign his crown, and betake himself to religious retirement; 'Oportet inter vitae negotia, et diem mortis, spatium aliquod intercedere,'[4] nevertheless, he was but an ill husband of his time. He was, throughout his life, making resolutions to rise at eight, no very early hour, and breaking them. The visits of idle, and some of them very worthless persons, were never unwelcome to him; and though they interrupted him in his studies and meditations, yet, as they gave him opportunities of discourse, and furnished him with intelligence, he strove rather to protract than shorten or discountenance them; and, when abroad, such was the laxity of his mind, that he consented to the doing of many things, otherwise indifferent, for the avowed reason that they would drive on time.

Of his visitors at this time myself was one, and having known the state of his mind at different periods, and his habitual dread of insanity, I was greatly desirous of calming his mind, and rendering him susceptible of the many enjoyments of which I thought him then in possession, namely, a permanent income, tolerable health, a high degree of reputation for his moral qualities and literary exertions, by which latter he had made a whole country sensible of its obligation to him, and, lastly, that he had as few enemies as a man of his eminence could expect. On one day in particular, when I was suggesting to him these and the like reflections, he gave thanks to Almighty God, but added, that notwithstanding all the above benefits, the prospect of death, which was now at no great distance from him, was become terrible, and that he could not think of it but with great pain and trouble of mind.

I was very much surprised and shocked at such a declaration from such a man, and told him, that from my long acquaintance with him, I conceived his life to have been an uniform course of virtue, that he had ever shown a deep sense of, and zeal for, religion, and that, both by his example and his writings, he had recommended the practice of it: that he had not rested, as many do, in the exercise of common honesty, avoiding the grosser enormities, yet rejecting those advantages that result from the belief of divine revelation, but that he had, by prayer, and other exercises of devotion, cultivated in his mind the seeds of goodness, and was become habitually pious. These suggestions made little impression on him: he lamented the indolence in which he had spent his life, talked of secret transgressions, and seemed desirous of telling me more to that purpose than I was willing to hear.

From these perturbations of mind, he had, however, at times, relief. Upon a visit, that I made him some months after, I found him much altered in his sentiments. He said that, having reflected on the transactions of his life, and acknowledged his sins before God, he felt within himself a confidence in his mercy, and that, trusting to the merits of his Redeemer, his mind was now in a state of perfect tranquillity.

In these discourses, he would frequently mention, with great energy and encomiums, the penitence of the man who assumed the name, and by that I must call him, of George Psalmanazar, a Frenchman, but who pretended to be a native of the island of Formosa, and a convert from paganism to Christianity, and, as such, received baptism. By the help of his great learning and endowments, he eluded all attempts to detect his impostures, but, in his more advanced age, became a sincere penitent, and, without any other motive than a sense of his sin, published a confession of them, and begged the pardon of mankind in terms the most humble and affecting. The remainder of his life was exemplary, and he died in 1763. The habitation of this person was in Ironmonger Row, Old Street, Middlesex, in the neighbourhood whereof he was so well known and esteemed, that, as Dr. Hawkes-worth once told me, scarce any person, even children, passed him without showing him the usual signs of respect. He was one of the writers of the *Universal History*, and, by his intercourse with the booksellers it was, as I conceive, that Johnson became acquainted with him.[5]

I mention the above particulars, as well to corroborate those testimonies of Johnson's piety already extant, as to refute the objections of many infidels, who, desirous of having him thought to be of their party, endeavoured to make it believed, that he was a mere moralist, and that, when writing on religious subjects, he accommodated himself to the notions of the vulgar: and also, because a certain female sceptic, of his acquaintance,[6] was once heard to say, that she was sure Dr. Johnson was too great a philosopher to be a believer.

From this digression, which I mean as an introduction to certain particulars of his behaviour in his last illness, hereafter related, I proceed to the future events of his life. In the year 1781, death put an end to the friendship that, for some years, had subsisted between him and Mr. Thrale, but gave birth to a relation that seemed to be but a continuation of it, viz. that of an executor, the duties of which office involved in it the management of an immense trade, the disposal of a large fortune, and the interests of children rising to maturity. For the trouble it might create him, Mr. Thrale bequeathed to him, as he did to each of his other executors, a legacy of two hundred pounds.

Dr. Johnson was not enough a man of the world to be capable alone of so important a trust. Indeed, it required, for the execution of it, somewhat like a board, a kind of standing council, adapted, by the several qualifications of the individuals that composed it, to all emergencies. Mr. Thrale wisely foresaw this, and associated with Johnson three other persons, men of great experience in business, and of approved worth and integrity. It was easy to see, as Johnson was unskilled in both money and commercial transactions, that Mr. Thrale's view, in constituting him one of his executors, could only be, that, by his philosophical prudence and sagacity, of which himself had, in some instances, found the benefit,[7] he might give a general direction to the motions of so vast a machine as they had to conduct. Perhaps he might also think, that the celebrity of Johnson's character would give a luster to that constellation, in which he had thought proper to place him. This may be called vanity, but it seems to be of the same kind with that which induced Mr. Pope to appoint Mr. Murray, now Earl of Mansfield, one of the executors of his will.

No sooner had this trust devolved on him, than he applied to me for advice. He had never been an executor before, and was at a loss in the steps to be taken. I told him the first was proving the will, a term that he understood not. I explained it to him, as also the oath that would be tendered to him, faithfully to execute it, to administer the testator's effects according to law, and to render a true account thereof when required. I told him that in this act he would be joined by the other executors, whom, as they were all men of business, he would do well to follow.

Johnson had all his life long been used to lead, to direct, and instruct, and did not much relish the thoughts of following men, who, in all the situations he could conceive, would have looked up to him: he therefore, as he afterwards confessed to me, began to form theories and visionary projects, adapted as well to the continuation and extension of the trade, which, be it remembered, was brewing, as the disposal of it; but in this, as he also acknowledged, he found himself at a loss. The other executors, after reflecting on the difficulty of conducting so large an undertaking, the disagreeableness of an office that would render them, in effect, tax gatherers, as all of that trade are, and place them in a situation between the public and the revenue, determined to make sale of the whole, and blew up Johnson's schemes for their commencing brewers, into the air. In the carrying this resolution into act, the executors had a great difficulty to encounter: Mr. Thrale's trade had been improving for two generations, and was become of such an enormous magnitude, as nothing but an aggregate of several fortunes was equal to; a circumstance, which could not but affect the intrinsic value of the object, and increase the difficulty of finding purchasers: of things indivisible exposed to sale, an estimate may be formed, till their value rises to a certain amount; but, after that, a considerable abatement from their intrinsic worth must be made, to meet the circumstance of a paucity of purchasers. This was the case in the sale of Pitt's diamond, which, in the ratio by which jewels are valued, was computed to be worth 225,000£. but, because only a very few persons were able to purchase it, was sold to the last king of France for little more than 67,000£.[8]

This difficulty, great as it was, Mr. Thrale's executors found the way to surmount: they commenced a negotiation with some persons of worth and character, which, being conducted on both sides with fairness and candour, terminated in a conveyance of the trade, with all its appendages, for which the consideration was, an hundred and thirty-five thousand pounds. Of this arduous transaction, Johnson was little more than a spectator, and, when called upon to ratify it, he readily acquiesced. There only remained for him to do justice to the memory of him, whom he could not but consider as both his friend and benefactor, and this he did, by an exercise of his talent, in the * monumental inscription.[9]

The death of Mr. Thrale dissolved the friendship between him and Johnson; but it abated not in the latter, that care for the interests of those whom his friend had left behind him, which he thought himself bound to cherish, as a living principle of gratitude. The favours he had received from Mr. Thrale, were to be repaid by the exercise of kind offices towards his relict and her children, and these, circumstanced as Johnson was, could only be prudent councils, friendly admonition to the one, and preceptive instruction to the others, both which he was ever ready to interpose. Nevertheless, it was observed by myself, and other of Johnson's friends, that, soon after the decease of Mr. Thrale, his visits to Streatham became less and less frequent, and that he studiously avoided the mention of the place or family.[10]

Having now no calls, and, as I believe, very little temptation, to become a sojourner, or even a guest, in the habitation of his departed friend, he had leisure to indulge himself in excursions to the city of his nativity, as also to Oxford; for both which places he ever entertained an enthusiastic affection. In the former, he was kindly received, and respectfully treated, by Mrs. Lucy Porter, the daughter, by her former husband, of his deceased wife, and in the latter, by the Reverend Dr. Adams, who had been his tutor at Pembroke College, and is now the head of that seminary. While he was thus resident in the university, he received daily proofs of the high estimation in which he was there held, by such members of that body as were of the greatest eminence for learning, or were any way distinguished for their natural or acquired abilities.

Besides the places above-mentioned, Johnson had other summer retreats, to which he was ever welcome, the seats of his friends in the country. At one of these, in the year 1782, he was alarmed by a tumour, by surgeons termed a sarcocele, that, as it increased, gave him great pain, and, at length, hurried him to town, with a resolution to submit, if it should be thought necessary, to a dreadful chirurgical operation; but, on his arrival, one less severe restored him to a state of perfect ease in the part affected. But he had disorders of another kind to struggle with: he had frequent fits of pain which indicated the passage of a gallstone, and he now felt the pressure of an asthma, a constitutional disease with him, from which he had formerly been relieved by copious bleedings, but his advanced age forbade the repetition of them.

In the beginning of the year 1782, death deprived him of his old friend and companion; he who had, for near forty years, had the care of his health, and had attended him almost constantly every morning, to inquire after the state of his body, and fill out his tea, the mute, the officious, and the humble Mr. Levett. Of this disastrous event, as soon as it happened, Johnson sent to his friend, Dr. Lawrence, the following account:

Jan. 17, 1782.

Sir,

Our old friend Mr. Levett, who was last night eminently cheerful, died this morning. The man who lay in the same room, hearing an uncommon noise, got up, and tried to make him speak, but without effect. He then called Mr. Holder the apothecary, who, though when he came he thought him dead, opened a vein, but could draw no blood. So has ended the long life of a very useful and very blameless man.

I am, Sir,
Your most humble servant,
Sam. Johnson.

I find in one of Johnson's diaries the following note:

January 20, Sunday. Robert Levett was buried in the churchyard of Bridewell, between one and two in the afternoon. He died on Thursday 17, about seven in the morning, by an instantaneous death. He was an old and faithful friend. I have known him from about 46. Commendari.—May God have had mercy on him. May he have mercy on me!

The grief which the loss of friends occasioned Johnson, seems to have been a frequent stimulative with him to composition. His sense of Levett's worth he expressed in the following lines, which may, perhaps, contribute, more than any one circumstance in his character, to keep the memory of his existence alive:

1

Condemn'd to hope's delusive mine,
    As on we toil from day to day,
By sudden blast, or slow decline,
    Our social comforts drop away.

2

Well tried through many a varying year,
    See Levett to the grave descend;
Officious, innocent, sincere,
    Of every friendless name the friend.

3

Yet still he fills affection's eye,
    Obscurely wise, and coarsely kind,
Nor, letter'd arrogance,[11] deny
    Thy praise to merit unrefin'd.

4

When fainting nature call'd for aid,
    And hov'ring death prepar'd the blow,

The vig'rous remedy display'd,
　The power of art, without the show.

5

In mis'ry's darkest caverns known,
　His useful care was ever nigh;
Where hopeless anguish pour'd his groan,
　And lonely want retir'd to die.

6

No summons mock'd by chill delay;
　No petty gain disdain'd by pride;
The modest wants of ev'ry day,
　The toil of ev'ry day supply'd.

7

His virtues walk'd their narrow round,
　Nor made a pause, nor left a void;
And sure the eternal Master found
　The single talent well employ'd.

8

The busy day, the peaceful night,
　Unfelt, uncounted, glided by:
His frame was firm, his pow'rs were bright,
　Though now his eightieth year was nigh.

9

Then with no throb of fiery pain,
　No cold gradations of decay,
Death broke at once the vital chain,
　And freed his soul the nearest way.

About the middle of June, 1783, his constitution sustained a severer shock than it had ever before felt: this was a stroke of the palsy, so very sudden and severe, that it awakened him out of a sound sleep, and rendered him, for a short time, speechless. As it had not affected his intellectual powers, he, in that cumbent posture to which he was confined, attempted to repeat, first in English, then in Latin, and afterwards in Greek, the Lord's Prayer, but succeeded in only the last effort, immediately after which, finding himself again bereft of the power of speech, he rang for his servant, and making signs for pen, ink, and paper, wrote and sent the following note to his friend and next-door neighbour, Mr. Allen the printer.

Dear Sir,
It hath pleased Almighty God this morning to deprive me of the powers of speech; and, as I do not know but that it may be his farther good pleasure to deprive me soon of my senses, I request you will, on the receipt of this note, come to me, and act for me, as the exigencies of my case may require.
I am, sincerely,
Yours,
S. Johnson.

Mr. Allen immediately rose to his assistance, and, in the morning, dispatched a message to Dr. Heberden and Dr. Brocklesby, who immediately came, and, in a few days, so far relieved him, that his speech became, to a good degree, articulate, and, till his organs began to tire, he was able to hold conversation. By the skill and attention of these two worthy persons, he was, at length, restored to such a degree of health that, on the 27th of the same month, he was able to water his garden, and had no remaining symptoms of disease, excepting that his legs were observed to be swollen, and he had some presages of an hydropic affection. These gave him some concern, and induced him to note, more particularly than he had formerly done,[12] the variations of the state of his health.

But bodily afflictions were not the only trials he had to undergo. He had been a mourner for many friends, and was now in danger of losing one, who had not only cheered him in his solitude, and helped him to pass with comfort those hours which, otherwise, would have been irksome to him, but had relieved him from domestic cares, regulated and watched over the expenses of his house, and kept at a distance some of those necessitous visitants, towards whom his bounty, though it had seldom wrought any good, had often been exercised.

This person was Mrs. Williams, whose calamitous history is related among the events recorded in the foregoing pages. She had for some months been declining, and during the doctor's late illness was confined to her bed. The restoration of his health made it necessary for him to retire into the country; but, before his departure, he composed and made use of the following energetic prayer.

Almighty God, who, in thy late visitation, hast shown mercy to me, and now sendest to my companion disease and decay, grant me grace so to employ the life which thou hast prolonged, and the faculties which thou has preserved, and so to receive the admonition, which the sickness of my friend, by thy appointment, gives me, that I may be constant in all holy duties, and be received at last to eternal happiness.

Permit, O Lord, thy unworthy creature to offer up this prayer for Anna Williams, now languishing upon her bed, and about to recommend herself to thy infinite mercy. O God, who desirest not the death of a sinner, look down with mercy upon her: forgive her sins, and strengthen her faith. Be merciful, O Father of mercy, to her and to me: guide us by thy holy spirit through the remaining part of life; support us in the hour of death, and pardon us in the day of judgment, for Jesus Christ's sake. Amen.

During his absence from London, viz. on the sixth day of September, 1783, Mrs. Williams was released from all her cares and troubles by an easy death, for which she was well prepared. The last offices were performed for her by those of her friends who were about her in the time of her illness, and had administered to her all the assistance in their power.

At his return to London, Johnson found himself in a forlorn and helpless condition: his habitual melancholy had now a real subject to work on, and represented his house as a dreary mansion. Solitude was ever ungrateful to him, and the want of a companion, with whom he might pass his evening hours, often drove him to seek relief in the conversation of persons in all respects his inferiors. To talk much, and to be well attended to, was, throughout his life, his chief delight: his vein of discourse, which has often enough been described, was calculated to attract the applause, and even admiration, of small circles; to him, therefore, a confraternity of persons, assembled for the purpose of free communication, or, in other words, a club, could not but be a source of pleasure, and he now projected one, which will hereafter be described. In every association of this kind, he was sure, unless by concession, to preside, and, *ex cathedra*, to discuss the subjects of inquiry and debate.

The death of Mr. Thrale, and Johnson's estrangement from the dwelling and family of this his valued friend, have already been mentioned: it remains to say of this event, that it was not followed by a total oblivion, on the part of his relict, of the intimacy that had subsisted between him and her husband, it appearing, that an intercourse by letters was still kept up between them. It was, nevertheless, easy to discover by his conversation, that he no longer looked on himself as a welcome guest at Streatham, and that he did but ill brook the change in his course of life that he now experienced. He had, for near twenty years, participated in most of those enjoyments that make wealth and affluence desirable; had partaken, in common with their owners, of the delights of a villa, and the convenience of an equipage; and had been entertained with a variety of amusements and occupations. In short, during the whole of that period, his life had been as happy as it had been in the power of such persons to make it.

That this celebrated friendship subsisted so long as it did, was a subject of wonder to most of Johnson's intimates, for such were his habits of living, that he was by no means a desirable inmate. His unmanly thirst for tea made him very troublesome. At Streatham, he would suffer the mistress of the house to sit up and make it for him, till two or three hours after midnight. When retired to rest, he indulged himself in the dangerous practice of reading in bed. It was a very hard matter to get him decently dressed by dinner time, even when select companies were invited; and no one could be sure, that in his table conversation with strangers, he would not, by contradiction, or the general asperity of his behaviour, offend them.

These irregularities were not only borne with by Mr. Thrale, but he seemed to think them amply atoned for by the honour he derived from such a guest as no table in the three kingdoms could produce; but, he dying, it was not likely that the same sentiments and opinions should descend to those of his family who were left behind. Such a friendly connection and correspondence as I have just mentioned, continued, however, between Johnson and the widow, till it was interrupted by an event that will shortly be related.

I have in his diary met with sundry notes, signifying that, while he was at Streatham, he endeavoured, by reading, to acquire a knowledge of the Dutch language, but that his progress in the study thereof was very slow.

It has been already related that, being seized with a paralysis about the month of June, 1783, he was so far recovered therefrom, as to entertain a hope, that he had nearly worn out all his disorders. 'What a man am I!' said he to me, in the month of November following, 'who have got the better of three diseases, the palsy, the gout, and the asthma, and can now enjoy the conversation of my friends, without the interruptions of weakness or pain!' —To these flattering testimonies I must add, that in this seeming springtide of his health and spirits, he wrote me the following note:

Dear Sir,
As Mr. Ryland was talking with me of old friends and past times, we warmed ourselves into a wish, that all who remained of the club should meet and dine at the house which once was Horseman's, in Ivy Lane. I have undertaken to solicit you, and therefore desire you to tell on what day next week you can conveniently meet your old friends.

I am, Sir,
Your most humble servant,
Sam. Johnson.
Bolt Court, Nov. 22, 1783.

Our intended meeting was prevented by a circumstance, which the following note will explain:

Dear Sir,

In perambulating Ivy Lane, Mr. Ryland found neither our landlord Horseman, nor his successor. The old house is shut up, and he liked not the appearance of any near it: he, therefore, bespoke our dinner at the Queen's Arms, in St. Paul's churchyard, where, at half an hour after three, your company will be desired today, by those who remain of our former society.

Your humble servant,

Dec. 3   Sam. Johnson.

With this invitation I cheerfully complied, and met, at the time and place appointed, all who could be mustered of our society, namely, Johnson, Mr. Ryland, and Mr. Payne of the bank. When we were collected, the thought that we were so few, occasioned some melancholy reflections, and I could not but compare our meeting, at such an advanced period of life as it was to us all, to that of the four old men in the *Senile Colloquium* of Erasmus. We dined, and in the evening regaled with coffee. At ten, we broke up, much to the regret of Johnson, who proposed staying; but finding us inclined to separate, he left us with a sigh that seemed to come from his heart, lamenting that he was retiring to solitude and cheerless meditation.

Johnson had proposed a meeting, like this, once a month, and we had one more; but, the time approaching for a third, he began to feel a return of some of his complaints, and signified a wish, that we would dine with him at his own house; and, accordingly, we met there, and were very cheerfully entertained by him.[13]

A few days after, he sent for me, and informed me, that he had discovered in himself the symptoms of a dropsy, and, indeed, his very much increased bulk, and the swollen appearance of his legs, seemed to indicate no less. He told me, that he was desirous of making a will, and requested me to be one of his executors: upon my consenting to take on me the office, he gave me to understand, that he meant to make a provision for his servant Frank, of about 70£. a year for life, and concerted with me a plan for investing a sum sufficient for the purpose: at the same time he opened to me the state of his circumstances, and the amount of what he had to dispose of.

In a visit, which I made him in a few days, in consequence of a very pressing request to see me, I found him labouring under great dejection of mind. He bade me draw near him, and said, he wanted to enter into a serious conversation with me; and, upon my expressing a willingness to join in it, he, with a look that cut me to the heart, told me, that he had the prospect of death before him, and that he dreaded to meet his Saviour.[14] I could not but be astonished at such a declaration, and advised him, as I had done once before, to reflect on the course of his life, and the services he had rendered to the cause of religion and virtue, as well by his example, as his writings; to which he answered, that he had written as a philosopher, but had not lived like one. In the estimation of his offences, he reasoned thus— 'Every man knows his own sins, and also, what grace he has resisted. But, to those of others, and the circumstances under which they were committed, he is a stranger; he is, therefore, to look on himself as the greatest sinner that he knows of.'[15] At the conclusion of this argument, which he strongly enforced, he uttered this passionate exclamation,— 'Shall I, who have been a teacher of others, myself be a castaway?'

Much to the same purpose passed between us in this and other conversations that I had with him, in all which I could not but wonder, as much at the freedom with which he opened his mind, and the compunction he seemed to feel for the errors of his past life, as I did, at his making choice of me for his confessor, knowing full well how meanly qualified I was for such an office.

It was on a Thursday that I had this conversation with him; and here, let not the supercilious lip of scorn protrude itself, while I relate that, in the course thereof, he declared his intention to employ the whole of the next day in fasting, humiliation, and such other devotional exercises, as became a man in his situation. On the Saturday following, I made him a visit, and, upon entering his room, observed in his countenance such a serenity, as indicated that some remarkable crisis of his disorder had produced a change in his feelings. He told me, that, pursuant to the resolution he had mentioned to me, he had spent the preceding day in an abstraction from all worldly concerns; that, to prevent interruption, he had, in the morning, ordered Frank not to admit anyone to him, and, the better to enforce the charge, had added these awful

words, 'For your master is preparing himself to die.' He then mentioned to me, that, in the course of this exercise, he found himself relieved from that disorder which had been growing on him,
and was become very oppressing, the dropsy, by a gradual evacua-
tion of water to the amount of twenty pints, a like instance
whereof he had never before experienced, and asked me what I
thought of it.[16]

I was well aware of the lengths that superstition and enthusiasm
will lead men, and how ready some are to attribute favourable
events to supernatural causes, and said, that it might favour of
presumption to say that, in this instance, God had wrought a
miracle; yet, as divines recognize certain dispensations of his
providence, recorded in the Scripture by the denomination of
returns of prayer, and his omnipotence is now the same as ever,
I thought it would be little less than criminal, to ascribe his late
relief to causes merely natural, and, that the safer opinion was,
that he had not in vain humbled himself before his Maker. He
seemed to acquiesce in all that I said on this important subject,
and, several times, while I was discoursing with him, cried out, 'It
is wonderful, very wonderful!'

His zeal for religion, as manifested in his writings and conversation, and the accounts extant that attest his piety, have induced
the enemies to his memory to tax him with superstition. To that
charge, I oppose his behaviour on this occasion, and leave it to
the judgment of sober and rational persons, whether such an unexpected event, as that above-mentioned, would not have
prompted a really superstitious man, to some more passionate
exclamation, than that it was wonderful.

He had no sooner experienced the ease and comfort which followed from the remarkable event above-mentioned, than he began
to entertain a hope, that he had got the better of that disease
which most oppressed him, and that length of days might yet be
his portion; he, therefore, sought for a relief from that solitude,
to which the loss of Mrs. Williams and others of his domestic
companions, seemed to have doomed him; and, in the same spirit
that induced him to attempt the revival of the Ivy Lane Club,
set about the establishment of another. I was not made privy to
this his intention, but, all circumstances considered, it was no

matter of surprise to me when I heard, as I did from a friend of mine, that the great Dr. Johnson had, in the month of December, 1783, formed a sixpenny club, at an alehouse in Essex Street, and that, though some of the members thereof were persons of note, strangers, under restrictions, for three pence each night, might, three nights in a week, hear him talk, and partake of his conversation. I soon afterwards learned from the doctor, the nature of, as also the motives to this institution, which, as to him, was novel, in this respect, that, as the presidency passed in rotation, he was oftener excluded from, than entitled to enjoy, that pre-eminence which, at all times, and in all convivial assemblies, was considered as his right.

The more intimate of Johnson's friends looked on this establishment, both as a sorry expedient to kill time, and a degradation of those powers which had administered delight to circles, composed of persons, of both sexes, distinguished as well by their rank, as by their talents for polite conversation. It was a mortification to them, to associate in idea the clink of the tankard, with moral disquisition and literary investigation; and many of them were led to question whether that pleasure could be very great, which he had rendered so cheap: they, however, concealed their sentiments, and, from motives of mere compassion, suffered him to enjoy a comfort, which was now become almost the only one of which he was capable; and this he did for the short space of about ten months, when the increase of his complaints obliged him to forego it.[17]

I have now brought him to the seventy-fifth year of his age, and the last of his life, in which two remarkable events occurred, the one whereof gave him great uneasiness, and the other, though much talked of, little or none. The time I am speaking of, is the year 1784, by about the middle whereof, he was, to appearance, so well recovered, that both himself and his friends hoped, that he had some years to live. He had recovered from the paralytic stroke of the last year, to such a degree, that, saving a little difficulty in his articulation, he had no remains of it: he had also undergone a slight fit of the gout, and conquered an oppression on his lungs, so as to be able, as himself told me, to run up the whole staircase of the Royal Academy, on the day of the annual dinner there. In short, to such a degree of health was he restored, that he forgot all his complaints: he resumed sitting to Opie for his picture, which had been begun the year before, but, I believe, was never finished,[18] and accepted an invitation to the house of a friend, at Ashbourn in Derbyshire,[19] proposing to stay there till towards the end of the summer, and, in his return, to visit Mrs. Porter, his daughter-in-law, and others of his friends, at Lichfield.

A few weeks before his setting out, he was made uneasy by a report, that the widow of his friend Mr. Thrale was about to dispose of herself in marriage to a foreigner, a singer by profession,[20] and with him to quit the kingdom. Upon this occasion he took the alarm, and to prevent a degradation of herself, and, what as executor of her husband was more his concern, the desertion of her children, wrote to her, she then being at Bath, a letter, a spurious copy whereof, beginning 'If you are not already ignominiously married,' is inserted in the *Gentleman's Magazine* for December, 1784. That this letter is spurious, as to the language, I have Johnson's own authority for saying; but, in respect of the sentiments, he avowed it, in a declaration to me, that not a sentence of it was his, but yet, that it was an *adumbration* of one that he wrote upon the occasion. It may, therefore, be suspected, that someone who had heard him repeat the contents of the letter, had given it to the public in the form in which it appeared.

What answer was returned to his friendly monition, I know not, but it seems that it was succeeded by a letter of greater length, written, as it afterwards appeared, too late to do any good, in which he expressed an opinion, that the person to whom it was addressed had forfeited her fame.[21] The answer to this I have seen: it is written from Bath, and contains an indignant vindication as well of her conduct as her fame, an inhibition of Johnson from following her to Bath, and a farewell, concluding— 'Till you have changed your opinion of —— let us converse no more.'

In this transaction, Johnson seemed to have forgotten the story of the Ephesian Matron, related by Petronius, but was, by this time, convinced that, in his endeavours to prevent an attachment, which he foresaw would be prejudicial to the interests of his friend's children, and fix an indelible disgrace on their mother, who was about to abandon them and her country, he had been labouring to hedge in the cuckoo. From the style of the last mentioned letter, a conclusion was to be drawn, that baffled all the powers of reasoning and persuasion:

> One argument she summ'd up all in,
> The thing was done, and past recalling; [22]

which being the case, he contented himself with reflecting on what he had done to prevent that which he thought one of the greatest evils that could befall the progeny of his friend, the alienation of the affections of their mother. He looked upon the desertion of children by their parents, and the withdrawing from them that protection, that mental nutriment which, in their youth, they are capable of receiving, the exposing them to the snares and temptations of the world, and the solicitations and deceits of the artful and designing, as most unnatural; and, in a letter on the subject to me, written from Ashbourn, thus delivered his sentiments:

Poor Thrale! I thought that either her virtue or her vice, [meaning, as I understood, by the former, the love of her children, and, by the latter, her pride,] would have restrained her from such a marriage. She is now become a subject for her enemies to exult over, and for her friends, if she has any left, to forget or pity.

In the mention of the above particulars, it is far from my design to reprehend the conduct of the lady to whom they relate. Being her own mistress, she had a right to dispose of herself, and is unamenable to any known judicature. Johnson, in his relation of executor to her husband, as also in gratitude to his memory, was under an obligation to promote the welfare of his family. It was also his duty, as far as he was able, to avert an evil which threatened their interests. What he endeavoured, for that purpose, is part of his history, and, as such only, I relate it.

While Dr. Johnson was in the country, his friends in town

were labouring for his benefit. Mr. Thrale, a short time before his death, had meditated a journey to Italy, and formed a party, in which Johnson was included, but the design never took effect. It was now conceived, by Johnson's friends, that a foreign air would contribute to the restoration of his health; and his inclination concurring with their sentiments, a plan was formed for his visiting the continent, attended with a male-servant; which was become so well known, that, as a lady then resident at Rome afterwards informed me, his arrival was anxiously expected throughout Italy. The only obstacle to the journey was, an apprehension, that the expense of it would be greater than his income would bear; and, to get over this difficulty, Sir Joshua Reynolds undertook to solicit an addition of 200£. to his pension, and to that end, applied to Lord Thurlow, who, as the public have been fully informed, exerted his endeavours for the purpose, but the application failing, he declared himself willing, upon the security of that pension of which Johnson was in possession, to advance him 500£.[23] This generous offer Johnson thought proper to decline by a letter, of which the following is an authentic copy, being taken from his own draft now in my hands.

My Lord,
After a long and not inattentive observation of mankind, the generosity of your lordship's offer raises in me not less wonder than gratitude. Bounty, so liberally bestowed, I should gladly receive, if my condition made it necessary, for, to such a mind, who would not be proud to own his obligations? But it has pleased God to restore me to so great a measure of health, that if I should now appropriate so much of a fortune destined to do good, I could not escape from myself the charge of advancing a false claim. My journey to the continent, though I once thought it necessary, was never much encouraged by my physicians; and I was very desirous that your lordship should be told of it by Sir Joshua Reynolds, as an event very uncertain, for, if I grew much better, I should not be willing, if much worse, I should not be able, to migrate.—Your lordship was first solicited without my knowledge; but, when I was told, that you were pleased to honour me with your patronage, I did not expect to hear of a refusal; yet, as I have had no long time to brood hope, and have not rioted in imaginary opulence, this cold reception has been scarce a disappointment; and, from your lordship's kindness, I have received a benefit, which only

men like you are able to bestow. I shall now live mihi carior, with a higher opinion of my own merit.

> I am, my lord,
>> Your lordship's most obliged,
>> Most grateful,
>> And most humble servant,

Sept., 1784.   Sam. Johnson.

An incorrect copy of the above letter, though of a private nature, found its way into the public papers in this manner. It was given to Sir Joshua Reynolds, unsealed, to be delivered to Lord Thurlow. Sir Joshua, looking upon it as a handsome testimony of gratitude, and, as it related to a transaction in which he had concerned himself, took a copy of it, and showed it to a few of his friends. Among these was a lady of quality,[24] who, having heard it read, the next day desired to be gratified with the perusal of it at home: the use she made of this favour was, the copying and sending it to one of the newspapers, whence it was taken and inserted in others, as also in the *Gentleman's* and many other magazines. Johnson, upon being told that it was in print, exclaimed in my hearing—'I am betrayed,'—but soon after forgot, as he was ever ready to do all real or supposed injuries, the error that made the publication possible.

Dr. Brocklesby was one of those physicians who would not encourage Johnson in a wish to visit the continent; nevertheless, to console him for his late disappointment, and that the supposed narrowness of his circumstances might be no hindrance to such a design, he made him a voluntary offer of 100£. a year, payable quarterly, towards his support abroad, but could not prevail on him to accept it.

His excursion to Ashbourn was less beneficial than he hoped it would be: his disorders began to return, and he wanted company and amusement. During his stay there, he composed sundry prayers, adapted to the state of his body and mind; and translated from Horace, lib. IV. the ode, 'Diffugêre nives, redeunt jam gramina campis,' in the words following:

> The snow, dissolv'd, no more is seen;
> The fields and woods, behold, are green;

The changing year renews the plain;
The rivers know their banks again;
The sprightly nymph and naked grace
The mazy dance together trace:
The changing year's successive plan,
Proclaims mortality to Man.
Rough winter's blasts to spring give way;
Spring yields to summer's sovereign ray;
Then summer sinks in autumn's reign;
And winter chills the world again;
Her losses soon the moon supplies,
But wretched Man, when once he lies
Where Priam and his sons are laid,
Is nought but ashes and a shade.
Who knows if Jove, who counts our score,
Will rouse us in a morning more?
What with your friend you nobly share,
At least you rescue from your heir.
Not you, Torquatus, boast of Rome,
When Minos once has fix'd your doom,
Or eloquence, or splendid birth,
Or virtue shall replace on earth:
Hippolytus unjustly slain,
Diana calls to life in vain;
Nor can the might of Theseus rend
The chains of hell that hold his friend.

Nov., 1784.

In his return to London, he stopped at Lichfield, and from thence wrote to me several letters, that served but to prepare me for meeting him in a worse state of health than I had ever seen him in. The concluding paragraph of the last of them is as follows: 'I am relapsing into the dropsy very fast, and shall make such haste to town that it will be useless to write to me; but when I come, let me have the benefit of your advice, and the consolation of your company.' [dated Nov. 7, 1784.] After about a fortnight's stay there, he took his leave of that city, and of Mrs. Porter, whom he never afterwards saw, and arrived in town on the sixteenth day of November.

After the declaration he had made of his intention to provide for his servant Frank, and before his going into the country, I had frequently pressed him to make a will, and had gone so far as to make a draft of one, with blanks for the names of the executors and residuary legatee, and directing in what manner it was to be executed and attested; but he was exceedingly averse to this business; and, while he was in Derbyshire, I repeated my solicitations, for this purpose, by letters. When he arrived in town he had done nothing in it, and, to what I formerly said, I now added, that he had never mentioned to me the disposal of the residue of his estate, which, after the purchase of an annuity for Frank, I found would be something considerable, and that he would do well to bequeath it to his relations. His answer was, 'I care not what becomes of the residue.'—A few days after, it appeared that he had executed the draft, the blanks remaining, with all the solemnities of a real will. I could get him no farther, and thus, for some time, the matter rested.

HE HAD scarce arrived in town, before it was found to be too true, that he was relapsing into a dropsy; and farther, that he was at times grievously afflicted with an asthma. Under an apprehension that his end was approaching, he inquired of Dr. Brocklesby, with great earnestness indeed, how long he might probably live, but could obtain no other than unsatisfactory answers: and, at the same time, if I remember right, under a seeming great pressure of mind, he thus addressed him, in the words of Shakespeare:

> Canst thou not minister to a mind diseas'd;
> Pluck from the memory a rooted sorrow,
> Raze out the written troubles of the brain,
> And with some sweet oblivious antidote,
> Cleanse the full bosom of that perilous stuff,
> Which weighs upon the heart?—
>
> *Macbeth.*

To which the doctor, who was nearly as well read in the above author as himself, readily replied,

> ——————— Therein the patient
> Must minister unto himself.[1]

Upon which Johnson exclaimed— 'Well applied:—that's more than poetically true.'

He had, from the month of July in this year, marked the progress of his diseases, in a journal which he entitled 'Aegri Ephemeris,' noting therein his many sleepless nights by the words, 'Nox insomnis.' This he often contemplated, and, finding very little ground for hope that he had much longer to live, he set himself to prepare for his dissolution, and betook himself to private prayer and the reading of Erasmus on the New Testament, Dr. Clarke's sermons, and such other books as had a tendency to calm and comfort him.

In this state of his body and mind, he seemed to be very anxious in the discharge of two offices that he had hitherto neglected to perform: one was, the communicating to the world the names of the persons concerned in the compilation of the *Universal History*; the other was, the rescuing from oblivion the memory of his father and mother, and also, of his brother: the former of these he discharged, by delivering to Mr. Nichols the printer, in my presence, a paper containing the information above-mentioned, and directions to deposit it in the British Museum. The other, by composing a memorial of his deceased parents and his brother, intended for their tombstone, which, whether it was ever inscribed thereon or not, is extant in the *Gentleman's Magazine* for January, 1785. The note ascertaining the names of the compilers of the *Universal History*, is inserted in the magazine for the preceding month.[2]

He would also have written, in Latin verse, an epitaph for Mr. Garrick, but found himself unequal to the task of original poetic composition in that language.

Nevertheless, he succeeded in an attempt to render into Latin metre, from the *Greek Anthologia*, sundry of the epigrams therein contained, that had been omitted by other translators, alleging as a reason, which he had found in Fabricius, that Henry Stephens, Buchanan, Grotius, and others, had paid a like tribute to literature. The performance of this task was the employment of his sleepless nights, and, as he informed me, it afforded him great relief.

His complaints still increasing, I continued pressing him to make a will, but he still procrastinated that business. On the twenty-seventh of November, in the morning, I went to his house, with a purpose still farther to urge him not to give occasion, by dying intestate, for litigation among his relations; but finding that he was gone to pass the day with the Reverend Mr. Strahan, at Islington, I followed him thither, and found there our old friend Mr. Ryland, and Mr. Hoole. Upon my sitting down, he said, that the prospect of the change he was about to undergo, and the thought of meeting his Saviour, troubled him, but that he had hope that he would not reject him. I then began to discourse with him about his will, and the provision for Frank, till he grew angry. He told me, that he had signed and sealed the paper I left him;—but that, said I, had blanks in it, which, as it seems, you have not filled up with the names of the executors.— 'You should have filled them up yourself,' answered he.—I replied, that such an act would have looked as if I meant to prevent his choice of a fitter person.—'Sir,' said he, 'these minor virtues are not to be exercised in matters of such importance as this.'— At length, he said, that on his return home, he would send for a clerk, and dictate a will to him.—You will then, said I, be *inops consilii*; rather do it now. With Mr. Strahan's permission, I will be his guest at dinner; and, if Mr. Hoole will please to hold the pen, I will, in a few words, make such a disposition of your estate as you shall direct.—To this he assented; but such a paroxysm of the asthma seized him, as prevented our going on. As the fire burned up, he found himself relieved, and grew cheerful. 'The fit,' said he, 'was very sharp; but I am now easy.' After I had dictated a few lines, I told him, that he being a man of eminence for learning and parts, it would afford an illustrious example, and well become him, to make such an explicit declaration of his belief, as might obviate all suspicions that he was any other than a Christian. He thanked me for the hint, and, calling for paper, wrote on a slip, that I had in my hand and gave him, the following words: 'I humbly commit to the infinite and eternal goodness of Almighty God, my soul polluted with many sins; but, as I hope, purified by repentance, and redeemed, as I trust, by the death of Jesus Christ'; and, returning it to me, said, 'This I commit to your custody.'

Upon my calling on him for directions to proceed, he told me, that his father, in the course of his trade of a bookseller, had become bankrupt, and that Mr. William Innys had assisted him with money or credit to continue his business— 'This,' said he, 'I consider as an obligation on me to be grateful to his descendants, and I therefore mean to give 200£. to his representative.'—He then meditated a devise of his house at Lichfield to the corporation of that city for a charitable use; but, it being freehold, he said— 'I cannot live a twelve-month, and the last statute of mortmain ³ stands in the way: I must, therefore, think of some other disposition of it.'—His next consideration was, a provision for Frank, concerning the amount whereof I found he had been consulting Dr. Brocklesby, to whom he had put this question— 'What would be a proper annuity to bequeath to a favourite servant?'— The doctor answered, that the circumstances of the master were the truest measure, and that, in the case of a nobleman, 50£. a year was deemed an adequate reward for many years' faithful service.—'Then shall I,' said Johnson, 'be *nobilissimus*; for, I mean to leave Frank 70£. a year, and I desire you to tell him so.'—And now, at the making of the will, a devise, equivalent to such a provision, was therein inserted. The residue of his estate and effects, which took in, though he intended it not, the house at Lichfield, he bequeathed to his executors, in trust for a religious association, which it is needless to describe.

Having executed the will with the necessary formalities, he would have come home, but being pressed by Mr. and Mrs. Strahan to stay, he consented, and we all dined together. Towards the evening, he grew cheerful, and I having promised to take him in my coach, Mr. Strahan and Mr. Ryland would accompany him to Bolt Court. In the way thither he appeared much at ease, and told stories. At eight I set him down, and Mr. Strahan and Mr. Ryland betook themselves to their respective homes.

Sunday 28th. I saw him about noon; he was dozing; but waking, he found himself in a circle of his friends. Upon opening his eyes, he said, that the prospect of his dissolution was very terrible to him, and addressed himself to us all, in nearly these words: 'You see the state in which I am; conflicting with bodily pain and mental distraction: while you are in health and strength, labour to do good, and avoid evil, if ever you hope to escape the distress that now oppresses me.'—A little while after,—'I had, very early in my life, the seeds of goodness in me: I had a love of virtue, and a reverence for religion; and these, I trust, have brought forth in me fruits meet for repentance; and, if I have repented as I ought, I am forgiven. I have, at times, entertained a loathing of sin and of myself, particularly at the beginning of this year, when I had the prospect of death before me; and this has not abated when my fears of death have been less; and, at these times, I have had such rays of hope shot into my soul, as have almost persuaded me, that I am in a state of reconciliation with God.'

29th. Mr. Langton, who had spent the evening with him, reported, that his hopes were increased, and that he was much cheered upon being reminded of the general tendency of his writings, and of his example.

30th. I saw him in the evening, and found him cheerful. Was informed, that he had, for his dinner, eaten heartily of a French duck pie and a pheasant.

Dec. 1. He was busied in destroying papers.—Gave to Mr. Langton and another person,[4] to fair copy, some translations of the Greek epigrams, which he had made in the preceding nights, and transcribed the next morning, and they began to work on them.

3d. Finding his legs continue to swell, he signified to his physicians a strong desire to have them scarified, but they, unwilling to put him to pain, and fearing a mortification, declined advising it. He afterwards consulted his surgeon, and he performed the operation on one leg.

4th. I visited him: the scarification, made yesterday in his leg, appeared to have had little effect.—He said to me, that he was easier in his mind, and as fit to die at that instant, as he could be a year hence.—He requested me to receive the sacrament with him on Sunday, the next day. Complained of great weakness, and of phantoms that haunted his imagination.

5th. Being Sunday, I communicated with him and Mr. Langton, and other of his friends, as many as nearly filled the room. Mr. Strahan, who was constant in his attendance on him throughout his illness, performed the office. Previous to reading the exhortation, Johnson knelt, and with a degree of fervour that I had never been witness to before, uttered the following most eloquent and energetic prayer:

Almighty and most merciful Father, I am now, as to human eyes it seems, about to commemorate, for the last time, the death of thy son Jesus Christ, our Saviour and Redeemer. Grant, O Lord, that my whole hope and confidence may be in his merits and in thy mercy: forgive and accept my late conversion; enforce and accept my imperfect repentance; make this commemoration of him available to the confirmation of my faith, the establishment of my hope, and the enlargement of my charity; and make the death of thy son Jesus effectual to my redemption. Have mercy upon me, and pardon the multitude of my offences. Bless my friends, have mercy upon all men. Support me by the grace of thy holy spirit in the days of weakness, and at the hour of death, and receive me, at my death, to everlasting happiness, for the sake of Jesus Christ.—Amen.

Upon rising from his knees, after the office was concluded, he said, that he dreaded to meet God in a state of idiocy, or with opium in his head; and, that having now communicated with the effects of a dose upon him, he doubted if his exertions were the genuine operations of his mind, and repeated from Bishop Taylor this sentiment, 'That little, that has been omitted in health, can be done to any purpose in sickness.' [5]

While he was dressing and preparing for this solemnity, an accident happened which went very near to disarrange his mind. He had mislaid, and was very anxious to find a paper that contained private instructions to his executors; and myself, Mr. Strahan, Mr. Langton, Mr. Hoole, Frank, and I believe some others that were about him, went into his bedchamber to seek it. In our search, I laid my hands on a parchment-covered book, into which I imagined it might have been slipped. Upon opening the book, I found it to be meditations and reflections, in Johnson's own handwriting; and having been told a day or two before by Frank, that a person formerly intimately connected with his master,[6] a joint proprietor of a newspaper, well known among the booksellers, and of whom Mrs. Williams once told me she had often cautioned him to beware; I say, having been told that this person had lately been very importunate to get access to him, indeed to such a degree as that, when he was told that the doctor was not to be seen, he would push his way upstairs; and having stronger reasons than I need here mention, to suspect that this man might find and make an ill use of the book, I put it, and a less of the same kind, into my pocket; at the same time telling those around me, and particularly Mr. Langton and Mr. Strahan, that I had got both, with my reasons for thus securing them. After the ceremony was over, Johnson took me aside, and told me that I had a book of his in my pocket; I answered that I had two, and that to prevent their falling into the hands of a person who had attempted to force his way into the house, I had done as I conceived a friendly act, but not without telling his friends of it, and also my reasons. He then asked me what ground I had for my suspicion of the man I mentioned: I told him his great importunity to get admittance; and farther, that immediately after a visit which he made me, in the year 1775, I missed a paper of a public nature, and of great importance; and that a day or two after, and before it could be put to its intended use, I saw it in the newspapers.[7]

At the mention of this circumstance Johnson paused; but recovering himself, said, 'You should not have laid hands on the book; for had I missed it, and not known you had it, I should have roared for my book, as Othello did for his handkerchief, and probably have run mad.' [8]

I gave him time, till the next day, to compose himself, and then wrote him a letter, apologizing, and assigning at large the reasons for my conduct; and received a verbal answer by Mr. Langton, which, were I to repeat it, would render me suspected of inexcusable vanity; it concluded with these words, 'If I was not satisfied with this, I must be a savage.' [9]

7th. I again visited him. Before my departure, Dr. Brocklesby came in, and, taking him by the wrist, Johnson gave him a look of great contempt, and ridiculed the judging of his disorder by the pulse. He complained, that the sarcocele had again made its appearance, and asked, if a puncture would not relieve him, as it had done the year before: the doctor answered, that it might, but that his surgeon was the best judge of the effect of such an operation. Johnson, upon this, said, 'How many men in a year die through the timidity of those whom they consult for health! I want length of life, and you fear giving me pain, which I care not for.'

8th. I visited him with Mr. Langton, and found him dictating to Mr. Strahan another will, the former being, as he had said at the time of making it, a temporary one. On our entering the room, he said, 'God bless you both.' I arrived just time enough to direct the execution, and also the attestation of it. After he had published it, he desired Mr. Strahan to say the Lord's Prayer, which he did, all of us joining. Johnson, after it, uttered, extempore, a few pious ejaculations.

9th. I saw him in the evening, and found him dictating, to Mr. Strahan, a codicil to the will he had made the evening before. I assisted them in it, and received from the testator a direction, to insert a devise to his executors of the house at Lichfield, to be sold for the benefit of certain of his relations, a bequest of sundry pecuniary and specific legacies, a provision for the annuity of 70£. for Francis, and, after all, a devise of all the rest, residue, and remainder of his estate and effects, to his executors, in trust for the said Francis Barber, his executors and administrators; and, having dictated accordingly, Johnson executed and published it as a codicil to his will.[10]

He was now so weak as to be unable to kneel, and lamented, that he must pray sitting, but, with an effort, he placed himself on his knees, while Mr. Strahan repeated the Lord's Prayer. During the whole of the evening, he was much composed and resigned. Being become very weak and helpless, it was thought necessary that a man should watch with him all night; and one was found in the neighbourhood, who, for half a crown a night, undertook to sit up with, and assist him. When the man had left the room, he, in the presence and hearing of Mr. Strahan and Mr. Langton, asked me, where I meant to bury him. I answered, doubtless, in Westminster Abbey: 'If,' said he, 'my executors think it proper to mark the spot of my interment by a stone, let it be so placed as to protect my body from injury.' I assured him it should be done. Before my departure, he desired Mr. Langton to put into my hands, money to the amount of upwards of 100£. with a direction to keep it till called for.

10th. This day at noon I saw him again. He said to me, that the male nurse to whose care I had committed him, was unfit for the office. 'He is,' said he, 'an idiot, as awkward as a turnspit just put into the wheel, and as sleepy as a dormouse.' Mr. Cruikshank came into the room, and, looking on his scarified leg, saw no sign of a mortification.

11th. At noon, I found him dozing, and would not disturb him.

12th. Saw him again; found him very weak, and, as he said, unable to pray.

13th. At noon, I called at the house, but went not into his room, being told, that he was dozing. I was further informed by the servants, that his appetite was totally gone, and that he could take no sustenance. At eight in the evening, of the same day, word was brought me by Mr. Sastres, to whom, in his last moments, he uttered these words 'Jam moriturus,' that, at a quarter past seven, he had, without a groan, or the least sign of pain or uneasiness, yielded his last breath.

At eleven, the same evening, Mr. Langton came to me, and, in an agony of mind, gave me to understand, that our friend had wounded himself in several parts of the body. I was shocked at the news; but, upon being told that he had not touched any vital part, was easily able to account for an action, which would else have given us the deepest concern. The fact was, that conceiving himself to be full of water, he had done that, which he had often solicited his medical assistants to do, made two or three incisions in his lower limbs, vainly hoping for some relief from the flux that might follow.

Early the next morning, Frank came to me; and, being desirous of knowing all the particulars of this transaction, I interrogated him very strictly concerning it, and received from him answers to the following effect:

That, at eight in the morning of the preceding day, upon going into the bedchamber, his master, being in bed, ordered him to open a cabinet, and give him a drawer in it; that he did so, and that out of it his master took a case of lancets, and choosing one of them, would have conveyed it into the bed, which Frank, and a young man that sat up with him,[11] seeing, they seized his hand, and entreated him not to do a rash action: he said he would not; but drawing his hand under the bedclothes, they saw his arm move. Upon this they turned down the clothes, and saw a great effusion of blood, which soon stopped— That soon after, he got at a pair of scissors that lay in a drawer by him, and plunged them deep in the calf of each leg— That immediately they sent for Mr. Cruikshank, and the apothecary, and they, or one of them, dressed the wounds— That he then fell into that dozing which carried him off.—That it was conjectured he lost eight or ten ounces of blood; and that this effusion brought on the dozing, though his pulse continued firm till three o'clock.

That this act was not done to hasten his end, but to discharge the water that he conceived to be in him, I have not the least doubt. A dropsy was his disease; he looked upon himself as a bloated carcase; and, to attain the power of easy respiration, would have undergone any degree of temporary pain. He dreaded neither punctures nor incisions, and, indeed, defied the trochar and the lancet: he had often reproached his physicians and surgeon with cowardice; and, when Mr. Cruikshank scarified his leg, he cried out— 'Deeper, deeper;—I will abide the consequence: you are afraid of your reputation, but that is nothing to me.'—To those about him, he said,—'You all pretend to love me, but you do not love me so well as I myself do.'

I have been thus minute in recording the particulars of his last moments, because I wished to attract attention to the conduct of this great man, under the most trying circumstances human nature is subject to. Many persons have appeared possessed of more serenity of mind in this awful scene; some have remained unmoved at the dissolution of the vital union; and, it may be deemed a discouragement from the severe practice of religion, that Dr. Johnson, whose whole life was a preparation for his death, and a conflict with natural infirmity, was disturbed with terror at the prospect of the grave. Let not this relax the circumspection of anyone. It is true, that natural firmness of spirit, or the confidence of hope, may buoy up the mind to the last; but, however heroic an undaunted death may appear, it is not what we should pray for. As Johnson lived the life of the righteous, his end was that of a Christian: he strictly fulfilled the injunction of the apostle, to work out his salvation with fear and trembling; [12] and, though his doubts and scruples were certainly very distressing to himself, they gave his friends a pious hope, that he, who added to almost all the virtues of Christianity, that religious humility which its great Teacher inculcated, will, in the fullness of time, receive the reward promised to a patient continuance in well-doing.

A few days after his departure, Dr. Brocklesby and Mr. Cruikshank, who, with great assiduity and humanity, (and I must add, generosity, for neither they, nor Dr. Heberden, Dr. Warren, nor Dr. Butter, would accept any fees) had attended him, signified a wish, that his body might be opened. This was done, and the report made was to this effect:

Two of the valves of the aorta ossified.
The air cells of the lungs unusually distended.
One of the kidneys destroyed by the pressure of the water.
The liver schirrous.
A stone in the gall bladder, of the size of a common gooseberry.

On Monday the 20th of December, his funeral was celebrated and honoured by a numerous attendance of his friends, and among them, by particular invitation, of as many of the literary club as were then in town, and not prevented by engagements. The Dean of Westminster, upon my application, would gladly have performed the ceremony of his interment, but, at the time, was much indisposed in his health; the office, therefore, devolved upon the senior prebendary, Dr. Taylor, who performed it with becoming gravity and seriousness. All the prebendaries, except such as were absent in the country, attended in their surplices and hoods: they met the corpse at the west door of their church, and performed, in the most respectful manner, all the honours due to the memory of so great a man.

His body, enclosed in a leaden coffin, is deposited in the fourth transept of the abbey, near the foot of Shakespeare's monument, and close to the coffin of his friend Garrick. Agreeable to his request, a stone of black marble covers his grave, thus inscribed:

SAMUEL JOHNSON, LL.D.
Obiit XIII die Decembris,
Anno Domini
MDCCLXXXIV,
Aetatis suae LXXV.[13]

NOTES

Introduction (pages vii–xxviii)

1. *Johnsonian Miscellanies*, ed. by George Birkbeck Hill, New York, Harper, 1897, II, 297–298.
2. Boswell, I, 190; II, 126. All references are to the Hill-Powell edition, which has been quoted by permission of the Clarendon Press.
3. *Critical Review*, June, 1787, p. 417; *Monthly Review*, July, 1787, pp. 68, 70; *European Magazine*, May, 1787, p. 313.
4. The two unidentified quotations are taken from clippings kept in a scrapbook by Samuel Lysons, a contemporary of Hawkins. The scrapbook is the possession of James L. Clifford.
5. *The Hamwood Papers of the Ladies of Llangollen and Caroline Hamilton*, ed. by Mrs. G. H. Bell, London, Macmillan, 1930.
6. Boswell, I, 26–28.
7. *Johnsoniana*, ed. by J. Wilson Croker, Philadelphia, Carey and Hart, 1842, p. 339.
8. *Old Kensington Palace and Other Papers*, New York, Oxford, n.d., p. 136.
9. Boswell, IV, 53.
10. *The Covent-Garden Journal*, June 2, 1752.
11. James L. Clifford in *New Light on Dr. Johnson* (ed. Frederick W. Hilles), New Haven, Yale University Press, 1959, p. 130.
12. Letter of William Cowper to Samuel Rose, Feb. 19, 1789, in *The Correspondence of William Cowper* (ed. Thomas Wright), New York, Dodd, 1904; John Bowyer Nichols, *Illustrations of the Literary History of the Eighteenth Century*, London, Nichols, Son, and Bentley, 1858, V, 213.
13. Harold Nicolson, *The Development of English Biography*, London, Hogarth, 1903, p. 97.
14. Letter to Samuel Rose, June 20, 1789.

Chapter One (pages 1–23)

1. Ecclus. chap. xliv. ver. 1, *et seq.* [Hawkins.]
2. Of this person, who yet lives in the remembrance of a few of his associates, little can be related but from oral tradition. He was, as I have heard

278

Johnson say, a man of great wit and stupendous parts, but of very profligate manners. He was chaplain to Lord Chesterfield during his residence at the Hague; but, as his lordship was used to tell him, precluded all hope of preferment by the want of a vice, namely, hypocrisy. It was supposed that the parson in Hogarth's "Modern Midnight Conversation," was intended to represent him in his hour of festivity, four in the morning. [Hawkins.]

3. Hawkins' date for Johnson's birth is according to the Julian calendar, which was replaced by the Gregorian in the mid-eighteenth century. Johnson's birthday is celebrated on September 18. Nathaniel was born in 1712.

4. The Jacobites supported the claim made to the English crown by the son and grandson of King James II.

5. This story, which Anna Seward of Lichfield contributed to the Gentleman's Magazine, is now considered apocryphal.

6. The young Sam Johnson was probably touched by the queen on March 30, 1712.

7. There are various versions of the duck poem. Johnson assured Boswell, however, that the poem had been written by his father. (Boswell, I, 40.)

8. The Reverend John Hunter was a stern disciplinarian. According to Johnson, Hunter beat his students "unmercifully." He did, however, have a considerable reputation for scholarship.

9. William Butt, who ventured this prediction, was the father of Cary Butt. Cary Butt became a leading surgeon in Lichfield. The King's Chaplain mentioned by Hawkins was the Reverend George Butt, grandson of William Butt.

10. This was Edmund Hector, Johnson's neighbor in Lichfield. Hector gave identical information to Boswell.

11. Johnson was suffering a severe attack of melancholia when he left Oxford in December, 1729.

12. Cornelius Ford's living was at Pedmore, near Stourbridge, in Worcestershire.

13. Hawkins seems to have been misinformed concerning the deceit he accuses Wentworth of practicing. John Wentworth, the headmaster of Stourbridge School from 1704–1732, was the son of Thomas Wentworth, of Salisbury. He matriculated at Corpus Christi College, Oxford, in May, 1692, when he was fifteen.

14. Young Andrew Corbet, whose father (Roger, not Andrew) was dead by this time, had been a friend of Johnson at Lichfield Grammar School. He was already enrolled as a gentleman commoner at Pembroke College, and, in order to have Johnson as a companion, offered to pay part of his college expenses. Johnson's parents accepted the offer and entered Johnson at Pembroke on October 31. Corbet, however, left Pembroke during the same week Johnson was entered, and never made good his offer of assistance. Commoners at Oxford paid all their fees. Gentlemen commoners paid double fees and were permitted to dine with the fellows.

15. A. L. Reade (Johnsonian Gleanings, V, 21–22) has identified the donor of the shoes as William Vyse, who later became Archdeacon of Salop.

16. The line is from Johnson's London.

17. John Meeke later became a fellow of Pembroke College.

18. The "Adversaria," which Johnson used as a kind of writer's notebook, also served the purpose mentioned here.

19. Johnson had through his life a propensity to Latin composition: he showed it very early at school, and while there made some Latin verses, for which the Earl of Berkshire, who was a good scholar, and had always a Horace in his pocket, gave him a guinea. [Hawkins.]

20. According to Boswell (I, 61), who had his information from Edmund Hector, Johnson was asked by Jorden to translate Pope's *Messiah* into Latin as a Christmas exercise. It was not a punishment. The title of the volume is *A Miscellany of Poems*.

21. This was Johnson's lifelong friend, John Taylor, who entered the church.

22. Although all of his early biographers believed that he completed his residence at Oxford, Johnson did not return to the university after he left it in December, 1729. Hawkins was misled into thinking that Dr. Adams became Johnson's tutor because he knew that Jorden had accepted a living in the church. Adams would have become Johnson's tutor if Johnson had returned to Pembroke to complete his residence.

23. Servitors in Oxford, sizars in Cambridge. [G. B. Hill.]

24. Some historical examples justifying Hawkins' opinion are omitted.

25. The maiden sisters mentioned by Hawkins were those of Cornelius Ford rather than of Johnson's mother. In the first edition of the *Life*, Hawkins had mistakenly identified Ford as Johnson's uncle. In correcting this relationship, Hawkins failed to notice that he was falling into another error.

26. Michael Johnson was buried at St. Michael's, in Lichfield, on December 7, 1731. He died in his seventy-fifth year.

27. The master at the time Johnson went to Market Bosworth was the Reverend John Kilby. The Reverend John Crompton became master upon Kilby's death in 1734.

28. Johnson's inheritance from his father amounted to nineteen pounds. Hawkins failed to note Johnson's correction of the diary entry.

29. Hawkins' summary of the book, along with quotations from it, is omitted.

30. Thomas Warren paid Johnson five guineas for this translation.

31. The proposal notifies, that subscriptions would be taken in by N. [Nathanael] Johnson, who had succeeded to his father's business. [Hawkins.] The Latin title of the edition has been omitted from the text.

32. Both editions of the *Life* mistakenly have "defect."

33. Floyer's piece is a letter published in the *Gentleman's Magazine* for April, 1734.

34. A prize of fifty pounds for the best poem 'on Life, Death, Judgment, Heaven and Hell.' [Hawkins.]

35. This letter, and Cave's answer to it, may serve to refute an assertion in an anonymous account of Johnson's life, that he was introduced to the acquaintance of Cave by Savage. [Hawkins.]

36. John Stow's *Survey of London* (1598) was edited and brought up to date by John Strype in 1720.

37. Both editions of the *Life* mistakenly give this date as 1734.

38. There is no evidence of this relationship. There were three Porter children: Lucy, Jervis, and Joseph.

39. Reade (VI, 44–45) has identified Johnson's student as Lawrence Offley, the son of Crewe Offley. Crewe Offley was first cousin to Sir Thomas Aston, whose daughter Magdalen married Gilbert Walmesley in 1736.

40. The following is the advertisement which he published upon the occasion:—'At Edial, near Lichfield, in Staffordshire, young gentlemen are boarded, and taught the Latin and Greek languages by Samuel Johnson.' *Vide Gent. Mag.* for 1736, page 418. [Hawkins.]

41. Not all of the inelegance of this letter, written in 1737, should be ascribed to Gilbert Walmesley. Hawkins' source—presumably one of the many versions of the letter published in the periodicals about the time of Johnson's death—was partly at fault. In his final sentence, Walmesley actually wrote, "If it should any way lie in your way I doubt not but you would be ready to recommend and assist your countryman."

42. Richard Knolles, *The General History of the Turks* (1603).

43. Hawkins' account of the historical background of Johnson's tragedy *Irene* is omitted.

Chapter Two (pages 24–52)

1. Perhaps Hawkins himself.

2. Mr. Moses Browne, originally a pencutter, was, so far as concerned the poetical part of it, the chief support of the magazine, which he fed with many a nourishing morsel. This person being a lover of angling, wrote piscatory eclogues; and was a candidate for the fifty pound prize mentioned in Johnson's first letter to Cave, and for other prizes which Cave engaged to pay him who should write the best poem on certain subjects; in all or most of which competitions Mr. Browne had the good fortune to succeed. He published these and other poems of his writing, in an octavo volume, Lond. 1739; and has therein given proofs of an exuberant fancy and a happy invention. Some years after he entered into holy orders. A farther account of him may be seen in the *Biographia Dramatica*, to a place in which work he seems to have acquired a title, by some juvenile compositions for the stage. Being a person of a religious turn, he also published in verse, a series of devout contemplations, called *Sunday Thoughts*. Johnson, who often expressed his dislike of religious poetry, and who, for the purpose of religious meditation, seemed to think one day as proper as another, read them with cold approbation, and said, he had a great mind to write and publish *Monday Thoughts*.

To the proofs above adduced of the coarseness of Cave's manners, let me add the following: he had undertaken, at his own risk, to publish a translation of Du Halde's *History of China*, in which were contained sundry geographical and other plates. Each of these he inscribed to one or other of his friends; and, among the rest, one 'To Moses Browne.' With this blunt and

familiar designation of his person, Mr. Browne was justly offended; to appease
him, Cave directed an engraver, to introduce with a caret under the line,
Mr. and thought, that in so doing, he had made ample amends to Mr.
Browne for the indignity done him.

Mr. John Duick, also a pencutter, and a near neighbour of Cave, was a
frequent contributor to the magazine, of short poems, written with spirit and
ease. He was a kinsman of Browne, and the author of a good copy of
encomiastic verses prefixed to the collection of Browne's poems above-mentioned.

Mr. Foster Webb, a young man who had received his education in Mr.
Watkins's academy in Spital Square, and afterwards became clerk to a
merchant in the city, was, at first, a contributor to the magazine, of enigmas,
a species of poetry in which he then delighted, but was dissuaded from it
by the following lines, which appeared in the magazine for October, 1740,
after a few successful essays in that kind of writing:

> Too modest bard, with enigmatic veil
> No longer let thy muse her charms conceal;
> Though oft the Sun in clouds his face disguise,
> Still he looks nobler when he gilds the skies.
> Do thou, like him, avow thy native flame,
> Burst thro' the gloom, and brighten into fame.

After this friendly exhortation, Mr. Webb, in those hours of leisure which
business afforded, amused himself with translating from the Latin classics,
particularly Ovid and Horace: from the latter of these he rendered into
English verse, with better success than any that had before attempted it,
the odes 'Quis multa gracilis te puer in rosa'; 'Solvitur acris hyems grata vice
veris, & Favoni,' 'Parcus Deorum cultor & infrequens'; and 'Diffugêre nives,
redeunt jam gramina campis'; all which are inserted in Cave's magazine. His
signature was sometimes Telarius, at others Vedastus. He was a modest, ingenious, and sober young man; but a consumption defeated the hopes of his
friends, and took him off in the twenty-second year of his age.

Mr. John Smith, another of Mr. Watkins's pupils, was a writer in the
magazine, of prose essays, chiefly on religious and moral subjects, and died of
a decline about the same time.

Mr. John Canton, apprentice to the above-named Mr. Watkins, and also
his successor in his academy, was a contributor to the magazine, of verses,
and afterwards, of papers on philosophical and mathematical subjects. The
discoveries he made in electricity and magnetism are well known, and are
recorded in the transactions of the Royal Society, of which he afterwards
became a member.

Mr. William Rider, bred in the same prolific seminary, was a writer in the
magazine, of verses signed Philargyrus. He went from school to Jesus College,
Oxford, and, some years after his leaving the same, entered into holy orders,

and became sur-master of St. Paul's school, in which office he continued many years, but at length was obliged to quit that employment by reason of his deafness.

Mr. Adam Calamy, a son of Dr. Edmund Calamy, an eminent non-conformist divine, and author of the abridgment of Mr. Baxter's history of his life and times, was another of Mr. Watkins's pupils, that wrote in the magazine; the subjects on which he chiefly exercised his pen were essays in polemical theology and republican politics; and he distinguished them by the assumed signature of 'A consistent protestant.' He was bred to the profession of an attorney, and was brother to Mr. Edmund Calamy, a dissenting teacher, of eminence for his worth and learning.

A seminary, of a higher order than that above-mentioned, viz. the academy of Mr. John Eames in Moorfields, furnished the magazine with a number of other correspondents in mathematics and other branches of science and polite literature. This was an institution supported by the Dissenters, the design whereof was to qualify young men for their ministry. Mr. Eames was formerly the continuator of the abridgment of the *Philosophical Transactions* begun by Jones and Lowthorp, and was a man of great knowledge, and a very able tutor. Under him were bred many young men who afterwards became eminently distinguished for learning and abilities; among them were the late Mr. Parry, of Cirencester, the late Dr. Furneaux, and Dr. Gibbons; and, if I mistake not, the present Dr. Price. The pupils of this academy had heads that teemed with knowledge, which, as fast as they acquired it, they were prompted by a juvenile and laudable ambition to communicate in letters to Mr. Urban.

To this account of Cave's correspondents might be added the celebrated names of Dr. Birch, who will be spoken of hereafter, Mrs. Carter, Dr. Akenside, the Rev. Mr. Samuel Pegge, who, by an ingenious transposition of the letters of his name, formed the plausible signature of Paul Gemsege; Mr. Luck, of Barnstaple in Devonshire; Mr. Henry Price, of Pool, in Dorsetshire; Mr. Richard Yate, of Chively, in Shropshire; Mr. John Bancks; and that industrious and prolific genius, Mr. John Lockman. [Hawkins.]

3. It appeared in the *Gentleman's Magazine* for October, 1749.

4. In 1727 Savage killed Mr. James Sinclair in a tavern brawl.

5. Sir Robert Walpole.

6. An anecdote concerning David Garrick and Charles Fleetwood, patentee of Drury Lane Theatre, is omitted.

7. Both editions of the *Life* print "in" for "on."

8. Johnson appears to have lived with Richard Norris when he was in London the year before, but not in 1738.

9. Johnson probably refers to his poem "Ad Urbanum."

10. Robert Dodsley, one of the leading booksellers of this period, is still known for the 12-volume edition of old plays which he published in 1744.

11. Hawkins' informant was incorrect. Dodsley paid Johnson ten guineas for *London*.

12. The correct date for this, as for the letter of Lord Gower which follows, is 1739.

13. The original letter of Lord Gower has never been traced. Hawkins probably adapted his text from one of the numerous printed versions, but it is not identical with any of those that are known.

14. Proposals for publishing it were advertised in the *Weekly Miscellany* of 21st Oct., 1738, in the following terms: 'Just published, proposals for printing the *History of the Council of Trent*, translated from the Italian of Father Paul Sarpi, with the author's life, and notes Theological, Historical, and Critical, from the French edition of Dr. Le Courayer. To which are added, observations on the history and notes; and illustrations from various authors, both printed and manuscript, by S. Johnson, in two volumes quarto.' [Hawkins.]

15. Only the surname was the same. The other translator of Father Paul's *History* was the Reverend John Johnson.

16. John Nichols, proprietor of the *Gentleman's Magazine* at the time of Johnson's death, insisted that only six sheets were printed. Sarpi's Italian biographer was Fulgenzio Micanzi.

17. See note 26 below.

18. Johnson translated the *Commentaire* of Crousaz. The translation of the *Examen* was the work of Elizabeth Carter.

19. *Impransus*—not having had breakfast.

20. The account of Warburton which follows is abridged.

21. Hawkins' next paragraph, describing an earlier satirical prophecy, is omitted.

22. Princess Sophia, Electress of Hanover, was the granddaughter of James I and the mother of George I.

23. At Boswell's request, Thomas Steele, one of the Secretaries of the Treasury, "directed every possible search to be made in the records of the Treasury and Secretary of State's office, but could find no trace of any warrant having been issued." (Boswell, I, 141–142). While Hawkins would thus seem to have been mistaken in saying that warrants were issued for Johnson's arrest, it is not at all unlikely that Johnson, having heard rumors of warrants or believing himself in danger, took the precaution of going temporarily into hiding. The Walpole ministry was accustomed to take stern measures against its critics. Just about this time a number of writers were imprisoned for their attacks upon it, and Johnson's highly inflammatory pamphlet could hardly have gone unnoticed.

24. *King Charles the First*, mentioned in the abridged account which follows, was written by William Havard in 1737.

25. A brief comment on Lord Bolingbroke is omitted.

26.

DIVINITY

A small book of precepts and directions for piety: the hint taken from the directions in the [Countess of] 'Morton's' [daily] exercise.

PHILOSOPHY, HISTORY, and LITERATURE in general.

History of Criticism as it relates to judging of authors, from Aristotle to the present age. An account of the rise and improvements of that art; of the different opinions of authors ancient and modern.

Translation of the *History* of Herodian.

New edition of Fairfax's translation of Tasso, with notes, glossary, &c.

Chaucer, a new edition of him, from manuscripts and old editions, with various readings, conjectures, remarks on his language, and the changes it had undergone from the earliest times to his age, and from his to the present. With notes explanatory of customs, &c. and references to Boccace and other authors from whom he has borrowed, with an account of the liberties he has taken in telling the stories, his life, and an exact etymological glossary.

Aristotle's *Rhetoric*, a translation of it into English.

A *Collection of Letters*, translated from the modern writers, with some account of the several authors.

Oldham's *Poems*, with notes historical and critical.

Roscommon's *Poems*, with notes.

Lives of the Philosophers, written with a polite air, in such a manner as may divert as well as instruct.

History of the Heathen Mythology, with an explication of the fables, both allegorical and historical, with references to the poets.

History of the State of Venice, in a compendious manner.

Aristotle's *Ethics*, an English translation of them with notes.

Geographical Dictionary from the French.

Hierocles upon Pythagoras, translated into English, perhaps with notes. This is done by Norris.

A book of letters upon all kinds of subjects.

Claudian, a new edition of his works, cum notis variorum in the manner of Burman.

Tully's *Tusculan Questions*, a translation of them.

Tully *De Natura Deorum*, a translation of those books.

Benzo's *New History of the New World*, to be translated.

Machiavel's *History of Florence*, to be translated.

History of the Revival of Learning in Europe, containing an account of whatever contributed to the restoration of literature, such as controversies, printing, the destruction of the Greek empire, the encouragement of great men, with the lives of the most eminent patrons, and most eminent early professors of all kinds of learning in different countries.

A *Body of Chronology*, in verse, with historical notes.

A table of the *Spectators*, *Tatlers*, and *Guardians*, distinguished by figures into six degrees of value, with notes giving the reasons of preference or degradation.

A collection of letters from English authors, with a preface giving some

account of the writers, with reasons for selection and criticism upon styles
remarks on each letter, if needful.

A collection of proverbs from various languages:—Jan. 6—53.

A *Dictionary to the Common Prayer* in imitation of Calmet's *Dictionary
of the Bible*. March—52.

A collection of stories and examples like those of Valerius Maximus. Jan
10—53.

From Aelian, a volume of select stories, perhaps from others. Jan. 28—53

Collection of travels, voyages, adventures, and descriptions of countries.

Dictionary of Ancient History and Mythology.

Treatise on the Study of Polite Literature, containing the history of learning, directions for editions, commentaries, &c.

Maxims, Characters and Sentiments, after the manner of Bruyère, col
lected out of ancient authors, particularly the Greek, with apophthegms.

Classical Miscellanies, select translations from ancient Greek and Latin
authors.

Lives of illustrious persons, as well of the active as the learned, in imitation
of Plutarch.

Judgment of the learned upon English authors.

Poetical Dictionary of the English Tongue.

Considerations upon the Present State of London.

Collection of Epigrams, with notes and observations.

Observations on the English language, relating to words, phrases, and
modes of speech.

Minutiae Literariae, miscellaneous reflections, criticisms, emendations, notes.

History of the Constitution.

Comparison of philosophical and Christian morality by sentences col
lected from the moralists and fathers.

Plutarch's *Lives* in English, with notes.

POETRY and works of IMAGINATION

Hymn to Ignorance.

The Palace of Sloth—a Vision.

Coluthus, to be translated.

Prejudice—a Poetical Essay.

The Palace of Nonsense—a Vision. [Hawkins.]

27. This was probably the Reverend John Taylor, for whom Johnson wrote
a number of sermons.

28. *Faction Detected* was published in 1743.

29. Boswell disputed this (I, 125, n.4); and Johnson himself confessed that
he had not met Savage when the poem was written. Savage, however, was
by no means unknown to Johnson, who addressed a Latin distich to him at
the very moment *London* was being published. The subscription was first
moved early in 1738, and Savage would not have been one to keep his plans
to himself. In view of the striking parallels between the circumstances of
Thales and Savage, it is difficult not to accept Hawkins' identification.

30. Proverbs, chap. xxiii, ver. 31. [Hawkins.]

31. Hawkins quoted all six stanzas of both Johnson's original and the English imitation.

Chapter Three (pages 53–67)

1. Hawkins' next paragraph, describing Edward Cave's device for resolving the anagrams, is omitted.

2. At this point Hawkins included two speeches in their entirety: that of Lord Chancellor Hardwicke on the motion to remove Sir Robert Walpole, and that of Lord Chesterfield on the bill for restraining the sale of spirituous liquors. Both speeches, with some brief comment by Hawkins, are omitted.

3. This speech is still occasionally attributed to Pitt. Its opening sentence is well known: "The atrocious crime of being a young man, which the honourable gentleman has with such spirit and decency charged upon me, I shall neither attempt to palliate nor deny. . . ." In a note Hawkins quoted this entire speech and the speech of Horatio Walpole, to which it was a reply.

4. Four paragraphs commenting on the Walpole ministry are omitted.

5. The bill was passed in February, 1743, but the debate was not reported in the *Gentleman's Magazine* until the end of the year. It should be noted that in a recent article in *PMLA* (March, 1959, pp. 77–78) Donald J. Greene identifies Johnson's hand in a debate published in the magazine in 1744.

6. At what part of the catalogue Oldys's labours ended and Johnson's begin I have no express authority for saying: It is related of Johnson, by a person who was very likely to know the fact, that he was employed by Osborne to make 'a catalogue of the Harleian Library,' and if not to make such remarks on the books as are above inserted, an ordinary hand would have done as well; but it required the learning of a scholar to furnish such intelligence as the catalogue contains. This is one of the facts on which I ground my assertion that Johnson worked on the catalogue: to discriminate between his notes and those of Oldys, is not easy; as literary curiosities, and as a specimen of a great work, they nevertheless deserve attention. [Hawkins.]

7. Approximately twelve pages of Hawkins' original text, comprising extracts from the Harleian Catalogue, are omitted.

8. Johnson's proposals, which Hawkins inserted in their entirety, are omitted.

9. Johnson told Boswell that this incident took place in his own room rather than in Osborne's shop.

10. Hai Ebn Yokdan is the hero of the medieval Arabic romance *Hai Ebn Yokdan*, written by Abi Joafar Ebn Tophail (d. 1185). The book, the theme of which is how the ideal man can be produced, was translated into Latin in 1671 and into English in 1674, 1686, and 1708.

11. The Foundling Hospital.

12. Lady Macclesfield, whom Richard Savage claimed to be his mother, made

a public confession of adultery in order to obtain her freedom from her husband.

Chapter Four (pages 68–89)

1. Both editions of the *Life* have 1734, apparently a mistake for 1736, when
August 27 fell on a Friday and when Johnson was conducting his school at
Edial. What Johnson meant by "the breakfast law" is not known.

2. In a note in his diary dated April 13, 1781.

3. Works of Francis Osborn, Esq; 8vo. 1673, page 151. [Hawkins.]

4. In the preface to his edition of Shakespeare, published in 1747.

5. The account of Lord Chesterfield which follows is abridged. The
"other hands" referred to above by Hawkins were those of Thomas Villiers,
later Earl of Clarendon, who took the manuscript to Chesterfield.

6. In Hawkins' time it was mistakenly assumed that Lord Chesterfield's
description of a "respectable Hottentot" was intended as a portrait of Johnson.

7. Lord Chesterfield matriculated at Cambridge.

8. This story, repeated frequently in Johnson's day, appears to have had no
basis in fact. Johnson informed Boswell (I, 257) that no particular incident
gave rise to his quarrel with Lord Chesterfield. Because of Chesterfield's continued neglect, Johnson resolved to "have no connection with him."

9. This most famous of Johnson's letters was first printed by Boswell (I,
261–263).

10. I have been unable to identify the "eminent painter now living."

11. Prologue to *The Winter's Tale* and *Catharine and Petruchio*. [Hawkins.]
The dramatic pastoral *Florizel and Perdita; or The Winter's Tale* and the farce
Catharine and Petruchio were both performed at Drury Lane Theatre on Jan-
uary 21, 1756.

12. *Ibid.* [Hawkins.]

13. Johnson's prologue, which Hawkins inserted in its entirety, is omitted.

14. It was customary for the author to receive the profits of every third performance.

15. Hawkins' statement is misleading. *The Vanity of Human Wishes* was
published in January, 1749, whereas *Irene* was not performed until the following month.

16. Mrs. Elizabeth Foster.

Chapter Five (pages 90–111)

1. Although Alexander Pope made him the hero of his second *Dunciad*,
Colley Cibber achieved a considerable reputation as actor, playwright, and
manager of Drury Lane Theatre. He was appointed Poet Laureate in 1730.
His son Theophilus, also a successful actor, wrote nothing of particular value.

2. Of the accounts which follow, those of Thomas Birch, John Campbell,
John Hill, Tobias Smollett, and Samuel Richardson are abridged.

3. Both editions of the *Life* mistakenly give Mrs. Cockburn's first name as Elizabeth.

4. I heard him once relate, that he had the curiosity to measure the circuit of London by a perambulation thereof: the account he gave was to this effect: He set out from his house in the Strand towards Chelsea, and having reached the bridge beyond the waterworks, he directed his course to Marybone, from whence pursuing an eastern direction, he skirted the town, and crossed the Islington road at the Angel. There was at that time no city road, but passing through Hoxton, he got to Shoreditch, thence to Bethnal Green, and from thence to Stepney, where he recruited his spirits with a glass of brandy. From Stepney he passed on to Limehouse, and took into his route the adjacent hamlet of Poplar, when he became sensible that to complete his design he must take in Southwark: this put him to a stand; but he soon determined on his course, for taking a boat he landed at the red house at Deptford, and made his way to Say's Court, where the great wetdock is, and keeping the houses along Rotherhithe to the right, he got to Bermondsey, thence by the south end of Kent Street to Newington, and over St. George's Fields to Lambeth, and crossing over to Millbank, continued his way to Charing Cross, and along the Strand to Norfolk Street, from whence he had set out. The whole of this excursion took him up from nine in the morning to three in the afternoon, and, according to his rate of walking, he computed the circuit of London at above twenty miles. With the buildings erected since, it may be supposed to have increased five miles, and if so, the present circumference of this great metropolis is about half that of ancient Rome. [Hawkins.]

5. "Campbell is a good man, a pious man," said Johnson. "I am afraid he has not been in the inside of a church for many years; but he never passes a church without pulling off his hat. This shows that he has good principles. I used to go pretty often to Campbell's on a Sunday evening, till I began to consider that the shoals of Scotchmen who flocked about him might probably say, when any thing of mine was well done, 'Ay, ay, he has learnt this of CAWMELL!' " (Boswell, I, 417–418.) Hawkins' account is adapted from one in the *New and General Biographical Dictionary* of 1784.

6. Hill received his doctorate from the University of St. Andrews.

7. *Pamela* was published in 1740; *Clarissa*, mentioned in the account of Richardson, was published in 1748, in seven volumes.

8. Hawkins' acid account, of course, obscures Fielding's achievements both as a writer and as a Justice of the Peace, in which office he presided with distinction over the court in Bow Street.

9. Of his conversation, his morals, and the sense he entertained of the clerical profession, a judgment may be formed by the following saying of Johnson's. See his works, Vol. XI, page 214. I was, says he, but once in the company of Sterne, and then his only attempt at merriment was the display of a drawing too grossly indecent to have delighted even in a brothel. [Hawkins.]

10. Hawkins' next paragraph (describing the authors of the *Universal History*) is omitted.

11. The article, quoted at length by Hawkins, is omitted. In addition, the account of Samuel Dyer which follows is abridged.

12. The attack on Havana was made in 1762. Of this event, Bennet Langton recalled Johnson writing to Topham Beauclerk as follows: "The Havannah is taken; a conquest too dearly obtained; for, Bathurst died before it." (Boswell, I, 242.)

13. *Works* (1787), IV, 289.

14. Hawkins' remarks on the medical profession are abridged.

15. The medical character, whatever it is now, was heretofore a grave one: it implies learning and sagacity, and therefore, notwithstanding Lord Shaftesbury's remark, that gravity is of the very essence of imposture, the candidates for practice, though ever so young, found it necessary to add to their endeavours a grave and solemn deportment, even to affectation. The physicians in Hogarth's prints are not caricatures; the full dress, with a sword and a great tie-wig, and the hat under the arm; and the doctors in consultation, each smelling to a gold-headed cane shaped like a parish-beadle's staff, are pictures of real life in his time, and myself have seen a young physician thus equipped, walk the streets of London without attracting the eyes of passengers. [Hawkins.]

16. To these observations on the profession of physic, and the fate of its practitioners, I here add an anecdote of no less a personage than Dr. Mead himself, who very early in his life attained to this station of eminence, and met with all the subsequent encouragement due to his great merit, and who nevertheless died in a state of indigence.

The income arising from his practice I have heard estimated at 7000£. a year, and he had one if not two fortunes left him, not by relations but by friends no way allied to him; but his munificence was so great, and his passion for collecting books, paintings, and curiosities, so strong, that he made no savings. His manuscripts he parted with in his lifetime to supply his wants, which towards his end were become so pressing, that he once requested of the late Lord Orrery the loan of five guineas on some toys, viz. pieces of Kennel coal wrought into vases and other elegant forms, which he produced from his pocket. This story, incredible as it may seem, Lord Orrery told Johnson, and from him I had it. [Hawkins.]

17. After the Jacobite uprising of 1745 under Prince Charles Edward (the "late adventurer"), a number of the leaders were executed for treason on Tower Hill.

18. In his essay on the fates of clergymen. [Hawkins.]

19. *Idler*, No. 36.

20. The conversation of the Rota Club, which flourished briefly during the Commonwealth period, was political. One of the Rota Club's chief principles (from which its name was probably derived) was that one-third of a commonwealth's governing body should be replaced each year.

21. Sonnet "To Cyriack Skinner," line 6.

Chapter Six (pages 112–144)

1. The town life had also received great improvements, which have since been further extended: public entertainments are now enjoyed in an immediate succession: from the play the company are generally able to get away by eleven, the hour of assembling at other places of amusement; from these the hour of retirement is three, which gives, till noon the next day, nine hours for rest; and after that sufficient time for a ride, auctions, or shopping, before five or six the dinner hour. Nor is this seeming indulgence and immoderate pursuit of pleasure so inconsistent with the attendance on public worship as it may seem: Methodism, or something like it, in many instances, makes them compatible; so that I have known a lady of high rank enjoy the pleasures of a rout, that almost barred access to her house, on the evening of a Sunday which she had begun with prayer, and a participation of the solemnities which at an early hour in that day, are constantly celebrated at St. James's Chapel. [Hawkins.]

2. Mandeville, whose Christian name was Bernard, was a native of Dort in Holland. He came to England young, and, as he says in some of his writings, was so pleased with the country, that he took up his residence in it, and made the language his study. He lived in obscure lodgings in London, and betook himself to the profession of physic, but was never able to acquire much practice. He was the author of the book above-mentioned, as also of *Free Thoughts on Religion,* and A *Discourse on Hypochondriac Affections,* which Johnson would often commend; and wrote besides, sundry papers in the *London Journal,* and other such publications, to favour the custom of drinking spirituous liquors, to which employment of his pen, it is supposed he was hired by the distillers. I once heard a London physician, who had married the daughter of one of that trade, mention him as a good sort of man, and one that he was acquainted with, and at the same time assert a fact, which I suppose he had learned from Mandeville, that the children of women addicted to dram-drinking, were never troubled with the rickets. He is said to have been coarse and overbearing in his manners where he durst be so; yet a great flatterer of some vulgar Dutch merchants, who allowed him a pension. This last information comes from a clerk of a city attorney, through whose hands the money passed. [Hawkins.]

3. The Bangorian Controversy resulted from a sermon delivered in 1717 by Benjamin Hoadly, in which he denied that Christ had delegated any authority to the church. Hoadly was Bishop of Bangor in Wales.

4. In 1713 Anthony Collins published A *Discourse of Free-thinking, Occasioned by the Rise and Growth of a Sect Call'd Free-thinkers.* Richard Bentley replied to Collins in his *Remarks upon a Late Discourse of Free-thinking.*

5. Number 46.

6. Excerpts from Johnson's "Adversaria" are omitted.

7. Some of Hawkins' comments on style are omitted.

8. In addition, Number 10 was written by Hester Mulso, afterwards Mrs.

Chapone. Letters in Numbers 15 and 107 are from unknown correspondents.

9. Jonathan Swift, 'The Grand Question Debated,' lines 161–162.

10. Although Johnson may not have criticized other individual works in the *Rambler*, a number of *Ramblers* may properly be called critical essays.

11. The comments on Milton in this paragraph, and the account of William Lauder which follows, are abridged.

12. John Payne, who was one of the book's publishers.

13. Dr. Samuel Swinsen, Johnson's godfather. Johnson was understandably disturbed to discover that his diagnosis of his own illness had been shown by his godfather to a number of people.

14. This was told him, but the fact is questionable. [Hawkins.] No eighteenth century translation of the *Rambler* into Russian has been discovered.

15. Both editions of the *Life* mistakenly have "grammar and purity."

16. That Johnson was the writer of the papers signed T, I assert on the authority of his "Adversaria," in which are the original hints of many of them in his own handwriting. [Hawkins.]

17. Johnson's essay, which Hawkins quoted in its entirety, a lengthy extract about Crichton from Sir Thomas Urquhart's ΕΚΣΚΥΒΑΛΑΤΡΟΝ, and additional comments by Hawkins, are omitted.

18. The account of Hawkesworth which follows is abridged.

19. Both editions of the life have "were." *Formosae*, cited by Hawkins below, means "beautiful." It can be noted here that Johnson was himself responsible for the mistaken date on Mrs. Johnson's gravestone (1753 rather than 1752).

20. *Paradise Lost*, III, 44.

21. Dr. John Taylor.

22. Posterity will wonder to be told, that a celebrated courtezan, Kitty Fisher, was of the number, and that, possibly having heard of the attempt of Laïs on Demosthenes, she once left her card at his house. [Hawkins.]

23. She was a violent Whig, and, by consequence, a declaimer for liberty, a particular in her character that induced Johnson to compliment her in the following elegant epigram:

> Liber ut esse velim, suasisti pulchra Maria,
> Ut maneam liber—pulchra Maria, vale!

thus translated by Richard Paul Jodrell, Esq.;

> When fair Maria's soft persuasive strain
> Bids universal liberty to reign,
> Oh! how at variance are her lips and eyes!
> For while the charmer talks, the gazer dies. [Hawkins.]

24. I have sometimes thought that music was positive pain to him. Upon his once hearing a celebrated performer go through a hard composition, and hearing it remarked that it was very difficult, Johnson said, 'I would it had been im-

possible.' As a science of which he was ignorant he contemned it. In the early part of my life I had collected some memoirs of Abbate Steffani, Mr. Handel's predecessor at the court of Hanover, and the composer of those fine duets that go under his name, with a view to print them, as presents to some musical friends: I submitted the manuscript to Johnson's perusal, and he returned it with corrections that turned to ridicule all I had said of him and his works. [Hawkins.]

25. He has been heard to remark, that since the disuse of smoking among the better sort of people, suicide has been more frequent in this country than before. [Hawkins.]

26. This story is too well attested for me to omit it; but it leaves it a question, how, with the defect of sight under which he laboured, he was capable of discerning beauty. He might possibly think it an indispensable requisite for her profession, and therefore conclude that she had it. [Hawkins.]

27. The account which follows is abridged.

28. Barber appears to have become Johnson's servant in 1752, shortly after the death of Mrs. Johnson.

29. That he was an habitual sloven, his best friends cannot deny. When I first knew him, he was little less so than Magliabechi, of whom it is said, that at meals he made a book serve him for a plate, and that he very seldom changed his linen, or washed himself. It is said of other scholars and men eminent in literature, of Leibnitz, Poiret, St. Evremond, and Pope, that they were alike uncleanly. Johnson, as his acquaintance with persons of condition became more enlarged, and his invitations to dinner parties increased, corrected, in some degree, this failing, but could never be said to be neatly dressed, or indeed clean; he affected to wear clothes of the darkest and dirtiest colours, and, in all weathers, black stockings. His wig never sat even on his head, as may be observed in all the pictures of him, the reason whereof was, that he had a twist in his shoulders, and that the motion of his head, as soon as he put it on, dragged it awry. [Hawkins.]

30. Mrs. Williams, who, with a view to the interest of her friend, was very attentive to the conduct of this his favourite, when she took occasion to complain to his master of his misbehaviour, would do it in such terms as these: 'This is your scholar! your philosopher! upon whom you have spent so many hundred pounds!' [Hawkins.]

31. An extensive account of Lord Melcombe's clients (Edward Young, James Ralph, Paul Whitehead, and the quack Dr. Thompson) is omitted.

32. Hawkins has distorted this account, which he obtained from the *Gentleman's Magazine*. No notes were exchanged between Johnson and Millar. As Boswell described the incident (I, 287), "when the messenger who carried the last sheet to Millar returned, Johnson asked him, 'Well, what did he say'—'Sir, (answered the messenger) he said, thank GOD I have done with him.' 'I am glad (replied Johnson, with a smile,) that he thanks GOD for any thing.'"

33. Johnson's letter, which Hawkins quoted as "a specimen of a fine Latin style," is omitted. The vice-chancellor was Dr. George Huddesford.

34. Johnson defined *Ocean* as "The main; the great sea. Any immense expanse." Hawkins, relying no doubt upon his memory, was probably thinking of the following sentence in Johnson's preface to the *Dictionary*: 'It is remarkable that, in reviewing my collection, I found the word "Sea" unexemplified.'

35. The number of the French Academy employed in settling their language. [Hawkins.]

36. From the original contract now in my hand, dated 18th June, 1746, between Johnson on the one part, and the two Knaptons, the two Longmans, Charles Hitch, Andrew Millar, and Robert Dodsley, on the other. [Hawkins.]

37. "The Speeches of Ajax and Ulysses," from Ovid's *Metamorphoses* (Book XIII, lines 27–28).

38. Additional comments by Hawkins on the wisdom of not replying to one's critics are omitted.

Chapter Seven (pages 145–167)

1. Hawkins was mistaken in attributing "The Apotheosis of Milton" to Johnson. It was written by William Guthrie.

2. The writers in this publication were, Christopher Smart, Richard Rolt, Mr. Garrick, and Dr. Percy, now Bishop of Dromore. Their papers are signed with the initials of their surnames; Johnson's have this mark **. [Hawkins.] The periodical was known as *The Universal Visiter and Memorialist*.

3. Hawkins' account of the controversy with Jonas Hanway is abridged.

4. The engagement was probably with John Payne, who was the proprietor of the *Universal Chronicle*. Newbery published the first collected edition of the *Idler* in 1761.

5. Mr. Langton, of Langton in Lincolnshire, the father of his much beloved friend Bennet Langton, Esq.; mentioned in the codicil to his will, and husband of the Countess Dowager of Rothes. [Hawkins.]

6. *Tatler*, numbers 72 and 114.

7. I find in his diary a note of the payment to Mr. Allen the printer, of six guineas, which he had borrowed of him, and sent to his dying mother. [Hawkins.] The note is dated Friday, March 15, 1765.

8. *Rasselas* was published by James and Robert Dodsley, from whom Johnson received £100. He received an additional £25 for the second edition, which was also published in 1759.

9. Hawkins' comments on *Rasselas* are abridged.

10. A disquisition by Hawkins on the proportions of columns is omitted.

11. Of his facility in composition, and the rapidity with which he wrote for the press, here follow a few instances: Savage's life, containing a hundred and eighty octavo pages, was the work of thirty-six hours. He was wont to furnish for the *Gentleman's Magazine* three columns of the *Debates* in an hour, written, as myself can attest, in a character that almost anyone might read. His preface to *The Preceptor*, and his 'Vision of Theodore,' were each the work of one sitting, as was also the first seventy lines of his translation

of the tenth satire of Juvenal, entitled, *The Vanity of Human Wishes;* and what is almost incredible, he never read his *Rasselas* but in the proofs which came to him from the press for correction. [Hawkins.] It should be noted that Johnson had somewhat more help with *The Idler* than Hawkins knew of. Twelve essays were contributed by others. Sir Joshua Reynolds was the author of three.

12. *Epicoene,* Act II, Scene I. "All discourses but my own afflict me," Morose confessed, just before issuing this injunction.

13. Excerpts from *Rambler* No. 1 and *Idler* No. 3 are omitted.

14. Doubtless Bennet Langton, whose learning, said Johnson, "never lies straight." (Boswell, IV, 225.)

15. The Reverend James Hervey's *Meditations and Contemplations* was published in 1748. Hawkins seems to have adapted the mock meditation which follows from Boswell's *Journal of a Tour to the Hebrides.*

16. In 1766 George Adams published *A Treatise Describing and Explaining the Construction and Use of New Celestial and Terrestrial Globes.* The dedication to King George III was written by Johnson.

17. Myself have heard, in the Church of St. Margaret, Westminster, sundry sermons, which I and many others judged, by the sentiments, style, and method, to be of his composition; one in particular, Johnson being present. The next visit I made him, I told him that I had seen him at St. Margaret's on the preceding Sunday, and that it was he who then preached. He heard me, and did not deny either assertion, which, if either had not been true, he certainly would have done. In his diary I find the following note: '77, Sept. 21. Concio pro Tayloro.' [Hawkins.]

Chapter Eight (pages 168–191)

1. Johnson was granted a pension in July, 1762.

2. 'PE'NSION. . . . An allowance made to any one without an equivalent. In England it is generally understood to mean pay given to a state hireling for treason to his country.'

3. Some of Johnson's friends, and all his enemies, would have been glad had he imitated the conduct of Andrew Marvell, who, in the reign of Charles II. upon the offer of any post under the government that would please him, and of a thousand pounds in money, made him in a message from the king by the Earl of Danby at a time when he wanted a guinea, refused both. But Johnson had no reason to practise such self-denial. Marvell, to be grateful, must have deserted his principles, and acquiesced in the measures of a corrupt court. Johnson, on the contrary, was in no danger, during such a reign as is the present, of being required to make a sacrifice of his conscience, and, being thus at liberty, he accepted the bounty of his sovereign. [Hawkins.]

4. Hawkins' account of Dr. Levett is abridged, chiefly by the omission of the article which Hawkins borrowed from the *Gentleman's Magazine* of February, 1785. The article was later identified as the work of George Steevens, but since it was printed in the magazine anonymously, Hawkins could hardly

have known that in using it he was incurring a debt to a man he had every reason to detest. Steevens' attacks upon Hawkins are briefly described in the introduction to this volume.

5. The account of Dr. Lawrence which follows is omitted.

6. 'Tom Hervey,' Johnson told Boswell, '. . . though a vicious man, was one of the genteelest men that ever lived.' (II, 341.)

7. Johnson's definition of *imbecility* ('weakness; feebleness of mind or body') makes clear that in the eighteenth century the word did not always carry the stigma it does today. 'Every Man naturally persuades himself,' Johnson wrote on June 1, 1770, 'that he can keep his resolutions, nor is he convinced of his imbecillity but by length of time, and frequency of experiment.' (Yale Edition of Johnson's Works, I, 133.) Hawkins uses the word similarly on page 87.

8. From this account of Goldsmith only a brief passage from *The Traveller* is omitted.

9. A parody of one of Goldsmith's stories prefaced in this way is contained in Sir Joshua Reynolds' *Portraits*, published by the McGraw-Hill Book Company in 1952.

10. Johnson told Boswell that he wrote eight of the last ten lines of *The Traveller* and that he obtained sixty pounds for Goldsmith for the manuscript of *The Vicar of Wakefield*.

11. This was *The Vicar of Wakefield*. For Johnson's account of the incident, see Boswell (I, 416).

12. Hawkins seems to have overestimated Johnson's faithfulness in attendance. On March 8, 1766, Johnson wrote to Bennet Langton: 'Dyer is constant at the Club, Hawkins is remiss. I am not over diligent.'

13. Perhaps Mrs. Elizabeth Vesey, who regularly entertained on days when the Club met (Boswell, III, 424, n. 3).

14. As I was the only seceder from this society, my withdrawing myself from it seems to require an apology. We seldom got together till nine: the inquiry into the contents of the larder, and preparing supper, took up till ten; and by the time that the table was cleared, it was near eleven, at which hour my servants were ordered to come for me; and, as I could not enjoy the pleasure of these meetings without disturbing the economy of my family, and foresaw the impossibility of preventing the subversion of our society by the admission of exceptionable persons, I chose to forego it. [Hawkins.] Sir Joshua Reynolds told Boswell, however, that Hawkins was so rude to Edmund Burke on one occasion that the club members were very cool to him at the next meeting, and he never attended thereafter.

15. C. N. Fifer, in an article in *Notes and Queries* for July, 1956, cites an engagement book of Sir Joshua Reynolds which indicates that the first meeting of the club was held on Monday, April 16, 1764. According to Boswell (I, 477), the club was founded soon after Johnson returned to London in February, 1764.

16. Garrick was admitted to the club, but not until 1773.

17. He assumed a right of correcting his enunciation, and, by an instance,

convinced Garrick that it was sometimes erroneous.—'You often,' said Johnson, 'mistake the emphatical word of a sentence.'—'Give me an example,' said Garrick.—'I cannot,' answered Johnson, 'recollect one; but repeat the seventh commandment,'—Garrick pronounced it—'Thou *shalt* not commit adultery.'—'You are wrong,' said Johnson: 'it is a negative precept, and ought to be pronounced thus: Thou shalt *not* commit adultery.' [Hawkins.]

18. Abel Drugger is a character in Ben Jonson's *The Alchemist*.

19. The remainder of the account of Garrick is abridged.

20. Thomas Davies published his *Memoirs of the Life of David Garrick, Esq.* in 1780.

21. George Lillo, *The London Merchant: or, The History of George Barnwell* (1731). *The London Cuckolds* was written in 1682.

Chapter Nine (pages 192–205)

1. Charles Churchill ridiculed Johnson as "Pomposo" in *The Ghost*. The "engagement to the public" was the edition of Shakespeare, referred to in Book 3 of Churchill's poem (Lines 801–806):

> He for subscribers baits his hook
> And takes their cash—but where's the book?
> No matter where—wise fear we know,
> Forbids the robbing of a foe;
> But what, to serve our private ends,
> Forbids the cheating of our friends?

2. Had Johnson been provoked to an exercise of his prowess on this occasion, it would not have been the first display of his resentment on the stage of the theatre. He was once with Garrick at the representation of a play in his native city of Lichfield, when, having taken his seat in a chair placed on the stage, he had soon a call to quit it. A Scots officer, who had no good will towards him, persuaded an innkeeper of the town to take it; and he did as he was bid. Johnson, on his return, finding his seat full, civilly told the intruder, that by going out it was not his intention to give it up, and demanded it as his right: the innkeeper, encouraged by the officer, seemed resolved to maintain his situation: Johnson expostulated the matter with him; but, finding him obstinate, lifted up the chair, the man sitting in it, and, with such an Herculean force, flung both to the opposite side of the stage, that the Scotsman cried out, 'Damn him, he has broke his limbs'; but that not being the case, Johnson having thus emptied the chair, and Mr. Walmsley interposing, he resumed his seat in it, and with great composure sat out the play.

Johnson had great confidence in his corporeal strength, and, from this and some other particulars in his life, I am inclined to think he was vain of it. Such foibles are not uncommon in the greatest characters. Sir Isaac Newton, at the age of fourscore, would strip up his shirt sleeve to show his muscular, brawny arm, and relate how dexterous he was in his youth at boxing. And an intimate friend of mine, a sergeant at law, of the first eminence in his profession, who had nearly lost the use of his feet, was used to relate to me his dancing whole nights, when a young man, without feeling the least weariness. [Hawkins.]

3. Mr. Garrick knew not what risk he ran by this offer. Johnson had so strange a forgetfulness of obligations of this sort, that few who lent him books ever saw them again. Among the books in his library, at the time of his decease, I found a very old and curious edition of the works of Politian, which appeared to belong to Pembroke College, Oxford. It was probably taken out of the library when he was preparing to publish a part of that author, viz. in 1734, and had been used as his own for upwards of fifty years. [Hawkins.]

4. "For the extraordinary elegance and usefulness of his writings."

5. See his life of Milton among the *Lives of the Poets*. [Hawkins.] The debate between Milton and Salmasius (Claude Saumaise) was occasioned by the execution of Charles I.

6. Johnson's *Prayers and Meditations* was first published in 1785.

7. The section which follows is abridged.

8. Johnson once told me, he had heard his father say, that, when he was young in trade, King Edward the Sixth's first liturgy was much inquired for, and fetched a great price; but that the publication of this book, which contained the whole communion office as it stands in the former, reduced the price of it to that of a common book. [Hawkins.]

9. In 1720 Thomas Brett published A *Collection of the Principal Liturgies Used by the Christian Church*. *Reasons for Restoring Some Prayers and Directions* was written in 1717 by Jeremy Collier, and was answered by Nathaniel Spinckes in the volume mentioned below.

10. Johnson in his early years associated with this sect of non-jurors, and from them, probably, imbibed many of his religious and political principles. [Hawkins.]

11. The Reverend George Strahan edited the *Prayers and Meditations*. Johnson had requested that the profits from the first edition be given to Bray's Associates, a society which supplied clerical libraries in America and established schools for Negroes there and elsewhere.

12. The *Ramblers* published on Saturdays were generally on religious or moral subjects. [Hawkins.]

13. He was accustomed on these days to read the Scriptures, and particularly the Greek Testament, with the paraphrase of Erasmus. Very late in his life he formed a resolution to read the Bible through, which he confessed to me he had never done; at the same time lamenting, that he had so long neglected to peruse, what he called the charter of his salvation. [Hawkins.]

14. 'March 3. I have never, I thank God, since New Year's Day, deviated from the practice of rising.

'In this practice I persisted till I went to Mr. Thrale's some time before Midsummer: the irregularity of that family broke my habit of rising. I was there till after Michaelmas.' [Hawkins.] Johnson made this diary entry in 1766.

15. Johnson's interview with the king took place in February, 1767. A full account is in Boswell (II, 33–42).

Chapter Ten (pages 206–228)

1. John, chap. ix. v. 4. [Hawkins.]

2. Hawkins refers to the difficulties arising from John Wilkes's libel of King George III in his paper *The North Briton* (1762) and a second libel printed in his scurrilous *An Essay on Woman*. Wilkes was expelled from parliament, was reelected and again expelled. When he was again reelected, the House of Commons declared his defeated opponent, Colonel Luttrell, the victor.

3. Perhaps "A Letter to Samuel Johnson, LL.D." published in the *Gentleman's Magazine* of February, 1770, and attributed to John Wilkes.

4. Anoon's *Voyage Round the World* was related by Richard Walter.

5. Part of the passage quoted by Hawkins is omitted.

6. The Prince of Wales later became George IV. The queen's house was Buckingham House, which occupied the same site as the present Buckingham Palace.

7. The epitaph for Jane Bell, quoted by Hawkins, is omitted.

8. 'Hawky is no doubt very malevolent,' Boswell wrote to his friend William Temple on March 5, 1789. 'Observe how he talks of me as if quite unknown.'

9. Both editions of the *Life* mistakenly have "seven."

10. Hawkins' comments on Johnson's trip to Scotland are abridged.

11. Johnson had required, that it should be deposited in either the king's or the marischal college at Aberdeen, and submitted to public inspection; but this was never done. [Hawkins.]

12. The original of this letter bears the date January 20, 1775. Hawkins obtained his text from William Shaw's *Authenticity of the Poems Ascribed to Ossian*.

13. Although Hawkins' source, like the original, has "imposture," both editions of the *Life* printed the word "imposition."

14. In the 1760's Thomas Chatterton published a number of his own poems, which he claimed to have been the work of a fifteenth century monk named Thomas Rowley. The controversy over Phalaris's epistles raged in the late seventeenth century, and involved such notable persons as Sir William Temple, Richard Bentley, and Jonathan Swift.

15. It is now generally accepted that the poems ascribed to Ossian were almost entirely the work of Macpherson.

16. Hawkins' comments on *The Patriot* and *Taxation No Tyranny* are abridged.

17. For the Bangorian Controversy see Chapter Six, note three. The Disciplinarian Controversy, which flourished in the late sixteenth and early

seventeenth centuries, grew out of the Puritans' opposition to the episcopal discipline of the established church.

18. The fellows of Magdalen College resisted King James's efforts to force a president upon them against their wishes. The seven bishops (including the Archbishop of Canterbury) took the lead in resisting King James's order that his Declaration for Liberty of Conscience be read to English congregations.

19. "Unmeaning words," Horace Walpole wrote in the margin of his copy of the *Life of Johnson*.

20. Quite the contrary. [Walpole.]

21. Hawkins refers here to William Pitt, first Earl of Chatham, whom Johnson attacked in his pamphlet *Thoughts on the Late Transactions Respecting Falkland's Islands*.

22. Hawkins' comments on general warrants are omitted.

23. This all who knew him can attest. His written compositions were also so correct, that he, in general, trusted them to the press without a revisal. *Rasselas* he never read till it was printed; and having written at Mr. Langton's room at Oxford, an *Idler*, while the post was preparing to set out, that gentleman would have perused it; but Johnson would not suffer him, saying —'You shall not do more than I have done myself.' [Hawkins.]

24. The English captured the Philippine Islands in October, 1762, and the property of the inhabitants of Manila was saved from plunder on condition that Spain pay a ransom of one million pounds. Half this sum was paid in money, but the other half was given in bills upon the Spanish Treasury which Spain refused to honor.

Chapter Eleven (pages 229–241)

1. The text of the diploma is omitted.

2. Johnson did keep a journal of his French tour. It was first printed in Boswell's *Life* (II, 389–401), and has been most recently reprinted in the first volume of the Yale Edition of Johnson's works.

3. I have some reason to think, that at his first coming to town, and while he had lodgings in the Strand, he frequented Slaughter's coffee house, with a view to acquire a habit of speaking French, but he never could attain to it. Lockman used the same method, and succeeded, as Johnson himself told me. [Hawkins.]

4. By a note in his diary it appears, that he laid out near thirty pounds in clothes for this journey. [Hawkins.] In the paragraph which follows, both editions of the *Life* mistakenly give 1769 as the year in which *The Good-natured Man* was acted.

5. Hawkins' account of Johnson's efforts in behalf of Dr. Dodd is abridged.

6. Johnson told Boswell that he had been in Dodd's company once.

7. The Bishop of London was Dr. Robert Lowth.

8. Hawkins probably refers to the Edinburgh edition by Gilbert Martin's Apollo Press.

9. Possibly Charlotte Lennox, who had been honored by the Ivy Lane Club and was well versed in French literature.

10. Although Johnson completed much of the work in 1778, the first four volumes were published in 1779 and the last six in 1781.

11. A Midsummer Night's Dream, Act V, Scene 1.

12. Milton's L'Allegro, line 129.

13. Mrs. Elizabeth Montagu, known as "Queen of the Blues," published An Essay on the Writings and Genius of Shakespear in 1769.

14. This section on Pope's epitaphs is abridged. The pamphlet to which Hawkins refers is The Universal Visiter.

15. It is still unpublished.

Chapter Twelve (pages 242–265)

1. It is printed at the end of the first volume of Dr. Calamy's abridgment of Mr. Baxter's history of his life and times. [Hawkins.] At the Savoy Conference of 1661, Puritan divines and bishops of the Church of England were unable to agree on changes in the Book of Common Prayer.

2. [James] Howell's Letters, Book II, letter 11. [Hawkins.]

3. Polemical and moral discourses, folio, 1657, page 25. [Hawkins.]

4. It is fit, that between the business of life, and the day of death, some space should intervene. [Hawkins.]

5. Johnson was used to visit this person, and would frequently adjourn with him from his lodging to a neighbourhood alehouse, and, in the common room, converse with him on subjects of importance. In one of these conversations, Johnson took occasion to remark on the human mind, that it had a necessary tendency to improvement, and that it would frequently anticipate instruction, and enable ingenious minds to acquire knowledge. 'Sir,' said a stranger that overheard him, 'that I deny: I am a tailor, and have had many apprentices, but never one that could make a coat till I had taken great pains in teaching him.' [Hawkins.]

6. I have not been able to identify the "female sceptic" mentioned by Hawkins.

7. A few years before Mr. Thrale's death, an emulation arose among the brewers to exceed each other in the magnitude of their vessels for keeping beer to a certain age, probably taking the hint from the great tun at Heidelburg. One of that trade, I think it was Mr. Whitbread, had made one that would hold some thousand barrels, the thought whereof troubled Mr. Thrale, and made him repeat, from Plutarch, a saying of Themistocles, 'The trophies of Miltiades hinder my sleeping'; Johnson, by sober reasoning, quieted him, and prevented his expending a large sum on what could be productive of no real benefit to him or his trade. [Hawkins.]

8. It was sold for £114,000. [Walpole.]

9. The text of the inscription is omitted.

10. It seems that between him and the widow there was a formal taking of leave, for I find in his diary the following note: '1783, April 5th, I took leave

of Mrs. Thrale. I was much moved. I had some expostulations with her. She said that she was likewise affected. I commended the Thrales with great good will to God; may my petitions have been heard!' [Hawkins.]

11. Both editions of the *Life* mistakenly have "letter'd ignorance."

12. Of his being seized with the palsy, I find in his diary the following note:

> June 16. I went to bed, and, as I conceive, about 3 in the morning, I had a stroke of the palsy.
> " 17. I sent for Dr. Heberden and Dr. Brocklesby. God bless them.
> " 25. Dr. Heberden took leave. [Hawkins.]

13. A letter of Johnson to Mrs. Thrale, dated April 15, 1784, indicates that the group met again at Johnson's on April 14.

14. This, and other expressions of the like kind, which he uttered to me, should put to silence the idle reports, that he dreaded annihilation. [Hawkins.]

15. I find the above sentiment in Law's *Serious Call to a Devout and Holy Life*, a book which Johnson was very conversant with, and often commended. [Hawkins.]

16. Johnson's letter of February 23, 1784, to his daughter-in-law, Lucy Porter, indicates that this event took place on Thursday, February 19.

17. Although the Essex Head Club had a rather less select membership than the "Literary Club," Johnson was hardly degrading himself in the company of its members, many of whom were persons of considerable note. 'I am sorry my father suffered himself to seem pettish on the subject,' wrote Laetitia-Matilda Hawkins in her *Memoirs* (I, 104): 'honestly speaking, I dare say he did not like being passed over.'

18. Hawkins doubtless meant that John Opie was unable to finish the portrait during the preliminary sittings of 1783. The completed portrait is reproduced as the frontispiece to this volume.

19. Dr. John Taylor.

20. Gabriel Piozzi, whom Mrs. Thrale married on July 25, 1784.

21. Although Johnson wrote Mrs. Thrale again on July 8, the letter to which Hawkins refers is the same letter of which an "adumbration" was printed in the *Gentleman's Magazine*. Mrs. Thrale replied on July 4 with the letter concluding 'till you have changed your opinion of Mr. Piozzi—let us converse no more. God bless you!'

22. Pope and Swift's *Miscellanies*, 'Phyllis or the Progress of Love.' [Hawkins.]

23. The offer above-mentioned has, in the first view of it, the appearance rather of a commercial than a gratuitous transaction; but Sir Joshua clearly understood at the making it, that Lord Thurlow designedly put it in that form: he was fearful that Johnson's high spirit would induce him to reject it as a donation, but thought that, in the way of a loan, it might be accepted. [Hawkins.]

24. Probably Margaret, Countess of Lucan.

Chapter Thirteen (pages 266–277)

1. Both quotations are from *Macbeth*, Act V, Scene 3.

2. The text of Johnson's memorial to his parents and brother is omitted.

3. Viz. 9 Geo. 2. cap. 36, which enacts, that no lands, tenements, &c. shall be given to any bodies politic, unless by deed indented, made twelve months, at least, before the death of the donor. [Hawkins.]

4. Young Mr. [John] Desmoulins. [J. W. Croker.] John Desmoulins was the grandson of Johnson's godfather, Dr. Samuel Swinsen.

5. He very much admired, and often in the course of his illness recited, from the conclusion of old Isaac Walton's life of Bishop Sanderson, the following pathetic request:

> Thus this pattern of meekness and primitive innocence changed this for a better life:—'tis now too late to wish, that mine may be like his; for I am in the eighty-fifth year of my age, and God knows it hath not; but, I most humbly beseech Almighty God, that my death may; and I do as earnestly beg, that, if any reader shall receive any satisfaction from this very plain, and, as true relation, he will be so charitable as to say, Amen. [Hawkins.]

6. George Steevens.

7. As I take no pleasure in the disgrace of others, I regret the necessity I am under of mentioning these particulars: my reason for it is, that the transaction which so disturbed him may possibly be better known than the motives that actuated me at the time. [Hawkins.]

8. *Othello*, Act III, Scene 4.

9. This incident was not recounted in the first edition; it was added after Hawkins had been accused of purloining Johnson's diaries. Although Hawkins' account is plausible (it was never disputed by any of the other persons present when the incident took place), it is interesting to note that in the first edition the events of the next day ("I again visited him") were dated December 6 rather than December 7. Whether Hawkins' memory had been suddenly refreshed, or whether he deliberately changed the date to make clear that he gave Johnson time "to compose himself," must remain a matter of conjecture.

10. How much soever I approve of the practice of rewarding the fidelity of servants, I cannot but think that, in testamentary dispositions in their favour, some discretion ought to be exercised; and that, in scarce any instance they are to be preferred to those who are allied to the testator either in blood or by affinity.* It was hinted to me many years ago, by his master, that he [Francis Barber] was a loose fellow; and I learned from others, that, after an absence from his service of some years, he married. In his search of a wife, he picked up one of those creatures with whom, in the disposal of themselves, no contrariety of colour is an obstacle. It is said, that soon after his marriage, he became jealous, and, it may be supposed, that he continued

so, till, by presenting him with a daughter of her own colour, his wife put an end to all his doubts on that score. Notwithstanding which, Johnson, in the excess of indiscriminating benevolence, about a year before his death, took the wife and her two children, into his house, and made them a part of his family; and, by the codicil to his will, made a disposition in his favour, to the amount in value of near fifteen hundred pounds. [Hawkins.]

11. This was Cawston, servant to William Windham.

12. Philippians, ii, 12.

13. Johnson's will, and a postscript on Francis Barber and a distant relation of Johnson (Humphrey Heely), are omitted.

INDEX